OTHER PASTS,
DIFFERENT PRESENTS,
ALTERNATIVE FUTURES

INDIANA UNIVERSITY PRESS
Bloomington & Indianapolis

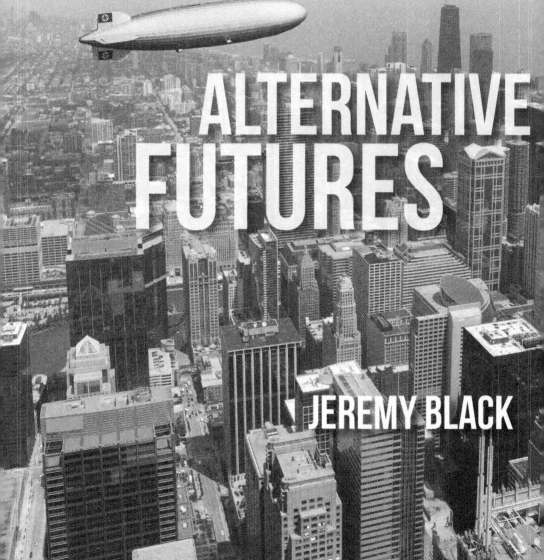

OTHER
DIFFERENT PASTS,
PRESENTS,
ALTERNATIVE FUTURES

JEREMY BLACK

This book is a publication of

Indiana University Press
Office of Scholarly Publishing
Herman B Wells Library 350
1320 East 10th Street
Bloomington, Indiana 47405 USA

Telephone   800-842-6796
Fax   812-855-7931

iupress.indiana.edu

The paper used in this publication meets
the minimum requirements of the
American National Standard for
Information Sciences—Permanence
of Paper for Printed Library Materials,
ANSI Z39.48-1992.

Manufactured in the
United States of America

Cataloging information is available
from the Library of Congress

ISBN 978-0-253-01697-3 (cloth)
ISBN 978-0-253-01704-8 (paperback)
ISBN 978-0-253-01706-2 (ebook)

1 2 3 4 5 20 19 18 17 16 15

FOR

Ginny and Peter Knott

Contents

Preface

The 2010s are a decade of commemorative anniversaries, most of which invite questions about whether other outcomes were possible and, if so, what would have happened. What if there had been no World War I or no Russian Revolution?—the latter incidentally an unlikely occurrence had there been no such war. What if Napoleon had won at Waterloo in 1815?; or if the Jacobites had won in 1715?; or if there had been no Bohemian Revolt leading to the outbreak of the Thirty Years' War in 1618?; or if Martin Luther had not nailed his complaints to the church door at Wittenberg in 1517?; or if Henry V had not won at Agincourt in 1415?; or Robert the Bruce at Bannockburn in 1314? Or if King John had not been obliged to accept Magna Carta in 1215?

The list can be readily extended, as well as varied by country and theme. The common element is the questioning of apparent certainties, or "known knowns," to quote Donald Rumsfeld. Indeed, "What if?" books today take a prominent role in airport bookshops, and have been a major publishing success over the last two decades.

Yet this approach, generally known as counterfactualism, has had only a limited impact in academic history and, more particularly, in historiography and the teaching of historical method. Indeed, there have been significant attacks on the counterfactual approach. This is unfortunate, as counterfactualism has much to offer. In this book, I offer a short guide to the subject, one that is designed to argue its value as a tool for public and academe alike. In particular, I focus on the role of counterfactualism in demonstrating the part of contingency, and thus human agency, in history, and on the critique the counterfactual approach necessarily offers to determinist accounts of past, present, and future, and therefore its value for teaching and research. I also discuss how counterfactualism can explain structural questions, notably how the modern world system took the form it did and does, and the form it might take in the future.

I have benefited first from the invitation to speak on this subject at a conference held at the Mershon Center at Ohio State University in 1997, and second from opportunities to offer counterfactual approaches to the American Revolution in lectures at Adelphi University, Assumption University, North Georgia University, the University of Washington, Rhode Island College, the University of Virginia Summer School, and the Lexington Historical Society. I also benefited from the opportunity to speak at the Fifth CECC International Conference on Culture and Conflict in Lisbon in 2013.

The comments of Pete Brown, Stan Carpenter, David Cohen, Strobe Driver, Bill Gibson, Stephen Morillo, Bill Purdue, Gavriel Rosenfeld, Richard Seaford, Dennis Showalter, Philip Woodfine, Neil York, and two anonymous readers on all or part of an earlier version proved most instructive. I also benefited from discussing the topic with Michael Axworthy, Jonathan Barry, Ian Beckett, Anthony Beevor, George Bernard, Richard Bernstein, John Blair, Rui Manuel Brás, Ahron Bregman, Michael Bregnsbo, Carl Bridge, Roger Burt, Stan Carpenter, James Chapman, Guy Chet, Jonathan Clark, Robert Cowley, Martin van Creveld, Michael DeNie, Kelly DeVries, Simon Dixon, Mike Dobson, David Ekserdjian, Warren von Eschenbach, Olavi Fält, Felipe Fernandez-Armesto, John France, Henry French, John Gaddis, David Gladstone, Jan Glete, Richard Hall, Richard Harding, Nick Henshall, Bob Higham, Michael Hochedlinger, Peter Hoffenberg, Jeff Horn, Tristram Hunt, Ronald Hutton, John Imber, Philippa Joseph, Henry Kamen, Janice Kaye, Tony Kelly, Brenda Laclair, John Lamphear, Karl de Leeuw, Jan Lemnitzer, Stephen Levine, Stewart Lone, Peter Lorge, Malcolm Mckinnon, John Maurer, Tim May, Rana Mitter, Anthony Musson, Ian Netton, Jeremy Noakes, William Olejniczak, James Onley, Mark Overton, Richard Overy, Marc-William Palen, Ryan Patterson, Mike Pavkovic, Murray Pittock, Arno Richter, Levi Roach, Andrew Roberts, Gijs Rommelse, Ralph Sawyer, Joe Smith, Christopher Storrs, Nigel Townson, Richard Toye,

Frank Turner, Hans van de Ven, Hilde De Weerdt, Chris Wickham, Peter Wiseman, and Adam Zeman. None is responsible for any errors in the book nor do they necessarily share the opinions offered, but much of the fun of this book has stemmed from the chance to discuss the subject with friends far and wide. I also benefited greatly from a variety of roles in "public history," not least in advising the UK Department of Education in 2013 on revisions to the National Curriculum.

An earlier, shorter study, *What If? Counterfactualism and the Problem of History,* was published by the Social Affairs Unit in 2008 and I would like to thank Michael Mosbacher for permission to use some of the material from that work. Bob Sloan has proved a most helpful editor for this book, and Eric Levy an exemplary copyeditor. It is a great pleasure to dedicate it to Ginny and Peter Knott, thoughtful friends with an interest in books.

Abbreviations

Add   Additional Manuscripts
AE   Paris, Ministère des Relations Extérieures
Ang   Angleterre
BL   London, British Library, Department of Manuscripts
CP   Correspondance Politique
FO   Foreign Office
LH   King's College London, Liddell Hart Library
NA   London, National Archives

OTHER PASTS,
DIFFERENT PRESENTS,
ALTERNATIVE FUTURES

1

INTRODUCTION

It was the meteorite that landed in the Western Approaches to the English Channel on the night of June 5–6, 1944, that doomed the long-planned Anglo-American invasion of Normandy. No fleet, especially one with heavily laden landing-craft, could have survived the resulting tidal wave, which was funneled up the Channel to devastating effect. By leaving the Germans in control of France, the total failure of this invasion attempt enabled them to concentrate on resisting the advance of the Red (Soviet) Army and to do so beyond April 1945 when Berlin might otherwise have fallen. As a result, the United States had the opportunity in August 1945 to drop on Berlin one of the two atomic bombs that were ready. The U.S. needed to do so to show that it could play a major role in overthrowing Hitler. However, with no Anglo-American ground forces yet in Germany, the Soviets were able, amidst the ruins of the Nazi regime, to occupy most of it. A Cold War frontier on the Rhine followed, as did a Communist bloc benefiting from the resources and capacity of the Ruhr industrial belt and from the revival of the German economy after World War II.

Well no. The idea of the "meteorite that ate D-Day" is not very helpful. A meteorite could have landed then, and its impact would have been totally devastating; the same being true for example of the British forces under General William Howe preparing to land on Staten Island in July 1776, launching the campaign to regain control of the Thirteen Colonies. Storms that were not due to meteorites, but that were seen as providential by the successful defenders, wrecked a Chinese invasion of Japan in

1274, and badly damaged Spanish fleets sent against Algiers in 1541 and England in 1588.

In the case of possible meteorites, as opposed to storms, in 1776 and 1944, it is not particularly helpful to discuss such possibilities as they were not considered by contemporaries, nor, indeed, were they at all probable. There were no signs that such possibilities affected planning. In contrast, weather forecasting did affect planning, with the British getting the forecasting at least partly wrong, whereas the Germans correctly forecast the poor conditions but drew the wrong conclusion that the Allies would not risk an invasion in choppy seas.[1]

A crucial value of counterfactualism is that it returns us to the particular setting of uncertainty in which decisions are actually confronted, made, and implemented. The meteorite theory is not helpful as it does not illuminate this uncertainty. There is no comparison, for example, between such counterfactuals for 1776 and 1944, and considering the more plausible counterfactual of the Soviet Union not attacking Japan (as it in fact did in 1945) and the effect upon the Allies' war with Japan, both in 1945 and subsequently.

Counterfactualism—conjecturing on what did not happen in order to understand what did, or, more precisely, the use of conditional assertions based on what is known not to have occurred—thus entails, or should entail, the disciplines of scholarship.[2] This is the case whether we are considering specifically crafted counterfactuals or the way that historians use counterfactuals as part of the "tools of the trade." Research to establish contemporary choices, and parameters and constraints, and informed analysis to assess them, are crucial, not least to the idea that "What was" and "What is" each incorporate "What might have been." The question "why," which is basic to history, cannot be adequately addressed without at least evaluating untaken roads.

More generally, discussions of historical causation are implicitly counterfactual, because they make assumptions, even though not usually articulated, as to what would have happened without the cause discussed. Aside from its role in history, counterfactualism also has a place in other disciplines, such as philosophy, sociology, political science, economics,[3] theology, geography, and literature, although they lack history's ability to act as a major subject of popular discussion as well as an academic discourse. In all subjects, counterfactuals offer a valuable logical tool, as well as play an important role in extending the grounded imagination.

As with other historical methods, however, there is no barrier in counterfactualism to less rigorous approaches, as all too many conversations in bars will reveal. These conversations about counterfactualism are relatively unhelpful, other than for establishing the content of public speculation. That might sound snooty or snobbish, which is not the intention, for this speculation, however misguided, is itself a matter of considerable interest as it can be a valuable guide to the public mood and can play a significant role in rumors.[4] The interest in counterfactuals, indeed, might be seen as an instance of the more general practice of history, with an iceberg tip (professionals would argue) of more rigorous study above a large base of historical beliefs and interests held and pursued every day.

This situation is a reminder that counterfactualism is a tool, capable of use in many contexts, rather than a position or a school of thought. Indeed, a discussion of varied options and likely outcomes is frequently one of the ways in which past, present, and future are understood, explained, and, as it were, advocated. Humans seem powerfully inclined to explore counterfactual ways of reasoning: like family history, there is a genuine constituency for it. As a consequence, these processes are a matter for discussion by historians.[5]

Politicians repeatedly tap into counterfactual speculation when they ask voters to imagine different pasts, presents, and futures. Thus, in the 2008 campaign for the Democratic nomination for president, Barack Obama pressed Americans to envisage a Washington without lobbyists or a United States without poverty, while Hillary Clinton, his leading rival, warned them about inexperience when her advertisement asked voters, "Who do you want answering the phone?" in the middle of the night if there were a national emergency.[6] The issue of inexperience represents a projection onto the unknown future of the situation in the present, a situation derived from the impact of the past. In turn, these concerns about the future provide a way to approach the present-day situation. Politicians communicate with the electorate in terms not only of what might and could be, but also of what might and could have been. Polling and policy presentation are linked to these alternatives. Moreover, psephology, the science of voting, draws heavily on counterfactuals.

All historians need to remember first that those in the past did not know what was going to happen, while we do, at least to a considerable extent, albeit an extent that varies greatly by individual and group. On the other hand, those in the past thought they knew what might happen, including what did not, while we do not know these thoughts, except indirectly through studying their records, which are frequently incomplete or nonexistent. Thus, part of our job should be trying to think of what possible outcomes were open at the time, in order to understand the thinking of those in the past, and, thereby, the reasons for how they acted. Counterfactualism provides a means to express real dilemmas, and understand both unfulfilled aspirations and lost moments of genuine crisis.

Linked to this is the consideration of the uses real historical actors have made of counterfactuals in order for us to explore not only their assumptions but also their political (and other) maneuvering. Counterfactuals, indeed, play an important role in political maneuvering and posturing,[7] specifically with the calculation of the likely moves and responses of others. This use of counterfactuals is taken further with the subsequent reconstruction by historical actors of their choices in the light of what actually did happen. A choice that works out, even if made for the wrong reasons, is then justified based on the results. Similarly, as with Tony Blair's justification in 2014 of the 2003 invasion of Iraq, a choice that comes out badly is reconstructed and excused or criticized, perhaps as determined by a more limited range of choices than in fact really existed when the choice was made. This very natural tendency to revise the history of individual choices in light of the results seriously complicates the historian's inquiry into historical decision making. An understanding of the options available therefore is important to the historian. The discussion of these options in terms of counterfactuals is both central to the evaluation of choices and policies, and natural.

The capacity for choice itself is a characteristic of the human species, with the developed frontal lobes providing the opportunity for the exercise of this facility. One of the defining human characteristics, and a fundamental human activity, is also the ability to imagine things otherwise than they are. This is achieved in part by detaching oneself from the here and now, and thereby conceiving of both past and future, or, rather, pasts and futures.[8] These processes are linked, as memory helps humans plan for the future, including how best to respond to future outcomes. The capacities employed in anticipating the future are broadly similar to those used when remembering the past (and amnesiacs tend to lose both). This is unsurprising as similar parts of the brain are activated.[9]

Such activity does not entail strain, but rather an imaginative effort. Counterfactualism, both by those directly involved and by others, can be seen as an aspect of this effort, not least because considering alternative pasts helps explain the past and, thus, fix memory. Counterfactualism in terms of alternative expositions is also an aspect of the close relationship for humans between history and story, and unsurprisingly so because of humans' interest in, and need for, telling stories as a way to process experience.[10]

Counterfactualism is not simply a subject of the past. It is as much the topic of discussion and planning now about both present and future. Indeed, in one respect, counterfactualism is an aspect of the process by which cultures produce versions of reality that prepare us for, protect us from, or conceal the social reality just ahead in what we call the future.[11] The concept of premediation, defined by Richard Grusin in 2010 as an anticipation, not by "getting the future right" ahead of time, but "by making futurity present," is relevant.[12] Thus, some products of culture, including counterfactual works but also those that lack any explicit or implicit counterfactual element, anticipate, and seek to anticipate, what will be the issues of the future.[13] Counterfactualism is about futurology as well as about considering the past; and aside from conceptual and methodological parallels, both are linked. Much of the methodology and vocabulary associated with the counterfactual approach take on their potency precisely because they are not employed solely for discussion about the past, but, instead, take a more central role in consideration of the future. Business planners assess the nature of the market, psephologists consider the result of the next election, strategists consider how best to implement policy and to plan for policy choices, and so on.

The exposition of alternative explanations about the past and present provides a key means of considering possible future trends.

A good example is provided by those, debating military procurement, who focus on possible threat-environments. For example, criticizing, in 2008, the British plan for two big aircraft carriers for the Royal Navy, Sir Michael Quinlan, permanent undersecretary of state at the Ministry of Defence from 1988 to 1992, accepted a counterfactual—"Recovering the Falklands [in 1982] would have been impossible without them," continuing, "But the scenario where carriers are essential is narrow." He subsequently offered both the cost-benefit analysis frequently seen in counterfactual exercises and the attempt to rank alternatives—albeit, as is generally the case, through assertion as much as clarification:

> Without the US, an operation dependent upon carriers yet not too tough for us has to fit a tight specification. . . . The task must be one that cannot be done, in the 2020s and 2030s, by systems such as unmanned aircraft [drones]. . . . And the operation must be so important to Britain that we cannot stand aside, as we have done for many conflicts.
>
> No one can prove that this scenario could never arise. But against its likelihood and importance we have to weigh its costs. . . . Abandoning the carriers would be painful for the Royal Navy, constituency and industrial interests, and procurement relationships with France. But in hard times for defence these are secondary considerations. The prime criterion must be strategic utility as compared with alternative resource uses.[14]

In the event, the option of canceling the carriers was in large part foreclosed by the high cancellation costs written into the contracts that were signed, allegedly in order to satisfy the constituency interest of the then prime minister, Gordon Brown. These costs helped ensure that the incoming government did not abandon the project.[15] Quinlan's use of the past (in the shape of drawing attention to the fact that Britain has stood aside in many conflicts) in order to support an assessment for the future is common, and reflects on the somewhat misleading nature of attempts to divine the future from the past. Moreover, it is instructive to see the stance adopted by a former senior civil servant who had been heavily involved in planning.

From such perspectives of present practicality, the likely consequences of past counterfactuals, for example of the Romans not invading and conquering much of what became Britain in the first century AD, may seem inconsequential and a distraction. Maybe so, but counterfactualism highlights the thesis that the most important lesson to learn from the past is indeterminacy;[16] and, therefore, that history is of value precisely because it can teach this lesson. That approach to history is a major theme of this book. The emphasis on indeterminacy can be combined with an argument about the very difficulty of knowing the past.[17]

There is also a serious danger with counterfactualism, and one that has encouraged some of the bitter criticism that has been made of the process. It is all too easy to transform the "What if?" into "If only," and to employ the latter to encourage a nostalgic approach that urges, explicitly or implicitly, a rewriting of the past in order to make another version seem not only possible but also, in part as a result, legitimate and desirable. Thus, aside from entertainment, the past becomes an aspect of present discontents and battles, feeding into a divisive empowerment through historicized grievance.

A good current example of this rewriting is provided by the regret, voiced and encouraged by Vladimir Putin and his allies in the 2000s and 2010s, about the collapse of the Soviet Union in 1990–91.[18] In their counterfactualism, Russia would have been stronger, and Eurasia more stable—from their point of view—had this collapse not occurred. This assertion is then employed to question the inevitability of the step; and that, in turn, serves as a comment on the present. Indeed, such attitudes played a significant role in Russian policy in Ukraine in 2014. There was also a more specific Russian response to the allocation of Crimea to Ukraine by Nikita Khrushchev, the Soviet leader, in 1954. Counterfactualism applied to that decision, for example the claim that he had been drunk, was employed in order to justify the return of Crimea to Russia in 2014.

Counterfactualism, presented as the study of what did not happen, has been strongly dismissed by prominent historians. In his influential *What Is History?* (1961), E. H. Carr described counterfactualism as a "parlor game," and E. P. Thompson, in *The Poverty of Theory* (1978), discussed it as "*Geschichtwissenschlopff,* unhistorical shit."[19] In 2005, Gavriel Rosenfeld, who does not share their reservations, in his important treatment of counterfactualism and the Third Reich, noted the persistence of deep-seated resistance by others based on epistemological, methodological, and moral objections.[20] In the case of Nazi Germany and other episodes, counterfactualism can be presented as representing one more attempt at an unwelcome relativism; although, in fact, that is not a necessary consequence of the method, or the intention of most practitioners.

Another criticism of counterfactualism is that, in giving importance to agency—usually the actions of a small number of individuals in specific conjunctures—it can explain large events by small causes. This is an approach that, for a number of reasons, is unwelcome to some commentators. Those who prefer "big, simple, linear metaphors" cannot be expected to appreciate such a stress on specific people and conjunctures. There is, in this, a general question of emphasis, in both historical content and historical method.[21] Conceding that counterfactualism is a protection against determinism, John Tosh nevertheless argued that this was "at the cost of elevating contingency to a disproportionate explanatory role."[22] The issue has also reached British school exams, as with question 3 in section B of the 2006 examination for the Edexcel Exam Board's Advanced Extension Award: "'Consideration of "What could have been" might be an entertaining activity, but it has no place for serious historical study.' How far do you agree with this view of counterfactual history?"

Moreover, to certain critics, counterfactualism might appear an aspect of what has been termed counterknowledge. The latter refers to the range of bogus beliefs that have been presented by critics as being particularly in evidence at present,[23] a range that may in part reflect the decline of Western ideologies. Damian Thompson has written powerfully in criticism of the present age as a "golden age of bogus history," and has argued that "the first duty of the scholar is to report things that did, rather than didn't, happen."[24] I fully agree with his criticism of "bogus history," but the purpose of this book is to define a sphere for counterfactualism, to differentiate it from such history, and to argue its value.

There is also the argument from politics. Richard Evans, professor of modern history at Cambridge from 2008 to 2014, has been robust in his denunciation of alternative histories, engaging against some of the foremost exponents of counterfactualism, notably Niall Ferguson, the editor of *Virtual History: Alternatives and Counterfactuals* (1997; an American edition followed in 1999).[25] His criticisms, many conceptual and methodological, were far from limited to politics, but Evans also helped politicize the issue by suggesting that those writing in this mode are on the political right, and intent, as a result of their conservatism, on rewriting the past.[26] In 2014, as the centenary of the beginning of World War I neared, Evans reopened his attack, delivering a book-length blast against counterfactualism. Others, including Ferguson, in contrast, repeatedly asked whether the war could have been avoided, and what would have happened had the war not occurred, or if Britain had not taken part. Moreover, they then used these questions to consider the value of counterfactual approaches.[27]

Of the other critics of counterfactualism, E. H. Carr, Eric Hobsbawn, and E. P. Thompson were also stalwarts of the Left. Indeed, a philosophical difference between left- and right-wing historians can be discerned insofar as the latter are much more prepared to embrace the concepts of individualism and free will, although these themselves are not without difficulties as explanatory concepts and methods. Much of the critique of counterfactualism from the Left reflects a resistance to the very idea, as opposed simply to its application. Ironically, some of these historians themselves used the method. For example, Carr and Hobsbawn mused on how things in the Soviet Union would have been different had Lenin lived longer, which was a way of expressing unease about Stalin.[28] This approach was taken further by many Trotskyites, eager to argue that the revolution would have followed a better path had Trotsky, not Stalin, succeeded Lenin.

However, possibly there was (and is) a reluctance on the Left to betray the Marxist tradition by eloping with such eminently liberal notions as individualism and free will. Free will is not the sole issue, because unpredictable *deus ex machina* events not involving free will, such as the sudden death of rulers or the meteor falling, are as much a blow against historical determinism.[29] So also with the impact of random microbial mutations, seismic eruptions, and unseasonal winds.[30]

In the *Guardian* on April 7, 2004, Tristram Hunt (from 2013 the shadow secretary of state for education in Britain), from the perspective of New Labour, argued, in "Pasting over the Past," that there was a right-wing political agenda in counterfactuals, as well as an ironic over-lapping with postmodernism and a bias in favor of individual choices and against social and economic structures: "It is no surprise that progressives rarely involve themselves, since implicit in it is the contention that social structures and economic conditions do not matter. Man is, we are told, a creature free of almost all historical constraints, able to make decisions on his own volition." Part of the reason that Evans appears to be so against counterfactualism is that it plays into the hands of dogmatic postmodernists, which is a different issue from that of left-right.

Prominent conservative politicians have certainly written counterfactuals. Linking American, British, and European history, Winston Churchill, writing in 1931, suggested that if the Confederate general Robert E. Lee had won (the subject of many counterfactuals[31]), Britain would have become Socialist while Germany dominated Europe.[32] Churchill himself was to be much the subject and agent of counterfactuals, both in serious works and in those that were explicitly fictional.

Newt Gingrich, one-time history professor (at the University of West Georgia) and, as Speaker of the House of Representatives from 1995 to 1999, a prominent Republican politician in the 1990s, as well as a failed candidate for the Republican nomination for the presidency in 2012, produced, with William Forstchen, a trilogy offering an alternative history of the Civil War: *Gettysburg* (2003), *Grant Comes East* (2004), and *Never Call Retreat: Lee and Grant; The Final Victory* (2005). The first has Lee win the battle, instead of the Union forces. This victory is followed by an advance on Washington, which is unsuccessfully attacked, before Baltimore is captured by the Confederates. In the event, Lee is defeated in the third volume, leading to the end of the Civil War in 1863. That poses a counterfactual for subsequent American history. Gingrich's volatile career itself offered room for counterfactual speculations.

The argument for a political agenda in counterfactual history, however, can be questioned. It may be the case that, for a particular contingency, a Left-Right dichotomy (the Left critiquing counterfactualism while the Right employs it) is appropriate. However, this is not true for counterfactualism as a whole, for three reasons. Firstly, there is no inherent reason why right-wing writers need focus on the past. The present and future might be of greater interest. Secondly, there is no inherent reason why left-wing writers need avoid counterfactualism. The question of what would have happened had Margaret Thatcher not been elected in 1979, or not been reelected in 1983 after the Falklands War of 1982, or been unsuccessful when confronted by the miners' strike in 1984–85, could just as plausibly be asked from the perspective of Left or Right. Indeed, after her death in 2013, left-wing criticism of her legacy in part adopted this perspective. Both Left and Right can have an interest in critiquing the present (as well as the past), and both can draw on the past (including counterfactual pasts) to do so. This is an issue that Evans fails to tackle adequately.

This point can be taken further by noting that the established Left-Right dichotomies do not apply in the same fashion to counterfactuals in all countries. In the United States, it was standard to ask what would have happened had George W. Bush, the Republican candidate, not been declared the winner of the 2000 presidential election. Chris Trotter's populist history of New Zealand, *No Left Turn: The Distortion of New Zealand's History by Greed, Bigotry and Right-Wing Politics* (2007), counterfactualizes from the left. International comparisons certainly challenge some of the standard national associations of ideas and policies with particular political parties.

Thirdly, and most significantly, it is also far from clear that such a Left-Right dichotomy is appropriate for most topics or indeed some types of history. Moreover, in discussing the political positioning of counterfactualism, it is important to underline the extent to which, contrary to the argument about the approach proving particularly conducive to conservative types of scholarship, it can be employed when discussing branches of history that are neither military nor political. This point is important to the argument of this book, and, indeed, is a theme in several of the chapters.

For example, there has been a systemic use of counterfactualism by some economic historians, as they seek to ascertain which factors were most pertinent in, for example, causing particular growth rates and spurts. A key instance of this cliometrics was *Railroads and American Economic Growth* (1964), Robert Fogel's assessment of the nature of American economic development had there been no railways.[33] In most cases, such arguments are not readily reducible to political alignments, although they still may have political dimensions. Fogel's work on railways was far less imbued with his liberal politics than his later *Time on the Cross* (1974). That was a distinctly politically engaged (but less counterfactual) econometric study of slavery in the United States. This had at its core, as a clinical evaluation, the cost to society of having African Americans in prison while ignoring the driving and underpinning issues of disempowerment and disenfranchisement which lead to African Americans' representing a large portion of the American prison population.

A lack of a political positioning for counterfactualism is generally true of the deep history of the distant past, in that, in most cases, this history scarcely abuts issues in present contention. Thus, to consider the likely impact of the slower spread, or later spread, of cereal cultivation from the Near East to Europe in about 6500 BC is a valuable adjunct to discussion of the consequence of this spread; but it scarcely accords with key issues in contemporary Left-Right debate. To bring the subject into the present, it is possible to evaluate alternative scenarios, such as a British National Health Service based on local authorities, rather than, as it was established in 1948, on control by central government, by using counterfactuals as well as comparative evidence. This issue and approach, again, are not inherently political or ideological.[34] Jeff Horn, an American economic historian of France, argues that counterfactuals "can illuminate a critical aspect" and has himself done so to ask the question, "Why didn't France enact laissez-faire policies and make the transition to an industrial society?"[35]

More generally, counterfactual history is a method, not an issue, and certainly not a political issue. Were politics to be the issue, then, ironically, counterfactualism could be reconceptualized in terms of tensions, even rivalries, within the historical profession. Indeed, a new counterfactualism could be offered. For example, "What if the profession (in country A) had been more or less right- or left-wing as far as historical methods are concerned, including the use of counterfactualism?"

Reactions to counterfactualism seem to be based on a confusion between its use heuristically (educationally) on the one hand, and its appeal to those with a particular view of history on the other. Heuristically, counterfactualism is, whether employed in relation to quantitative social science history (Fogel et al.) or qualitatively (as has tended to be the case in most recent versions, and in its popular manifestation), a valuable device to force historians and the public to consider systematically the relative importance of a range of factors in determining a particular historical path. Counterfactualism does so by requiring them to assess how the presence or absence of a particular factor might have altered both the balance of events and the path-dependent interplay of those factors. Interestingly, in this respect, counterfactualism can appeal to those seeking strongly causal models of historical explanation, and across a wide range of approaches to history, in terms of both topics (economic, political, etc.) and techniques (quantitative, narrative, etc.).

On the other hand, counterfactualism is also deployed in opposition to the once highly influential practice of deterministic history. Instead, counterfactualism is employed both in support of a view of history which emphasizes the contingent, underdetermined character of historical change, and to undermine any sense of the inevitability of the actual historical outcome. Counterfactualism, therefore, is centrally linked to contingencies and conjunctures, and all three pose challenges to deterministic approaches. By and large, this undermining of any sense of necessity has tended to appeal largely to historians working on those aspects of history where contingent events and human actions are most intuitively central, such as political and military history. This is the case whether their emphasis is on structured contingency or on a more random contingency. By stressing the contingent, notably unintended, consequences, counterfactualism, however, can have the paradoxical consequence of challenging both determinism and, indeed, in some cases, the significance of human choices.

Alternative futures are much more likely than alternative pasts to take an explicitly political stance, because the former are frequently based on a partisan assessment of the present, while alternative histories focus on a rewriting of the past, whether or not this suits the discussion of the present and would-be future or has a particular political slant. Thus, at the time of the bitter controversy in Britain over the Jewish Naturalisation Act of 1753,[36] critical newspaper writers used a depiction of Britain a century later in order to suggest that this modest piece of legislation would lead to a total transformation of the country into a Jewish state, with compulsory circumcision and other measures. The act was repealed. Benjamin Disraeli, who was to be prominent a century later as conservative chancellor of the exchequer in 1852, 1858–59, and 1866–68, and prime minister in 1868 and 1874–80, was heavily criticized for his Jewish background, in which he indeed took pride, but he had been baptized into the Church of England at age twelve and, as a politician, was a regular Christian worshiper.[37] Ironically, his father, Isaac D'Israeli, had published on counterfactuals, arguing, in "Of a History of Events Which Have Not Happened," that it was necessary to appreciate the role of accident.[38]

At a very different level from the newspapers of 1753, Edward Gibbon, the most prominent Anglophone historian of the eighteenth century, suggested, in a famous aside in his *The History of the Decline and Fall of the Roman Empire* (1776–88), that Moorish victory at the battle of Poitiers around 732 AD might have led to the conquest of Christian Europe and the teaching of Islam in Oxford. The latter was a gibe at the misplaced pomposity of his old university: "A victorious line of march had been prolonged above a thousand miles from the rock of Gibraltar to the banks of the Loire; the repetition of an equal space would have carried the Saracens to the confines of Poland and the Highlands of Scotland: the Rhine is not more impassable than the Nile or the Euphrates.... [T]he Koran would now be taught in the schools of Oxford, and her pulpits might demonstrate to a circumcised people the truth of the revelation of Mohammed."

Gibbon's speculation, which was to be taken up by Arnold Toynbee,[39] reflects the continual role of war in counterfactual speculation, because battles can indeed seem to be turning points. In hindsight, Poitiers could be presented as demonstrating the credentials of the Carolingian dynasty to be the lay head of Christendom (Charlemagne, the grandson of the victor at Poitiers, Charles Martel, indeed was crowned emperor at Rome in 800), as well as the crucial role of France in protecting Christendom, a theme that French writers were to play up. The scholarly analysis is more skeptical and also unsettled. The eighth-century Arab expedition has been presented more recently as a raid, but it has also been argued that the battle was important as the Arab force was substantial, and that its victory could have reinforced the pattern of Christian cooperation with the Arabs which, in turn, would have helped the latter maintain a presence in France.[40] Gibbon's aside was an echo of Voltaire's speculation about the invading Persians under Xerxes defeating the Greeks at Salamis in 480 BC instead of being routed. Barry Strauss, a specialist on the subject, has argued that even Persian victory at Salamis might not have changed the course of history all that much.[41]

To some critics, the military focus of much counterfactualism[42] weakens the case for it, but the merits of the counterfactual approach can be debated without having to discuss military history.[43] Indeed, for his part, Gibbon placed military developments in a context that put them at a remove from the one-battle-settles-all approach. His account invited counterfactuals, because, in looking to the future and asking if the "Barbarian" invasions of Europe could be repeated, Gibbon offered an explanation in which cultural change took precedence over the chance of battle: "Cannon and fortifications now form an impregnable barrier against the Tartar horse; and Europe is secure from any future irruption of Barbarians; since, before they can conquer, they must cease to be barbarous. Their gradual advances in the science of war would always be accompanied, as we may learn from the example of Russia,[44] with a proportionable improvement in the arts of peace and civil policy; and they themselves must deserve a place among the polished nations whom they subdue."[45]

Thus, the possibilities of battle were played out within a predetermined cultural context. Progress in the form of science apparently allowed advanced and settled societies to employ a military technology that multiplied the effectiveness of their soldiery. Adopting the stadial account (history in stages) also seen with some other Enlightenment historians, Gibbon saw this progress as crucial in enabling such societies to restrict military service to specialized forces, and thus to free the rest of society for productive activity and civilized pursuits. Progress therefore secured and benefited from military modernity, an analysis that apparently could be applied in Europe, and then on the global scale, to narrow the impact of any counterfactual historical path.

Yet, far from that analysis replacing the contingencies of counterfactualism with some type of determinism, this development itself involved choice. Indeed, the willingness and ability of other states to adopt Western means and modes of warmaking varied considerably, Japan proving more successful than China.[46] Gibbon, however, also argued that, in what he saw as the unlikely event of civilization collapsing in Europe, "Europe would revive and flourish in the American world, which is already filled with her colonies and institutions."[47] There is a distant echo of this in the discussions of possible German victory in Europe in World War II (a frequent counterfactual) being counteracted by the United States, which is the theme, for example, of a counterfactual argument from Holger Herwig.[48]

More generally, the interaction between the specifics—whether of battle, politics, or inventions, themselves unpredictable—and unpredictable contextual developments is of key interest when considering counterfactual propositions and scenarios. The common theme is a challenge to determinism, and this theme can help explain the political positioning of counterfactualism. Where the dominant determinist account is of the Left, then counterfactualism can appear right-wing, but the converse is also true. Right-wing determinisms for example have been based on notions of national and/or ethnic exceptionalism: X was/is bound to happen because we were/are superior, an approach that calls out for counterfactual speculation of the type, "What if there had been failure?" as such failure would undermine such determinism and exceptionalism.

A useful analogy is offered by geopolitics. Due to the role in the 1930s of Karl Haushofer, Professor of Geopolitics at Munich University, who had close links with the Nazi regime,[49] this subject was associated with the Right and it was subsequently discredited as a result. Yet, there was no necessary relationship between geopolitics and Fascism, and an alternative left-wing geopolitics has been developed more recently.[50]

Whereas the political placing of the counterfactual approach can therefore be queried, a very important aspect of counterfactual studies is their explicit awareness of the role of the scholar as interpreter, which provides a point of contact with postmodernism. A stress on this role draws on the task of the historian in organizing material and asking questions, but takes it a stage further, and indeed frequently a considerable stage further. As such, it is appropriate to add the explicit authorial voice, rather like that of Henry Fielding in his novels *Joseph Andrews* (1742) and *Tom Jones* (1749). By so doing, the role of the scholar as organizer of questions is made clear, and the counterfactualism can be introduced and discussed in a helpful manner.

Yet Fielding's novels also captured the sense of indeterminacy and chance held by contemporaries. The twentieth-century films of these novels, *Tom Jones* (1963) and *Joseph Andrews* (1977), presented them as jolly romps, with the many unexpected twists of the plots being essentially contrivances to move the stories along and to obtain comic effect. There was also, on Fielding's part, however, an attempt to show the folly of the self-serving human search for control. Instead, he emphasized the role of Providence; not as excuse for an inactive contemplation of Divine Grace, but rather as a counterpart to good human activity that itself reflects the divine plan. Parson Adams is presented in *Joseph Andrews* as an exemplary individual, not least when, oblivious to his own safety, he hastens to the aid of the heroine, Fanny Adams, who is resisting rape. This attempted act symbolizes the brutal role of chance. Fanny declares that she had "put her whole trust in Providence," and Adams sees himself as the means of Providential deliverance. Their views are at once humorous and deadly serious: the vehicles of divine judgment might be comic, but it alone could save the innocent from malign fate in the shape of unhappy coincidence and the wretched designs of the sinful. Furthermore, the role of Providence, alongside the explicit interventions of Fielding as author-narrator, demonstrated the need for readers to be cautious in anticipating events, passing judgment, and predicting the plot. Readers were thus instructed in a humility to match that of the benign characters depicted.

Emphasizing the role of the scholar as interpreter can focus attention on a postmodernist dimension to counterfactualism; not that that is the sole philosophy/methodology that is at issue. Indeed, counterfactualism is a common and accepted practice within philosophy. A stress on postmodernism, which is classically linked to radical thinkers, an irony noted by Tristram Hunt (see discussion above), helps counter the charge that those interested in counterfactualism are primarily reactionaries reluctant to accept the process or results of change.

More generally, the idea of history as offering questions, rather than providing "the answer," is underlined by counterfactualism. This approach is particularly valuable given the general tendency, in popular and official history but also in some academic history, to provide "the answer" and to shape the narrative accordingly. This misplaced, if not pernicious, certainty, is challenged, if not unpicked, by the reminder of other possible narratives, of various answers, and of the difficulty of providing a definitive answer, all reminders offered by counterfactualism.

To take a wider perspective, the question "What if?" is very heuristic and should remain in dialogue with "Why?" and "How?" Counterfactuals, moreover, must be included in "Why?" and "How?" explanations if these explanations are to be true to their historical moments. This argument and that in the previous paragraph can be linked to shifts in the history of political thought. The cultivation of counterfactual awareness is in the general spirit of Michael Oakeshott's skeptical revision of political "traditions": from Whiggish determinism to a pragmatic accretion or accumulation of choices made from among contingencies. Oakeshott, professor of political science at the London School of Economics from 1950 to 1969 and an influential, largely conservative thinker in the Anglophone world, resented, in particular, the notion that a political "tradition" was driven, by *a priori* assumptions, to an unalterable destination. Rather, to him, a political "tradition" was the accretion of what people actually had done and thought. Oakeshott adopted a skeptical approach to systematization.[51]

Aside from the challenge that counterfactualism poses to teleological assumptions, as well as to the explanatory complacency buried deep in public culture, it also poses a challenge to scholarly assessments. The counterfactual approach outlined undermines the Whiggishness of national schools of historiography.[52] More specifically, it also queries the attempt—seen, for example, in Linda Colley's influential study *Britons: Forging the Nation 1707–1837* (1992), as well as in many other historical studies—to discern a national mood or identity, however manufactured, and to give this mood or identity explanatory force. This new version of the *zeitgeist* (spirit of the age) approach is contested by counterfactualism, for the latter necessarily places weight on a pluralism of attitudes and possible outcomes, and on the ability of this pluralism to qualify and challenge supposedly hegemonic discourses.[53]

Counterfactual approaches also query schematic accounts of international relations in systemic terms, for example those advanced by many political scientists, and also by historians, such as Paul Schroeder, influenced by such theories.[54] Moreover, a counterfactual approach to domestic politics and outcomes challenges scholars of international relations who tend to treat states as building blocks and, therefore, to underrate the extent, role, and potential of domestic debate over foreign policy.[55] Thus, counterfactualism can perform the valuable intellectual purpose of questioning the re-creation of the concept of determinism in the shape of supposedly dominant ideas and/or systems. As such, counterfactualism makes explicit what any good historian would do anyway.

The tensions that encouraged the use of counterfactualism, as well as criticism of it by E. H. Carr, E. P. Thompson, and others, are therefore still relevant in the different historiographical world of the 2010s. Determinism has been reconceptualized and reapplied, away from the social-economic fundamentals of Marxism and, instead, at the service of a range of approaches. Each, however, can be challenged by employing counterfactual methods. This challenge is valuable, not so much in terms of any attempt to overthrow entire interpretative models and strategies, but rather to encourage a refinement in their use. Counterfactualism, indeed, contributes both to the humane skepticism toward method and to the openness to pluralism in interpretation that ought to be at the heart of historical enquiry. Counterfactualism is a valuable intellectual exercise that identifies those events that served as turning points and those factors that truly shaped the course of events. Used within these confines, it is repeatedly valuable, but counterfactualism, although a useful tool, cannot stand alone as historical analysis. While it is a method of identifying the critical or deciding factor, counterfactualism is not academically helpful as a stand-alone practice, although that can yield interesting and thoughtful stories and reflections.

2

A PERSONAL NOTE ON LIFE AND TIMES

One of the great pleasures of being a "nuts and bolts" historian is that every so often my intellectual betters explain what I am doing. The French playwright Molière phrased it better when, in his comic masterpiece *Le bourgeois gentilhomme* (1670), he gave the ridiculous, fictional Monsieur Jourdain the line, "Il y a plus de quarante ans que je dis de la prose sans que j'en susse rien" (For more than forty years I have been speaking prose without knowing it) (act 2, scene 4). In light of the critique of counterfactualism by Richard Evans,[1] I have discovered that I have been "liberal Whiggish" or "conservative, pessimistic," if not a "young fogey," for I have employed counterfactuals,[2] frequently lecture in the United States on the topic "Could the British have won the American War of Independence?" (not "should"—more interesting, but outside my competence), and have discussed, on radio and in print, the topic of "What if, instead of turning back toward Scotland, the Jacobites had advanced on London from Derby in December 1745?"

I have no particular sympathy for Jacobites, nor for George III when defeated by the Americans, nor would I like the French to have beaten the British in their struggle for dominance in 1688–1815, all of which are counterfactuals addressed in chapter 6. Instead, my interest comes from the material I work on. The history of diplomacy, war, and government is not, as suggested by Evans, "very narrow," or only "about events," and, contrary to the criticism of some, they include "processes, structures, cultures, societies, economies, and so on." Indeed, far from being only about events, diplomatic history in particular is sometimes approached in schematic and structural terms. However, that is an approach that faces problems, for it is difficult to spend a long time reading the documents without being returned to the sense of uncertainty which those who created them faced.[3] For example, speculating on possible outcomes, diplomats did, and still do, counterfactualism all the time. It is indeed part of their job description. Furthermore, it is necessary to probe this uncertainty in order to understand contemporary debates about policy, for example toward China or Iran, and to make evaluations about the competence of ministers, diplomats, and commentators.

When I was writing *Parliament and Foreign Policy in the Eighteenth Century* (2004) and trying to evaluate the role of Parliament and consider the quality of its debates, this process did rather require considering what would have happened had the role of Parliament been less prominent. There were also more specific counterfactuals, such as considering whether the Anglo-Russian Ochakov crisis of 1791 would have been handled differently had Parliament not been in session, as, for example, it was not during the Anglo-French Dutch crisis of 1787. This issue is of recent relevance, as the question of how far, in 1791, opposition in Parliament helped end the plan of the British government and its allies to attack Russia offers an interesting prefigurement to the 2013 crisis over Syria. Moreover, in order to assess speeches in Parliament and other representative assemblies, it is necessary to consider the practicality of the policies that were suggested by speakers. In contrast, part of the problem with the discussion of many texts by specialists in political thought or rhetoric is that they tend to focus on intellectual coherence, rather than practical application. As a reminder of the counterfactual offered by different historical approaches—"What if I tackle, or tackled, it this way?" —it is instructive to approach a period from different perspectives, for example by considering it both chronologically and thematically.

Taking a different tack, given the apparent role of counterfactuals in modern politics, it is appropriate to ask why the past was any different. "Is choice only for the present?" is a question that emerges from the way the past is frequently presented, for example in the Whiggish and teleological confidence of the television narratives of British history. This question, of whether choice is apparently restricted to the present, indeed provides a pertinent way to pose questions for historical research.

Leave aside for the moment the travesty of democracy in Florida in 2000, and the varied possible consequences of a President Gore in office during the terrorist attacks of September 11, 2001, and the subsequent crises in American relations with Afghanistan and Iraq,[4] or of a Republican in office at the time of the Syrian crisis of 2013. To take, instead, Britain in recent decades, the striking coal miners might have failed against Edward Heath, the Conservative prime minister, in 1974, but succeeded against Margaret Thatcher in 1984–85. The disclosure of government documents reveals that the Thatcher government considered a military response when the dockers came out in support of the miners. Moreover, had there been no means of exploiting natural gas or oil in the North Sea, the consequently lower government revenues would have put great pressure on Thatcherite public finances, making it harder to cut taxes, as she did, and thus encourage the expansion of the private sector. It is instructive to contrast Britain with the majority of European states, which lacked this resource: "What if Britain in the 1980s had had only the economic and fiscal opportunities of France?" How far, in short, was policy (which was very different in the cases of Thatcher and François Mitterrand, the President of France from 1981 to 1995) responsible for differences, and how far resources?

Alternatively, the earlier exploitation of the North Sea oil might have weakened the position of the British coal industry (as well as removed the need to invest in nuclear power) and also possibly saved the reputation of the Labour government of Harold Wilson by permitting it to avoid the devaluation of sterling in 1967, or even enabled Heath to see off the miners' strikes. Had Heath done so, he would probably not have lost office in 1974 or been replaced by Thatcher as party leader in 1975. She offered a more radical set of attitudes and policies than he did. The ability of the Thatcher government, in early 1985, to state that, thanks to healthy electricity supplies, including from France, there would be no power cuts, helped speed the demise of the miners' strike.

Again, by calling a general election in late 1978, as he was strongly pressed to do, James Callaghan, Wilson's successor as the Labour Prime Minister, might have thwarted Thatcher, not least by preempting the strikes of the "winter of discontent" (1978–79) which created a strong and deserved impression of governmental failure. This is a counterfactual that has frequently been offered, and one that challenges the right-wing narrative about the necessity of Thatcher. A similar counterfactual linked to electoral timing arises from Gordon Brown's decision not to hold a general election in 2007 soon after he became Prime Minister by succeeding Tony Blair as party leader. He could well have won then, instead of losing in 2010.

Moreover, by not invading the Falklands in 1982, the course followed by previous *juntas,* the Argentinian military might have denied the then-unpopular Thatcher the opportunity to regain the domestic political initiative through victory. This is a counterfactual used to challenge the idea of Thatcher as successful and Thatcherite domestic policies as appropriate, but, conversely, one also employed to emphasize her achievement in defeating the Argentinians. Thatcher might also have been killed by the IRA (Irish Republican Army), either during the Conservative Party conference at Brighton in 1984 when a bomb exploded in the hotel in which she was staying,[5] or elsewhere.

By failing to remove Thatcher in 1990 (and she nearly won the necessary margin on the first ballot of the party's MPs), the Conservatives might have helped Labour to victory in the election two years later as Thatcher was more unpopular than her successor, John Major, at least until after the election, the results of which were close. As a result, Labour would have been left to bear the burden of the recesssion of the 1990s and the Maastricht debate on European convergence, helping a reunited Conservative Party to return to power in 1997, if not earlier.[6] This is a counterfactual that British politicians have discussed with me.

By refusing to support the United States in its war with Iraq in 2003, Blair would have faced a very different international situation, which might have affected the domestic political debate about Britain's relations within Europe. In turn, in March 2008, President George W. Bush defended that war by posing the instructive counterfactual of what would have happened had Saddam Hussein remained in power. A confusion of outcomes was suggested by Bush's claim that the invasion had led to Al-Qaeda's being driven from Iraq, when in fact it was only established there during the post-invasion chaos. That very confusion throws some light on his motivation and ability.

The sum of these "What ifs?" is that these processes are fragile and largely involve luck and circumstances. The counterfactuals also point out how much events hang on contingencies. For example, the militancy of the petrol-supply dispute in Britain in 2000, which momentarily posed the most serious public order crisis the Blair government faced, owed much to the extent to which farmers had been badly and recently affected by events, notably agricultural diseases. A number of the leaders of the blockades of the petrol depots were hauliers with farms, who seemed doubly hit.

The British electoral system could also have been changed, as the parties of the center—Liberals, Social Democrats (SDP), and, later, Liberal Democrats—demanded, producing the "realignment of British politics" pressed for in the SDP's founding Limehouse Declaration in 1981. Labour's failure in the Euro-elections in 1999, the first national election in Britain under a system of proportional representation, led the Labour government, however, to abandon its commitment to holding a referendum on proportional representation (PR) before the next general election. There was a limit therefore to Blair's drive for a "New Britain." Had such a system been introduced then, or earlier, as the Liberals and Liberal Democrats pressed for as the price of their political support, it is likely that all British governments thereafter would have been coalitions (rather than, fortuitously, that formed in 2010). It is probable, therefore, that centrist tendencies and politicians would have been dominant. Such a dominance would have dramatically changed the history of both the individual political parties and the country itself.

The wider impact of such a "high political" change is less clear, and the experience of Scotland and Wales, once their separate electoral systems had been established after the referenda following Labour's victory in 1997, is not necessarily indicative of what would have been the British situation. There might have been, as is normal with systems of PR, a fragmentation of political parties, as well as an entry into mainstream politics of hitherto marginal groups that would have given a particular voice to political extremists, such as the British National Party, and perhaps to different ethnic groups. The impact of PR, or, for that matter, the existing electoral system, on social and economic developments is less clear. Aside from PR, the role of contingency in British politics was made abundantly clear in 2013–14 by speculations about the likely consequences of the Scottish vote on independence in September 2014 and about a possible electoral breakthrough for the UK Independence Party (UKIP), which did very well in the elections to the European Parliament in May 2014.

Such counterfactuals in my lifetime were one part of the active consideration of possibilities and are not merely idle retrospective speculation. At any one moment, various developments seemed possible to people in the past, and the sole guarantee was that what was going to happen was not known. Contingency, and therefore counterfactualism, can also be extended to aspects of history that are not usually tackled through the "What if?" approach. It is possible to consider different developments in British public culture, for example those arising from policies toward media regulation. In an instance of a nostalgic "What if?" but also a reflective one, the prominent left-wing Labour politician Tony Benn argued that the possibility of Socialism in Britain was greatly lessened by the introduction, as a result of the Television Act of 1954, of commercial television the following year, with the advertising it carried. In the case of the environment and transport, the consequences of more stringent restrictions on building on greenfield sites, and of heavier fuel prices, invite counterfactual consideration which is not idle, as such options play a major role in economic modeling and social planning.

These options also affect the nature of the city of Exeter, where I live. Exonians frequently consider what their city would have been like had the *Luftwaffe* not gone destructively and murderously town planning in 1942: "What would Exeter have been like but for the Blitz?" is a classic instance of nostalgic counterfactualism. At the same time, much of the more reflective discussion, in Exeter and elsewhere, includes a consideration of how far the character of postwar town planning was responsible for part of the subsequent urban malaise, and whether the situation would have been improved had there been no such planning. Thus, the counterfactual approach can be more hard-edged than a simple concern with the bombing might suggest.

The pedagogical value of counterfactual approaches, handled carefully, was driven home to me when, at the age of fourteen, we role-played the Congress of Vienna (1814–15) at school. The coursework entailed keeping a congress diary, recording the doings of particular delegations as well as the proceedings of negotiating sessions, and also writing an essay explaining why our peace terms were different from those actually negotiated. I was given the nonvoting role of Charles Maurice de Talleyrand, French foreign minister and the chief French delegate, on the basis that I was the sole pupil who knew anything about the subject. As at Vienna in 1814–15, it proved possible, in practice, for the French to exploit divisions between the victorious Allies, although there were not the conflicts between the Allies that broke out in other simulations of the congress held at the same school.[7] Nevertheless, far from these conflicts proving the failure of the simulation method, they underlined tensions that were very much felt by participants in the congress, particularly Anglo-Austrian concern about Russian-backed Prussian territorial demands on Saxony, concern that caused a marked deterioration in relations among the powers in the winter of 1814–15. For our replay, the principal French task was that of ensuring that Prussian territorial claims and gains were as distant as possible from France's German frontier: for example Anhalt and Mecklenburg, rather than the Rhineland acquired at the actual congress.

We went on at school to replay the negotiation of the Paris Peace Conference/Treaty of Versailles (1919), but less successfully. The contrast is instructive for the pedagogic value and drawbacks of counterfactualism. For Vienna, we essentially followed the ground rules of negotiation, not least by trying, in part through observing norms of conduct, to derive maximum mutual advantage while pursuing national goals, and by essentially observing the bounds of practicality. But, at Versailles, the "Italian" delegation ignored such norms in favor of trickery. Using lines of longitude to define colonial boundaries in Africa, and relying on other delegates' not checking the longitudes, the delegation drew that of Libya to include the British-run Suez Canal and therefore all of Egypt, which was a counterfactual too far, one that defeated its purpose by being implausible. At school, this result, once revealed, led to the collapse of the Peace Conference. The responsibility, alas, was all mine.

In geography at school there was also replaying, both of the course of Anglo-Saxon settlement in England in the fifth to ninth centuries and also, at greater length, of the spread of the railway across the American

West. Each play was linked to the modeling of change in order to explain it, notably in terms of the relationships between physical and economic features. Each involved a process of choosing between options and ascertaining the likely consequences. The spread of the railway across the West is itself the subject of a board game.

Going back, and without suggesting any equivalent with their use in teaching, thinking about counterfactuals leads me to realize that they were also part of my leisure. I wrote the lengthy history of an imaginary country, a classic opportunity for counterfactualism (and one complicated by including the names of real historical figures). Board games were also a longstanding enjoyment, and a key introduction to counterfactualism. In particular, I owned two Avalon Hill war games: 1914 and Stalingrad. These board games invited one to replan and refight, while at the same time trying to simulate key aspects of both episodes, which is most difficult in the case of the role of surprise. War games can be seen as callous, given that large numbers of troops die with the throw of a die, but they also provide opportunities for learning through consideration of the range of plausible options. This was especially the case with the more complex game, 1914 (produced in 1968), as the counterfactuals had to be explained in the game's manual. A role of the die could not suffice. The introduction to the manual for the Standard Game announced, "Through Avalon Hill's extensive research and simplified adaptation of modern 'wargame' techniques (as practiced by present general staffs and such 'think tanks' as the RAND Corporation) you can put yourself in a situation remarkably similar to the one in August 1914. You can change history."

The Advanced Game offered greater complexity in its attempt to recapture more of the elements of the original campaign. The options included rules designed to offer such features as simultaneous movement, the information gap, and the impact for operations on the western front of developments on the eastern front. Moreover, as the manual for this section noted, "numerous minor military and political factors could have altered the outcome of the 1914 campaign. In order to incorporate these into the game as simply as possible we have included ten Game Variation Cards for each side." These variation cards included factors such as rebellion in French North Africa, which would have lessened opportunities to send reinforcements to mainland France. Rebellions among the Muslim colonial subjects of its opponents were one of the reasons why Germany sought the aid of the Ottoman sultan, who, indeed, proclaimed a *jihad* (holy war).

War-gaming after the event can be compared instructively to war games held before a conflict. The gaming of alternative scenarios to aid military planning has played a major role since the rise of general staffs and formal military education in the late nineteenth century. An elaborate war game held by the British in 1905 considered a German attack on France via Belgium and how far a BEF (British expeditionary force) would help thwart the Germans. The conclusion, that a BEF would stop German victory, helped determine the start of Anglo-French staff-talks.[8]

Visiting the Strategy and Policy Department of the American Naval War College in Newport, Rhode Island, on many occasions, I have been struck by how much the instructors employed counterfactualism in their teaching and in the exercises given to the students. As John Maurer, the chair of the department from 2005 to 2013, put it, this was not a case of impossibles, of the type "What if Pericles [ca. 495–429 BC] had had atomic weaponry?"—interesting as it might be to assess their possible consequences for the Peloponnesian War between Athens and Sparta (431–404 BC)—but of exercises based on options available in the past. Maurer argued that these exercises were of great value educationally, as well as of considerable interest to the students.[9] They were forced to think strategically, to consider alternative courses of action, approaches, or options, and to consider all factors and dynamics in order to craft the strategy and resultant military operations most likely to establish the conditions whereby the policy objective could be achieved. Through this process of critical analysis, the idea was then to choose the most achievable or rational course of action.

Counterfactual thinking permits the imagining of alternate realities or possibilities as a learning tool for strategic thinking. This enables the avoidance of the pitfalls of overly restrictive dogma or doctrine that all too often result in inappropriate and unsustainable strategies. Military thinking is full of failed strategies and operations based on limited and unimaginative thinking. Counterfactuals aid in creating patterns of analytical thinking that can hopefully overcome limited, doctrinaire thinking.

At Vanderbilt, Peter Lorge uses simulations in a co-taught course in which the decision making is role-played by student teams which receive secret information that includes their strategic preferences: "So, for example, we do China's entry into the Korean War [in 1950], and the teams are China, America, North Korea and Russia. The rules of the game are engineered to reproduce what happened in history. If the students play optimally, then they should move immediately to a negotiated settlement at the 38th parallel. Usually they play sub-optimally, fight, expend a lot of resources and then end up at the 38th parallel. On a few occasions we get nuclear war."[10]

Learning through considering alternatives and options is more generally true of military history. Consider the three attacks on Quebec between 1759 and 1776. Comparisons with the failure of the French in 1760 and of the Americans in 1775–76 throw light on British success in 1759, and vice versa (see chapter 7). At the start of the 1748 campaigning season, Giovanni Zamboni, a diplomat in London, raised the issue of how British policy might change if victories were not won that year.[11] More generally, comparative history involves counterfactualism as an integral part of the drawing of comparisons.

My own research repeatedly underlines the extent of choice in foreign policy and the degree to which structural factors affected, but did not determine, these choices, and also did not determine resource availability and international responses. This perspective is linked to the issue of how far success and failure are inherent in a particular situation. Arguing that different outcomes were in fact possible, and adopting the counterfactual approach, it is reasonable to consider whether Louis XIV of France (r. 1643–1715) could have thwarted William III of Orange's plans to invade England in 1688, or whether greater effort could have sustained and strengthened the promising French positions in India and North America in the early 1750s. For geographical, cultural, and political reasons, France was different from Britain as an economy, a society, and a state, but this difference did not predetermine consequences in the military or diplomatic spheres (see chapter 6).

The archival dimension is pertinent here. For example, the personalization of policy by contemporary commentators offered a different impression from that created by the discussion, by both some contemporaries and subsequent scholars, of policy in terms of the apparent predictabilities of mechanistic concepts of an international system, most prominently that of the balance of power. In practice, the close relationship in the seventeenth and eighteenth centuries between foreign policy and the volatile world of court politics encouraged a perception of flux in international relations among most contemporary commentators. This was a perception imbued with, indeed expressed through, counterfactual options and speculations, one that is totally ignored by the ordered presentation of policy of the period in much academic writing. This scholarship subordinates contingency and personality to the predictabilities of national interests and the dominant role of the international system and international norms.[12] However, this approach did not match the experience of contemporaries. As an instance of the views of a well-informed contemporary, John, Viscount Perceval, a British politician with links to the government, observed in 1726,

> France and the Emperor[13] have no ground of quarrel neither has Spain any claim on France, only a resentment for sending home the Lady,[14] which surely ought not to be an occasion to raise Mars[15] out of his sleep, but there is a spirit of Don Quixotism remaining there which joined with Italian revenge[16] provokes them to insist that Monsr le Duc[17] be removed from the management of affairs, if Frejus[18] have credit enough it may be brought about, and that may produce a new scene. France may grow cool in her alliance with us having no farther use of it, and we together with Prussia be left to renew our friendship with the Emperor and Spain as well as we can. If the Dutch acceed to our alliance[19] as is everyday expected,[20] it will be of service, poor and unprepared as they are, and then we may talk big in the ensuing Parliament against the Ostend trade,[21] but otherwise I cannot think we shall take violent resolutions in that affair, especially if it be that there is so great spirit raised against this French treaty, that it will require all the ministry's attention to allay it without permitting them to look to things abroad. But I have been so used to see these violent gusts end in a calm.[22]

The issue of how best to understand and conceptualize this very volatile international world was eased for Perceval by a resort to counterfactualism, which, apart from anything else, reflected (and reflects) the weakness of the attempt to understand, explain, and guide by means of the concept of the balance of power, which is a systemic approach. There is a clear contrast between Perceval's account, which is multi-faceted and personality-driven, and systemic analysis based on mechanistic concepts approached in a unilinear fashion.

More generally, in teaching, research, and writing, there is a degree of at least implicit counterfactualism all of the time. Crucially, for the point of this book, this degree of counterfactualism is inherent to the structure as well as the details of the subject. To focus on an aspect of a topic, for example the causes of World War I, is to pose a silent counterfactual to the range of other aspects that are on offer: "If I/we consider the causes this way, will it work?"[23] This was abundantly clear in 2014 when the causes of the war were extensively debated in Britain. To take a specific, if a scholar writes, "Churchill's notorious 'Gestapo' radio broadcast attacking the Labour Party contributed to his defeat by Labour in the 1945 British general election," then the scholar is implying that had he not made it, or had he said something different, his defeat by Clement Attlee would have been less severe. However much counterfactual approaches might seek to make a distinctive impression for commercial or other reasons, they do not contrast with this, because they simply entail stating this proposition in a more formal way—"What if Churchill had not made his 'Gestapo' broadcast?"—and then telling a story about the possible consequences.[24]

As most historians employ implicit counterfactuals readily and without problems, it is inappropriate to be overly critical of the formal kind, even though they can often become somewhat repetitive and silly, as well as overdetermined in the sense that an initial event is varied but then alleged consequences are somewhat rigidly drawn. Looked at differently, however unhelpful or harmless "What if?" books may be, they can serve to draw attention to assumptions that are often made without explicit thought. As Ian Kershaw, like Evans a noted historian of Nazi Germany, pointed out, "Historians implicitly operate with short-range counterfactuals in terms of alternatives to immediate important occurrences or developments. Otherwise, they are unable fully to ascertain the significance of what actually did take place."[25]

Implicit counterfactuals are even more clearly involved in choosing and organizing material for publication. The very scope and content of what we read as history is shaped by commercial and readership considerations. A counterfactual approach can suggest to us how different published history might easily be. This element of choice and organization is very much the case with works covering large portions of the past, as it is necessary to determine what to include and to decide how best to do so. Drawing on personal experience, it is instructive to note the compromises involved, as they highlight the "What ifs?" centered on other choices. For example, when editing *The Seventy Great Battles of All Time* (2005), my first proposal to the publisher sought to avoid the usual Eurocentric approach and attempted to give due weight to the different parts of the world. It included, for example, the battles of Nehavend, Atlakh/Talas River, Ain Jalut, Nicopolis, Varna, Tunu, Chaldiran, Alcazarquivir, Tondibi, Jao Modo, Gulnabad, Karnal, Cesmé, Nezib, Nanjing, and Gundet (there should be a reader prize for those who can locate and date each one). All of these, however, were discarded, as the publisher understandably pressed the case for more well-known, usually European, battles on commercial grounds, although the availability of information on some of the extra-European battles was also a factor.

It is instructive to contrast the choice in this volume with that in other similar works, for example recent ones by Williamson Murray and Richard Overy, and to consider the impression created by the choice made. So also with the different editions of books for particular national markets. Thus, the American edition of Overy's *The Bombing War: Europe 1939–1945* (2013) made significant cuts, which led to a greater focus on the Anglo-American Combined Bomber Offensive against Germany than in the original British edition, which devoted considerable space to the situation on the eastern front.[26]

The same process of publisher choice clearly affects other projects, and this very much opens up the "What if?" question focused on the possibilities of a different coverage. Such a scope for choice is rarely explicitly acknowledged in projects, but it can be seen with some works.

These acknowledgments should remind readers of the more general process at play. Thus, the preface to Charles Paullin's *Atlas of the Historical Geography of the United States* (1932), which is still the best book on the subject, commendably drew attention, detailed attention, to the percentage of space devoted to particular categories of topic, and was also explicit about the issues confronted. For example: "On Plates 61–67A space was economized by marking on the same maps both colonial and state boundaries and the locations of towns and cities. . . . Perhaps somewhat more graphic effect might have been achieved had it been practicable to separate the two elements—political units and cities—and to employ a greater range and variety of symbols to distinguish the towns and cities according to size."[27]

The range of possible depictions can also be illustrated by comparing, for example, earlier and later editions of the same work, as with *Pützger's Historischer Schul-Atlas,* the leading German school atlas for over a century, or the *Times Atlas of World History,* which is now in its seventh edition,[28] albeit now titled *The Times Complete History of the World.* The latter is different in many respects from the first edition, not least with its greater coverage of Africa and Korea. An active process of choice—"What if we map this?" and "What if we map it this way?"—has taken place. These choices reflect issues of opportunity, market, and intellectual cohesion, each of which can prove the basis for counterfactuals in such projects. However, in taking such an approach, what are not seen are ideas for maps that, in the end, are discarded, and therefore the "What if?" of likely audience response to new images is not fully probed.[29]

To return to the personal example, in writing the text and drafting the maps for the *Cambridge Illustrated Atlas of Warfare II: Renaissance to Revolution 1492–1792* (1996), I produced a draft map of India in the eighteenth century that was designed to show the peripheral nature of the European impact in the first six decades of that century. The standard north-south map of India, instead, places a premium on European penetration, making the relationship between India and the surrounding seas apparently central: India appears primarily as a peninsula, and eyelines focus on Delhi from European coastal positions, such as Bombay, Calcutta, Goa, Madras, and Pondicherry. In employing these names, we leave aside the "What if we use the current Indian names, such as Mumbai, instead of Bombay? How far will the readers understand them and/or prefer them?" The customary maps also indicate only European victories, particularly those of the forces of the British East India Company under Robert Clive at the battles of Arcot (1750) and Plassey (1757). Moreover, these maps organize the space and time of the map in terms of British annexations with different colors, for example, for British acquisitions under Clive, Hastings, Cornwallis, and Wellesley.[30]

In contrast, the major theme of my draft map was the contested succession to the Mughal Empire by a number of expansionist powers. Britain and France, or, rather, their East India Companies, were two; but there was also the Maratha Confederation, the Nizam of Hyderabad, the Nawabs of Bengal and the Carnatic, and the Sultan of Mysore. To show this, as well as the impact of successful invasions of northern India by Nadir Shah of Persia in 1739 and by the Afghans in the late 1750s, culminating, near Delhi, in the third battle of Panipat in 1761, I designed a perspective in which India opened up from the Khyber Pass, with a central alignment thence via Delhi. What if India is presented thus? Well, the coastlines appeared more peripheral, an impression that can be accentuated depending on the projection and perspective employed. To compound the impact, I wanted to include not only battles that did not involve the British, such as the third battle of Panipat, the largest battle fought in India that century, as well as Nadir Shah's nearby victory over the Mughals at Karnal in 1739; but also British defeats, for example at the hands of the Marathas in 1779 (Wadgaon), and Mysore (Perumbakam) in 1780 and 1782 (Coleroon River), as well as the unsuccessful British advance on Mysore in 1791. Adopting a very different cartographic language, allocating space on the basis of equal-population mapping rather than the conventional equal-area mapping, would have reinforced the point being made by the orientation of the map, and notably with the focus on northern India. Marketing considerations militated, or, rather, were held to militate, against these maps, as with those focusing on the view from Scotland that I proposed for my *Culloden and the '45* (1990). Yet, this issue poses a "What if?" that is difficult to address, because counterfactuals linked to the method of explication assume an understanding of likely audience response that, in fact, is lacking.

A focus on explanation reminds us of the significance of audience, and this should be a key element in the discussion of academic methods; although, equally, it should not be the sole element. Speculative history has the appeal not only of being enjoyable to many readers, but also of sharpening the critical-thinking skills of students and others, about choices and options. Crucially, the existence of both choices and options is underlined.

At the same time, the very discussion of possible teaching methods, both in the profession and among the public, underlines options, and thus creates counterfactuals, focused on the likely consequences. "What would be the result if history were taught in a certain fashion?" was very much the issue in controversy over the draft National History Standards in the United States in 1994,[31] and also in discussion about the content of history education in Britain. The latter has become more contentious since the 1990s, with complaints from both sides of the political spectrum. As an instance, what would be the consequences if history were taught in Britain as suggested in the following letter published in the *Guardian* in 2008? "It's a shame that some of the main reasons for the invisibility of white working-class culture are ignored," the correspondents wrote. "First and foremost is the education system. Take history lessons. Very little is focused on the stories of ordinary people. A lot of time is spent on the Tudors and Stuarts, very little on the Levellers, Diggers or any mass movements of working people. Little is taught about the success of the trade unions in the industrial revolution and the great gains they made for future generations."[32]

This question is an appropriate conclusion to this chapter—not because I agree with this letter, which indeed mistakes politicized mass movements (and not always even "mass" movements) for the history of "ordinary people" (in practice, the overlap was limited and the aspirations of the population were as much expressed in conservative loyalties, or religious activism, as in radicalism; in particular, the Diggers of 1649 were highly atypical). More significant is the manner in which the letter reminds readers of the variety of ways of engaging with the past, as indeed did the controversy in England in 2008 about engaging more at the school level with the national story, an issue that was to recur in 2013 as the revised National Curriculum was debated. In 2013, aside from major differences over method, the respective weight to be given to British, European, and non-European history was debated.[33] To treat counterfactualism, as is sometimes done, as an aberration from a clearly established and authoritative historical tradition (for both research and teaching) is inaccurate for it takes the latter at its own estimation. This approach is mistaken whatever the politics of the situation and irrespective of the approved historical method.

3

TYPES OF HISTORY

In his history of Rome, Livy (Titus Livius, ca. 59 BC–17 AD) offered what has become the classic instance of counterfactualism in ancient literature. In book 9, sections 17–19, he considered what would have happened had Alexander the Great of Macedon (r. 336–323 BC), the greatest conqueror then known, lived longer, instead of dying young in Babylon, and had used this opportunity, having vanquished the Persian empire to the east, to turn west and invade Italy. In doing so, Livy was departing from the norm in ancient literature in order to respond to Greek claims that Alexander would have succeeded against the Romans. Livy was therefore challenging the counterfactualism (Alexander could have conquered Rome) of others. Clearly uneasy, Livy felt it necessary, at the outset, to explain why he had introduced "ornamental digressions" that provided "agreeable bypaths for the reader."[1] Livy felt able to reassure his Roman readers that the might of Rome would have proved invincible. He commented on the quality of the Roman generalship of the age, and argued that Alexander had become degenerate as a result of his absorption of Persian culture. This argument, directed against the Hellenistic rivals of Rome in Livy's lifetime, such as Cleopatra's Egypt, was also a warning to Rome about the dangers of empire, a theme that was to be taken up in the late eighteenth century by the British historian Edward Gibbon. Advancing a structural interpretation, Livy also contrasted the achievements of one man, Alexander, with those of the Romans, a people in its four hundredth year of warfare. He argued, moreover, that Roman numbers, weaponry, and formations were superior, and that Rome was resilient and, in addition, as a sign of respective strengths, had subsequently defeated the Macedonians at Cynoscephalae (197 BC) and Pydna (168 BC).[2] The Romans had gone on to conquer Macedon and Greece. In this section, Livy anticipated part of the modern discussion of counterfactualism. He also captured the tension between individual circumstances, specifically Alexander's ability, and those that were more "structural," in this case the shape of Rome's military culture.

Earlier, the famous Greek historian Herodotus (ca. 485–425 BC) depicted the debate among the Athenian generals about whether to fight the Persian invaders in 490 BC. Herodotus had Miltiades the Younger, who masterminded the Greek victory, press Callimachus, the Polemarch, who, in the event, had the casting vote, by outlining what was at stake: "If we forbear to fight, it is likely that some great schism will rend and shake the courage of our people till they make friends of the Medes [Persians]; but if we join battle before some at Athens be infected by corruption, then let heaven but deal fairly with us, and we may well win in this fight."[3]

This was not really a counterfactual, but instead a reminder, within the narrative, of what was at stake. A clearer instance was the discussion of the second Persian invasion, that under Xerxes, the emperor, in person, in 480 BC. The Athenians had the option of making peace with the Persians, as some Greek states did, but chose not to, and Herodotus gives them credit by pointing out what would have happened if they had made the easier choice. He notes, however, that his praise would displease many, as he was writing in about 430 BC, at the height of the unpopularity of the Athenian empire over the Aegean:

> The professed intent of the king's march was to attack Athens, but in truth all Hellas [Greece] was his aim. This the Greeks had long since learnt, but not all of them regarded the matter alike. Those of them that had paid tribute of earth and water to the Persian were of good courage, thinking that the foreigner would do them no harm; but they who had refused tribute were sore afraid, since there were not in Hellas ships enough to do battle with their invader, and the great part of them had no stomach for grappling with the war, but were making haste to side with the Persian.

Here I am constrained perforce to declare an opinion which will be displeasing to most; but I will not refrain from uttering what seems to me to be true. Had the Athenians been panic-struck by the threatened peril and left their own country, or had they not indeed left it but remained and surrendered themselves to Xerxes, none would have essayed to withstand the king by sea. If, then, no man had withstood him by sea, I will show what would have happened by land: though the Peloponnesians had built not one but many walls across the Isthmus [of Corinth] for their armour, yet the Lacedaemonians [Spartans] would have been deserted by their allies (these having no choice or free will in the matter, but seeing their cities taken one by one by the foreign fleet), till at last they would have stood alone; and so standing they would have fought a great fight and nobly perished. Such would have been their fate; or it may be that, when they saw the rest of Hellas would have been subdued by the Persians. For I cannot perceive what advantage could accrue from the walls built across the isthmus, while the king was master of the sea. But as it is, to say that the Athenians were the saviours of Hellas is to hit the truth. For which part soever they took, that way the balance was like to incline; and by choosing that Hellas should remain free they and none others roused all the rest of the Greeks who had not gone over to the Persians, and did under heaven beat the king off. Nor were they moved to desert Hellas by the threatening oracles that came from Delphi and sorely dismayed them, but they stood firm and were bold to abide the invader of their country.[4]

Counterfactualism, however, was uncommon in classical historiography. This may well have reflected a sense that historians focus on what did happen and did not see their job as including commentary on things that did not happen. There was also on the part of the Romans a tendency to think in the teleological fashion, not least as the republic and, then, empire expanded. More specifically, it may be the case that the absence of reliable and prompt news at the time encouraged a pattern of waiting for news, a pattern that discouraged thinking about alternatives.

The nature of historical fact may well have been relevant. The uncertainty of facts possibly affected the turn to counterfactuals. Ancient historians made things up to add to their narratives—to add interest or to add information that their sources were lacking. Such "inventions" were not thought wrong at all, but the contemporary audience readily accepted them, provided they were within the conventions of being plausible. Hence many speeches by generals were made up, with the content based on what a general would or should have said. Some items were attributed to more than one person, either due to uncertainty or because they could have reasonably been applied to both.

There are also issues for modern scholars, notably the role of myth in early history. The period of the kings in early Roman history was regarded as fact during the Roman period, but it was largely myth, perhaps built on a few true elements. This creates problems for modern counterfactuals, for example, "If the early Roman kings had been better, the republic may not have been created." This issue would imply that counterfactuals are best considered only in certain circumstances.[5]

THE NATIONAL DIMENSION

A focus on variations in the appeal of counterfactualism across cultures and countries serves to emphasize how much of the academic and popular discussion of counterfactualism is confined to its recent and current use in Britain and the United States (on which see chapter 1), as well as in other Anglophone countries. In Australia, for example, G. V. Portus published a set of six counterfactual essays in the 1940s, while Geoffrey Blainey, one of Australia's most prominent historians, mounted a counterfactual argument about northern Queensland secession in *A Land Half Won* (1989), and elsewhere spoke on what would have happened if Australia had been French. There are also several counterfactual pieces in Craig Wilcox and Jenny Aldridge's *The Great War: Gains and Losses* (1995). And Geoffrey Bolton, another leading Australian historian, wrote on what would have happened if Herbert Evatt's Australian Labor Party had won the 1954 election and there had not been a Menzies era: Robert Menzies was prime minister from 1939 to 1941 and 1949 to 1966. *What If?* (2006), edited by Stuart Macintyre and Sean Scalmer, addresses counterfactualism in Australian history.

In New Zealand, a 2005 conference led to the publication of *New Zealand as It Might Have Been*. Presented as "an exercise in disciplined creativity,"[6] this collection ranged widely to include recent politics as well as origins (What if the Maori had not been made British subjects in 1840?), war (What if Japan had invaded New Zealand in 1942?), infrastructure (What if Robert Muldoon's "think big" energy projects had never been constructed?), and sport (What if the New Zealand All Blacks had not won the final rugby test against the South African Sprinboks in 1981?). This approach was presented "as a way both of identifying alternative possibilities and of offering a different means of understanding what actually did happen at pivotal moments in New Zealand's national experience."

The extent to which the national experience of individual states, and also the broader international experience, is shaped by specific events invites counterfactual discussion. Indeed, the national experience of particular states is frequently framed in terms of such alternatives. As a result, counterfactualism, explicitly or implicitly, plays a role, notably in the Anglophone world, in revisionist approaches to national history. Moreover, the use of counterfactualism is a charge leveled against revisionists. This is the case, for example, in Ireland, where it has been one of the many made against the revisionist school of Irish history, particularly Roy Foster. There are important counterfactual explorations of early twentieth-century Irish history as part of the bitter debates over the subject.[7]

Far less attention has been devoted to counterfactualism in non-Anglophone countries in the present day, or indeed in different historiographical traditions. This contrast raises the question as to whether counterfactual arguments are a normal part of how human minds work, or whether counterfactualism can only be a product of a free society characterized by liberalism and, in particular, a stress on individualism and free will; as opposed to societies where the stress is on fatalism, especially in the shape of providentialism. The element of choice can still play a role in the latter as the bad human conduct that leads to divine intervention can be discussed in these terms. If the liberal/illiberal distinction is adopted, then counterfactualism, in many respects, equates with a belief in human agency as opposed to structure. This agency extends to religious interpretations of free will. As Neil York, a Mormon historian, put it to me in 2008, God might choose a course for a person but that individual has the choice to ignore this course, which is a widespread proposition. Religious people can believe in counterfactualism even if the context is different from secular interpretations. More generally, to ask "Why?" implies a counterfactual if the answer involves human agency and choice. Counterfactualism is thus most conducive only to certain types of secular and religious thought. The possibility of different outcomes indeed can be regarded as blasphemous, as well as unwelcome, and this can be the case in both religious and secular interpretations.

Modern Pagan traditions do not use counterfactuals and nor, in their essentials, do Christian histories, as opposed to histories about Christianity. There is an awareness that had Constantine, the first Roman emperor to promote Christianity, lost the battle of the Milvian Bridge (312), or had the emperor Julian "the Apostate" not marched so far into Persian territory in 363, being defeated there and ending the chance of reversing Christianity in the Roman Empire, Christianity would probably not have become the dominant European religion. In practice, Constantine defeated Maxentius, believing that his victory was the work of the Christian God, while Shapur beat Julian. However, this issue is not generally explored by religious writers.[8]

Any reimagination of the origins of Islam would have been regarded as highly blasphemous in Muslim societies and would have rendered the author liable to death. Counterfactualism does not play a significant role in Muslim historiography, although Ibn Khaldun (1332–1406), the author of a history of the Arabs and of an introduction to history, despite coming from a supposedly fatalist culture, indulged freely. Shiism, moreover, is postulated on counterfactuals: notably, the question of what would have happened if Ali (d. 661), who is held by Shias to have been the true successor of his cousin and father-in-law, Muhammad, had succeeded the latter as second Caliph, and if martyrs had survived.

There is also a long-established Arab historical counterfactual relating to the devastating Mongol storming of Baghdad in 1258, a storming referred to by Saddam Hussein in 2003 when he sought, unsuccessfully, to rally support against the American-led coalition that invaded Iraq. The debate centers on whether Muslim civilization would have remained stronger, and the (Persian) Gulf a key area of trade, but for this invasion, with all sorts of consequences in terms of the balance between Islam and the West. Another Arab counterfactual focuses on the question of what if there had been no Israel or no Western support for Israel, both linked to the question of what if there had been no Holocaust.

Counterfactuals played a role in Ottoman (Turkish) historiography, as in the comment in Ibrahin Pecevi's *History* after his description of the Ottoman campaign in Hungary in 1596, which resulted in the conquest of Eger and the (completely unexpected) victory over the Habsburgs at Mezö-Kerésstés. He claimed that if the sultan (Mehmed III, r. 1595–1603) had remained with the army for the following campaigning season, it would have conquered Hungary and gone on to conquer Vienna. In the event, the Ottomans found it difficult to sustain their position during the winter, and Ottoman political problems corroded army discipline. Pecevi's comment clearly reflects a belief in the totemic powers of the sultan, whose presence on the battlefield was supposed to ensure victory. This comment may not have been full-fledged counterfactual history, but it indicates a sense of unpredictable developments. Whether Vienna would have fallen anyway is unclear, not least due to the serious logistical strains of operating from distant Ottoman bases.[9] In 1597, there was no battle of note when the Ottomans advanced anew, while the Austrians regained Gÿor; and renewed Ottoman advances in 1598 and 1599 led to sieges, but no decisive developments. That was the pattern for the rest of the war, which ended in 1606.

The Mongols do not appear to have thought in counterfactual terms. The idea that Tengri (Heaven) had bequeathed the Earth to Chinggis Khan (d. 1227) and his offspring developed under Chinggis's successor, Ogodei (r. 1229–41), and this succession myth did not encourage counterfactual thought. Nevertheless, there was room for specific counterfactuals, as in the letter from the Ilkhan Khan Hülegü (ca. 1217–65) to Louis IX of France, a potential ally, suggesting that the Mongols would have defeated the Mamluks of Egypt and held on to their conquest of Syria if there had been sufficient pasture for their horses. The context was that for much of the Ilkhanid period (1258–1353), the Mongols always saw the loss of Syria, where they were defeated by the Mamluks in 1260, 1281, and 1312–13, as temporary, and there was a confidence that they would regain it when they were ready.[10]

Counterfactual reasoning is common in Indian and Chinese logic and had a place in Chinese historiography. It played an important part in one of the standard historical genres (the *lun,* or exposition), in which imperial elites had to try their hand at passing the civil service examinations. Counterfactuals were a common way of framing examination questions from the Tang period (619–907 AD) onward. In addition, they were a standard part of the soul-searching kind of history that tended to be written upon major military defeat or following the fall of a dynasty. In modern times, counterfactual reasoning figures into Chinese apologies for modernization, Westernization, Christianization—the standard pattern is: if we would have followed a track that was abandoned at some point in the past, we would have ended up modern or stronger or Christian, or whatever the case may be. At the turn of the twentieth century, Liang Qichao and others argued that it had been the Manchus who had destroyed China's vitality after they conquered it in the mid-seventeenth century, an approach which can also be read as a "What if the Manchus hadn't occupied China?" scenario. There was also the "sprouts of capitalism" argument of the 1950s to 1970s. The main dogma, held not least by the Communist dictator Mao Zedong (1893–1976, r. 1949–76), was that China had begun to develop capitalism in the early modern period, but that these sprouts were extinguished by Western imperialism. The implicit position, sometimes made explicit, was that if the British had not begun the Opium Wars (1839–42, 1857–60), China would not have experienced its last two dismal centuries, and thus that an anti-Western policy was crucial for China and helped ground Communist legitimacy.

Nevertheless, there has not been any serious attempt in China to engage in "What if?" type histories, with the case fully thought through. In part, this may be because the Chinese, steeped in what did happen, are very keen on getting things in what they see as the right order. The Chinese government does not encourage discussion of alternatives in recent or current Chinese developments. However, Chinese official and public interest in the 2000s in the comparative development and historical fate of empires opened up opportunities for counterfactual speculation as different trajectories were discerned. This process was taken further in the 2010s when Chinese expansionism in the East and South China Seas was discussed in historical contexts, both Chinese and non-Chinese.

In modern Japan, among academic historians, there is an extreme respect for documents, with great swaths of documents often reprinted in the text of historical works and the authors merely appending some brief comment about their relevance. This respect for documents is a major barrier to the appeal of counterfactual studies. Yet, respect for documents does not rule out counterfactualism, because they can point to plans that were not but might have been implemented, or to debates as to what action or response to take. In the case of 1937 and 1941, there are significant counterfactuals over Japanese policy and strategy. Ishiwara Kanji, chief of the Operations Section of the Japanese general staff, had warned that an invasion of China would result in an intractable commitment, with victory unobtainable and withdrawal impossible. However, more aggressive views had prevailed. He was transferred from the general staff in 1937 and the attempt he encouraged to secure German mediation was abandoned in January 1938.[11]

Counterfactualism is foreign to African concepts of history, which are dominated by the oral mode of transmitting history. Historical renderings change, but not in "What if?" terms. John Lamphear informs me that, as a mental exercise, he tried to express the concept to himself in Kiswahili, the East African language in which he is most fluent, and that he found it nearly impossible to do so. Insofar as some contemporary Africans engage in "What if?" historical speculation, this can be seen as one of the many ways in which Western perspectives and methodology have been grafted onto African thought.

Within the Western tradition itself there has been no consistency in the acceptance and use of counterfactualism. Religion, and ideology more generally, played a role in the response, as did national traditions. The use of the question "Why?" implying alternatives was not central in medieval exposition, though it was employed, for instance in documents by Pedro IV of Aragon (r. 1336–87). Medieval people could and did use (implicit) counterfactuals to project future possibilities when making choices; they could and did use the same counterfactuals when describing how past decisions were made; and they could use them to describe normative processes of decision making. Intellectual and legal thought involved the consideration of alternatives, while explanations of divine retribution for sins invited the counterfactual, "If only he had not sinned."

The question "What if?" probably had limited resonance for people anxiously attempting to discern the workings of Providence, but, then again, there were attempts to influence or appropriate greater forces through white or black magic and these attempts represented a conviction that developments could be changed. Intercession for those in Purgatory represented an attempt to counteract (and thus change) the impact of the past, and to extenuate this past through prayer and good works. Moreover, even in the early medieval chronicles that most frequently emphasize religious considerations, historical actors exercise free will. Occasionally, the Holy Spirit will intervene and make people do things, but this is a special intervention and a miraculous occasion. Thus, St. Gregory, bishop of Tours (ca. 538–94), in his *Historia Francorum*, has the Holy Spirit move the Franks to agree to Clovis's proposal to convert to Christianity in 493, but Clovis was free to choose. In later chronicles Providence tends to play a role similar to that assigned it by the novelist Henry Fielding in the eighteenth century (see chapter 1). Thus, fatalism was limited and there was a role for human free will.

More recently, Communist historiography, which can also be seen as an instance of implied theology, did not employ counterfactualism, which helps account for the Left-Right difference of views mentioned in chapter 1. However, the frequently employed notion of false consciousness can be seen as a significant implied counterfactual as it argues that working-class activism would otherwise have been stronger. Moreover, the idea of the revolution as under threat invites counterfactuals focused on success in overcoming challenges.

There have also been major contrasts at the national level, with counterfactualism more pronounced in Anglophone than in non-Anglophone cultures. This may owe something to the degree to which the history of the British and American peoples is one of breaking traditions and striking out in new directions, especially in regard to such developments as intellectual freedom, rule or law, constitutionalism, and property rights. Counterfactualism can be seen as an aspect of the ability to think and create beyond hidebound traditions and conformism.

German historiography, with its nineteenth-century legacy, the Hegelian emphasis on history as the unfolding of an idea, and the classic Rankean focus on the facts, on studying only what happened (what might be termed factualism), has had scant room for counterfactualism. There were few German counterfactual works prior to the mid-1960s. The same is true for countries influenced by and sharing in German historiography, such as Austria, the Netherlands, and Sweden. The German system of study still does not encourage such exercises. In part, this reflects a disciplinary conservatism in Germany in which traditional theories and existing camps are well entrenched. New approaches can be a threat, and counterfactuals are annoying at best and dangerous at worst.[12] Dutch academic historians hardly ever use counterfactual perspectives because they feel their arguments and claims should be based on verifiable empirical research. Although Dutch scholars increasingly express themselves in English, their methodology is still very much Rankean.[13]

Yet, the more recent recovery of interest in the "Third Germany," the smaller states other than Austria and Prussia and their role in the seventeenth to nineteenth centuries,[14] offers an explicit or implicit counterfactual based on German development as a federal system, and not as a state organized by Prussia. This counterfactual, which draws on a traditional analysis of the only way for middle-rank German powers to try to prevent Austrian and Prussian hegemony, provides a critique of the idea of a German *sonderweg* (unique path) predicated on the role of Prussian militarism. At the same time, like many counterfactuals, this one can be seen, at least in part, as a rewriting of the past in terms of the present: a modern, decentralized federal Germany seeks a suitable and validating heritage, both in terms of a rejection of the more centralized and authoritarian German experience of 1871–1945 and in order to ground the present system in the legitimacy of the past. Complicating this are the arguments that German unification under Prussia did not have to take its subsequent form and direction, that Prussian identity was more contingent than much of the criticism directed against it would suggest, and that a Prussian Germany did not have to lead to Nazism.[15] Looked at differently, a counterfactual history of the twentieth century for Germany would require confronting the pernicious choices that were made, whether deliberately and consciously or, simply, by not acting.

In France, the key historiographical development of the twentieth century, the *Annales* school, did not have any place for counterfactualism. Instead, this school very much offered an emphasis on environmental constraints. Counterfactualism, a "périlleux" method, has limited appeal to other French historians.[16] In France and Germany, Marxisante ideas were also particularly influential among historians, and this influence encouraged varying degrees of determinism. These ideas also played a role in Britain, but had less sway there in part because the profession was more fractured in terms of ideological and institutional politics. In Latin America, counterfactualism does not play a major role. In a culture whose writers and readers made much of "magic realism" this situation is not because of an inability to think of different pasts, presents, and futures, but rather due to a difficulty in giving these suggestions substance.

It would be misleading, however, to suggest that counterfactualism is limited to the Anglophone world. For example, at least two books on Finnish history have been published from the counterfactual point of view, including M. K. Niemi ja Ville Pernaa's edited volume *Entäs jos... Vaihtoehtoinen Suomen historia* (What if ... The alternative history of Finland) (2005). This book however, had little impact. In the 1990s, most Danish historians would dismiss counterfactualism as stuff and nonsense, but by the late 2000s it had become a genre which was actually being written by professional historians, and even those historians who did not write counterfactual history still discussed counterfactual possibilities in their works. Anthologies with counterfactual approaches to important events in Danish history were published, for example, "What would have happened in connection with the fall of royal absolutism in Denmark in 1848 if it had not happened as peacefully as it did?" Furthermore, Danish historians employing traditional approaches came in their conclusions to discuss alternative possibilities of how things might have turned out, instead of solely considering the way they did actually turn out.

Yet, there is often little to match the situation in Britain and the United States. For example, the Swedes have not engaged with counterfactualism to anywhere near the same extent. It is instructive that a book on counterfactuals in Spanish history, *Historia virtual de España, 1870–2004: Qué hubiera pasado si?* (Virtual history of Spain, 1870–2004: What if?) (2004) was edited by a British scholar: Nigel Townson. The collection includes essays on what would have happened if Spain had avoided war with the United States in 1898, if the republican parties had been united in the 1933 elections, if Spain had entered World War II, if Carrero Blanco, Franco's prime minister and a potential strongman, had not been murdered by the Basque terrorist group Eta in 1973, and if Spain had not joined in the Iraq war in 2003. One of the chapters considers whether the Spanish Civil War (1936–39) would have been avoided had the socialist Indalecio Priesto accepted the premiership in May 1936; the answer is, quite possibly. The impact of the Spanish Civil War and of Franco in the Spanish imagination and on recent Spanish history is such that the majority of the chapters relate directly or indirectly to one or the other. Counterfactualism offered a way to address these issues and this impact, which was seen immediately after Franco died in 1975, for, the following year, two books, Fernando Díaz-Plaza's *El desfile de la victoria* and Jesús Torbado's *En el día de hoy,* offered counterfactuals based on Republican victory in the Civil War. To complicate the situation, in Spain under Franco (r. 1939–75), as in Eastern Europe under the Communists, much historiography focused on advancing clearly ideological positions, such as backing Franco or supporting the Catholic Church. In practice, the consequence was an imaginary history for Spain that was to some extent a form of counterfactual history.

For Portugal, much of the counterfactualism focuses on the twentieth century with other outcomes based on different pasts. Whereas some Portuguese commentators argue that the country developed too rapidly, jumping stages, others regret that the development was not sufficiently fast to keep up with other leading Western states. The latter theme becomes an aspect of the debate about Portuguese history and prospects, as it focuses on a critique of Salazarism and related right-wing authoritarian options from the 1920s to the 1970s. More generally, the many "accidents" in Portuguese history encourage an interest in counterfactualism.[17]

For Israel, there are key questions relating to the origins of the state and to relations with the Arabs, and these are often expressed in counterfactual terms. What if there had been no Holocaust? Would there have been an Israel? What if, in May 1948, David Ben-Gurion, the first prime minister of Israel, had not declared a state? There are those who insist that the invasion of the Arab armies could have been avoided by changing the timing of independence, and that the proclamation of the state on May 14, 1948, was unnecessary. By postponing the declaration of the Jewish state—a state that in any case already existed in terms of institutions, armed forces, and so on—Israel might have reached an accommodation with the Arabs. Conversely, what if, in 1948, Israel had "completed the job" and, as it could have done, thrown out the remaining six hundred thousand Palestinians? What if Menachem Begin had not replaced Yitzhak Rabin in 1977: would there have been peace with Egypt? What if Israel had not bombed the Iraqi reactor in 1981? What if Rabin had not been assassinated in 1995: would the peace process have been strengthened? What if Arafat had negotiated with a genuine willingness to reach a solution? What if Israel had lost the Six-Day War in 1967, a question that was the subject of a book published soon after?

THE THEMATIC DIMENSION

To turn from national to thematic history, Livy's contrast between individual circumstances and more structural factors points the way toward variations in the modern use of counterfactualism. In particular, it has much more purchase in political than social history,[18] which reflects not so much the nature of counterfactualism, as developments in social history. Neither of the uses of counterfactualism outlined in the introduction—educational or in deliberate opposition to determinism—have made it especially attractive to social and cultural historians, whether they come from various of the branches of social constructionism or from the linguistic turn into postmodernism. These historians have been more interested in uncovering the "differences" and otherness of the actual past, rather than in imagining or modeling different pasts. So, although they have shared with all recent forms of professional history a distrust of any "Whiggish history," their objection to it has focused more on its misassignment of the motive forces and meanings of historical change than on its necessitarian or deterministic model. Their preferred heuristic method has not been the counterfactual experiment (seen as rather "scientistic" in its Fogelian form (see discussion below), and rather old-fashioned in its populist form), but rather the hermeneutic method. Ronald Hutton observed in 2013, "I know of not a single counterfactual study with respect to paganism, and my kind of cultural history does not lend itself as well to them as military and diplomatic history."[19]

The closest that sociocultural history has come to the counterfactual approach has been in the area of microhistory, and in the revival of narrative insofar as it has occurred. The former stresses the notion that, in a highly complex world of many competing processes and forces, it is easier to uncover the actual interplay of those forces by looking in detail at specific historical locales rather than through the conventional (macro) level of history. In a sense, this process is substituting a different form of experimentation into historical causation—based on the forensics of particular cases, rather than the quantitative accumulation of evidence to identify causal patterns. An instructive extension of this approach was provided by Chris Wickham in his study of early medieval Europe. He offered an English case study that was "frankly speculative, indeed partially invented," a hypothetical reconstruction of a village society called Malling, which is amplified by brief mention of four other (unnamed) local villages with different social politics, before concluding, "This account is invented, but it does represent a picture, plausible to me at least, of how village societies worked and change in England."[20] The use of such an approach in a scholarly work by a leading historian (subsequently Chichele Professor of Medieval History at Oxford), published by a major academic publisher (Oxford University Press), is instructive, in that the invented village provides not only a means of explication but also, by this means, a form of comparative discussion that offers possibilities for a type of research as well as for explication. Malling, however, is a paradigm rather than a counterfactual. Rather like historical geographers modeling settlement patterns, and seeking to investigate processes through these models, Wickham constructs an ideal picture of reality, seeking to crystallize the characteristics of many places. He does not go counter to the facts.

Microhistory can be regarded as not lending itself to counterfactualism, because causation is largely dropped in favor of small-scale reconstruction. Nevertheless, as actually presented, microhistorical study can often be seen to support a sense of the contingencies of the historical process and can also encourage a sense of multiple historical pasts (locally distinctive) which, in effect, act as an equivalent to the counterfactual past pitted against a supposedly singular historical reality. Similarly the revival of narrative, notably from the 2000s, as a prestigious mode of historical presentation in Western academic circles (it never died in any other circles) can easily lead to an emphasis on historical actions and choices, and, thus, on counterfactuals.

As a technique in social history, however, counterfactual history is rarely used. Thus, questions such as "What would have happened had there never been an Elizabethan Poor Law?" valid as they are, in this case for the study of sixteenth-century England, are not posed. This lack of counterfactualism reflects the conventions of the subject, but involves more than that, and may be primarily because many subjects in social history tend to be tackled thematically, rather than chronologically, and with an emphasis on trends rather than events. Therefore, in these cases, considering a counterfactual probably would not work as well as it does as a technique of assessing the sufficiency of links within a broadly chronological causal chain, where one discrete event or decision might be said to lead more directly to another.

It is also possible that the modest role of counterfactualism in social history arises because agency there tends to be attributed to groups, rather than to individuals or small cohorts. Given the decline of class explanations in scholarship, it then becomes more difficult to attribute decisive agency in the way generally required for a counterfactual. For example, although valid, the question "What would have happened if the middle classes in eighteenth-century Britain or North America had preferred coffee to tea?" does not quite work, because it is difficult to imagine the "middle classes" making a decisive collective decision. Thus, we may ask if the cast, in this and other comparable cases, may be too large for counterfactuals, not least because social changes tend to be the outcome of large numbers of independent and not-always-known variables. The question also arises of whether there was even such a thing as the "middle class" except as a historical contrivance. On the other hand, the theme of individuals making decisions is of particular relevance for theories of economic change that place an emphasis on patterns of consumption. These patterns have changed and it is appropriate to employ counterfactuals, such as the one in this paragraph, in order to understand their impact. Moreover, patterns of consumption can be linked to policy choices. "What would have happened if William Pitt the Elder (who, as first Earl of Chatham, headed a ministry from 1766 to 1768) had halved the excise duty on coffee, while doubling it on tea?" does work easily, because we can relate the decision to the agency of a single, significant individual.

Similarly, Robert Page profitably examined the implications of a further period of Labour government in Britain from 1951 to 1964, continuing the control begun in 1945. He argued that such a continuation (and Labour won more votes than the Conservatives in the general election of 1951, though not those of 1955 and 1959) would not have led to a second-stage attempt to create a Socialist country, including by means of a large-scale redistribution of wealth. Page did so by drawing attention to the awareness within the Labour Party of limited public support for such policies. Instead, he saw a more pragmatic attitude as likely. Yet, at the same time, Page suggested that longer Labour governance would have helped embed the welfare culture in British society, and that this would have influenced the strategies of future Labour governments, making it harder for them to push for reforms that challenged the welfare state.[21] This contribution was related to the debate about Labour policies under Tony Blair, prime minister from 1997 to 2007, and, specifically, to the discussion of how far they are linked to a coherent long-term element in Labour attitudes and policy.[22] By considering the counterfactual, Page appeared to present Blair as out of line with postwar Labour principles, as well as show the relevance of counterfactualism for debates on the Left, notably in establishing norms.

A variable is presented with the argument that if, as was widely believed likely at the time, Winston Churchill and the Conservatives had won the general election of 1945, this would have led to a more selectivist welfare state than the collectivist form that was to be introduced by Labour from 1945. A comparison of the 1944 Education Act with the National Health Service established by Labour in 1948 suggests that this might well have been the case. At the same time, such counterfactuals underline the number and complexity of variables involved in politics, and thus the difficulty of predicting outcomes from different choices. A very different type of social history—that of the response to alleged witchcraft in early modern Europe—revealed the value of employing different criteria in order to study variations in persecution.[23]

ECONOMIC HISTORY AND COUNTERFACTUALISM

Turning to economic history, economic theory would in principle allow for counterfactualism, but economists and economic historians have made only limited use of it. They usually compare the evolution of different cases, rather than ask the question of whether a different decision or an event would have placed one case on another trajectory. Yet, counterfactuals do occur, and to a greater extent than for social history, in the more econometric end of the subject, where various elements are reduced to numerical variables. Counterfactual history became particularly popular in the 1960s when the American New Economic Historians, or Cliometrics School, took it on board as a way of applying economic theory to the past. They were developing an initial idea from World War II that was as much practical as economic. During this conflict, military strategists were asked what damage might be inflicted upon the German economy if the Allies managed to knock out the entire German railway network. The answer was, not much. Counterfactual methods were thus employed "counter" to the facts; the result was a methodology that was able to question one of the Allies' main war weapons—strategic bombing. The apparent postwar embarrassment of the British government and its failure to acknowledge the work of Bomber Command in 1943–45 were related to the ethics as well as the effectiveness of this policy. Two longstanding, though different and not morally equivalent, debates have involved counterfactuals: "Should the Allies have bombed the rail lines to Auschwitz?" and "Were the Allies right to bomb Dresden?"[24] Returning to the issue of practicalities, the concept of opportunity, notably the opportunity to use resources and to hit targets, greatly complicates the analysis of bombing.

As economic historians more than most others claim to have practical minds—not least minds that are open to the insights of other professionals—it is perhaps small wonder that it was they who brought counterfactualism into the mainstream academic arena with gusto. Robert Fogel's study of railways in the American Industrial Revolution, *Railroads and American Economic Growth* (1964), was the classic usage of counterfactual economic modeling. Fogel was critical of economic historians, such as Joseph Schumpeter and W. W. Rostow, who based their assumptions about the value of the railways on descriptions (rather than analyses) of what railways did. This descriptive approach seemed to lack rigor as it revealed nothing about the impact of railways in hardheaded economic terms. Fogel claimed, instead, that it was necessary to ask what an economy would have looked like if there had been no railways. What did the country save by having best-practice technology—that is, railways as opposed to roads or canals? What, in other words, were the "social savings" attached to having railways? By constructing models that removed the railways from the economies of America (in the case of Fogel) and Britain (in the case of Fogel's follower, G. R. Hawke), the following quantitative conclusion was reached: that in America the benefit amounted to just 4 percent of national income, and in Britain to between 7 and 11 percent. Critics, however, claimed that the removal of a key factor can change the situation so dramatically that one is not talking about the same situation.

Fogel went on to consider counterfactuals and slavery. In *Without Consent or Contract: The Rise and Fall of American Slavery* (1990), Fogel introduced political elements in order to show that slavery was not stopped by economic factors: rather than finding slavery unprofitable or inconsistent with industrialization, he emphasized the contingent nature of American politics in the late 1850s and early 1860s.

The counterfactual approach has been employed in other areas of study from economic history, such as the debate over the failure of British entrepreneurs in the last quarter of the nineteenth century, when American and German economic competition had pushed Britain off the top spot in the world. In an influential book, *English Culture and the Decline of the Industrial Spirit* (1981), the American historian Martin Weiner encapsulated a then-common explanation of British industrial failure. He argued that entrepreneurs, risk-takers, had failed to build on the innovations and successes of their fathers' and grandfathers' generations. Scapegoats were required, and Weiner, along with Marxists such as Eric Hobsbawm, was happy to blame the men who let their family companies go to seed. Weiner viewed this declining spirit as the result of middle-class self-improvement; it seemed that the sons of Victorian Britain's Thomas Gradgrinds (Gradgrind is a hard-working character from Charles Dickens's 1854 novel *Hard Times*) had been spoiled by public schools, shooting parties, and life in the country. This shift in values led to a diminishing interest in the family firm and a failure to make the most of opportunities. Thus, by the 1880s, British firms were based on old labor-intensive methods and old technology, and were importing American managers to turn them around. Critics of the "entrepreneurial failure" approach, however, have shown, using counterfactual methods, that British industry was not in fact a victim of failed management. They argue that British managers actually had a rational attitude toward improvement and labor. As skilled labor in Britain, unlike that in America, was cheap and plentiful, there was less need to invest in expensive new technologies. Moreover, Britain's economy continued to grow quite healthily in this period, and it was only the sheer size and recent development of the American and German economies that made Britain's eclipse inevitable. Britain's decline, in short, was actually relative and not absolute.[25]

Looked at differently, counterfactuals in economic history rely on isolating factors in order to establish their significance. These are then considered within regression analyses to see whether or not their presence or absence makes a measurable difference to the outcome—of phenomena such as the Industrial Revolution, the Agricultural Revolution, the "Great Divergence" between European and Asian economic growth,[26] demographic trends, etc. Thus, in Mark Overton's study of early modern English probate inventories, regression analyses were employed to see which variables appeared to exert the greatest influence over the possession or absence of an item in a household. Overton found, for example, that the presence of a mirror was influenced much more strongly by whether or not the household was in Cornwall or Kent than by whether or not the household was wealthy. In Overton's regression analysis, county location exerted a statistical significance between four and nine times greater than wealth level.[27]

On the global scale, and with a specific engagement with counterfactualism, William McNeill asked, "What if Pizarro had not found potatoes in Peru?" when he conquered it for Spain in the 1530s. As is the norm with counterfactuals, he presented this as a key variable, even though, as he pointed out, "Pizarro himself, and the ruffians he led, would have thought such a question absurd." At the same time, the value of this counterfactual is that McNeill explained the importance of particular crops to European development, concluding that "potatoes from Peru were essential for fueling the swarming human biomass that sustained Europe's imperial ventures."[28] Mention of the potato leads to the counterfactual "What if the Irish potato crop had not failed in the 1840s?" At least in the short term, British and Irish demographics would have been very different.

HEALTH AND DEMOGRAPHICS

Medical history provides another field for counterfactuals, as it is possible to isolate key elements and also to ascertain what might have happened had these varied. Counterfactual work on disease in the West Indies, notably on yellow fever and malaria, has indicated that but for these diseases, migration would have led to a British New World that was demographically dominated by the West Indies. If migrants thither had multiplied at the same rate as emigrants to the mainland, their population by 1760 would have been nearly 3 million, compared with only 1.7 million in British North America, while if the rate had been the same as that of migrants to the southern plantation colonies in North America, the figures would have been equal. Conversely, death rates in North America comparable with those in the British West Indies would have left a mainland population of fewer than two hundred thousand whites in 1760, of whom only fifty thousand would live in the northern colonies. The race balance is also subject to counterfactuals. Higher white death rates ensured that Jamaica could not become a settler society with a large, locally born white population.[29] To take a different approach, had migrants ceased arriving in British North America, then the ability of the colonies to expand at the expense of the Native Americans could be questioned, or, phrased as a counterfactual, "What if the flow of migrants had ceased . . . ?" The importance of continued migration from Europe as a whole was captured by the historian David Quinn in a thoughtful counterfactual, in which he highlighted the importance of Europe's industrial dynamics by asking what would have happened had this growth ceased in the mid-eighteenth century:

> All the intrusive settlement patterns in Asia—and such as there were in Africa as well—might well have faded out as a result of indigenous attrition had it not been for the industrialising powerhouse into which Europe turned from the later eighteenth century. . . . [It is] probable that the settlement patterns already established in Mexico, Peru, probably the Plate and a few other regions could have sustained themselves without the addition of capital sustenance or anything more than residual trade with Europe. . . . Virginia might not have the internal resources or will to carry her people across the mountain chain. . . . When we come to Pennsylvania, New York, and above all Massachusetts . . . the tradition of an expanding self-reliance and of the balance of urban and rural interests together with the differentiation of skills in their population and the habit of capital-accumulation, could quite probably have enabled them, strengthened by their own merchant marine, to become the heirs of a great part of the east central part of North America, perhaps to the Mississippi. The biggest question mark would lie over the capacity of the indigenes [Native Americans] to stage something of a come-back once European settlements had ceased to be bolstered by officials and soldiers and by increasing numbers of emigrants. . . . [30]

Like many counterfactuals by scholars who have carried out considerable research on a topic, this is more than a passing curiosity. It is a reminder that the past is a matter of steps, rather than a smooth process; and, more specifically, that the strength and nature of the transoceanic European presence were to a considerable extent, if not primarily, the products of developments within Europe (a theme returned to in chapters 5 and 6). Alongside the deployment of military power and the exercise of political authority, demographic and economic movements provided the dynamism that ensured that the multifarious links between Europe and its outer world remained potent.

A more difficult challenge is posed by the question, "What if there were no Black Death?"—the plague epidemic of 1346–51.[31] This question is made more problematic because population growth rates in Eurasia had already been hit by adverse conditions in the early fourteenth century, although without the consequences that were to stem from the Black Death. Moreover, assuming away diseases, while highlighting different population growth rates, perhaps does not establish the possibility of a genuine alternative past as convincingly as assuming different decisions by leaders does. Instead, this is the type of situation that brings counterfactualism up against environmental-structural constraints.

CULTURAL HISTORY

Turning to cultural history, it is possible to see counterfactuals across types and genres. In the case of painting, the failure of the Dutch Revolt against Philip II of Spain (r. 1556–98) that broke out in the 1560s might have ensured that there was less or no Dutch genre painting, for example still lifes, and likewise middle-class portraits. Instead, there might have been a focus on court and church themes, as in the Spanish Netherlands (essentially modern Belgium), the area Spain regained from the 1570s to the 1600s in its struggle to suppress the revolt. Patronage and the nature of the art market would have played a different role alongside stylistic influences. This thesis can be impacted within another counterfactual about the cultural and artistic consequences of the failure or absence of a Protestant Reformation.

To take cinema, there are counterfactuals in regard to aspects of technology, i.e., "Would things have happened differently if particular developments had or had not taken place as they did?" One counterfactualism relates to origin: if the film taken of Leeds Bridge by Louis le Prince in 1888 had survived, the origin of the medium of film might now be placed seven years earlier than the accepted date of 1895. Moreover, there has been much debate since the 1970s over the standard teleological narrative of film history, a sort of Whiggish version which sees the history of film as developing inevitably toward the model of classical Hollywood cinema—a view advanced by early historians in the 1930s such as Lewis Jacobs and Paul Rotha. This approach tends to assume that because the medium developed as it did, it was inevitable that it would do so, but this was challenged by revisionists such as Tom Gunning and Charles Musser, who argued, instead, that the rise of the narrative film came about through a range of cultural and industrial determinants and was not necessarily an inevitable outcome. If it were not for the existence of the classic nineteenth-century novel and Victorian stage melodrama, film might have adopted conventions from elsewhere: the Lumière films of the 1890s, for example, were actualities (what we now call documentaries), rather than fictional story films. If there is a particular period in which film might have developed in other ways, it is the early period.

Perhaps the biggest "What if," however, involves external impact on the film industry, specifically, "What if World War I had not happened?"[32] It was the war that created the conditions in which the American film industry rose to a position of global economic and cultural hegemony that it has maintained ever since by wrecking most European film industries, some of which, such as the French, British, German, and Swedish, were severely affected by the war. There were prolific production industries in Europe before 1914, but filmmaking almost halted in Britain and France after the outbreak of war, and when it picked up again, American imports had filled the gap. Germany was largely isolated for most of the war with nowhere to export her films. Sweden exported a lot of films to Germany before the war, but lost this market in 1914. Although European film industries recovered after World War I, the Americans had already established themselves as the global "brand leaders" by this time. Other industries have been competing from a position of inferiority ever since.

In stylistic and content terms, there were also counterfactuals. This was particularly so in the shape of the self-conscious counter-cinema, for example Jean-Luc Godard's *À bout de souffle* (1960), that challenged normative, mainstream, classical cinema.

There are also plenty of "What ifs?" revolving around casting decisions. For example, would Humphrey Bogart have become such a big star if George Raft had not turned down *High Sierra* and *The Maltese Falcon*? What would *Casablanca* have been like with Ronald Reagan and Ann Sheridan? Or *The Bridge on the River Kwai* with David Lean's first choice for Colonel Nicholson—Charles Laughton—or the Bond films with

David Niven as the first Bond? He was Ian Fleming's choice and that of a poll of the British public by the *Daily Express*. Would Fred Astaire have made a comeback if Gene Kelly hadn't broken his ankle playing touch football before shooting began for *Easter Parade*? Lux Radio Theatre and other radio series adapted famous films with different casts, but still using recognized stars, which provides us with a veritable alternative history of the "golden age" of Hollywood.

Similar approaches can provide counterfactual episodes, themes, or histories for other spheres of culture, for example opera or the novel. At the same time, counterfactuals in literary studies are relatively few. There are some "suppose X had met Y, then Z would never have happened" moments, but they are strictly on the margins and are often considered suppositious in the absence of fact, rather than advanced on the basis of the knowledge of actual events. A different form of alternative is offered by authors who write continuation novels in the style of others, developing the history and character of the latters' fictional creations, as P. D. James did for Jane Austen, Sebastian Faulks for P. G. Woodhouse, and Kingsley Amis, Faulks, William Boyd, and others for Ian Fleming. Counterfactualism does not play much of a role in the history of art, although it can be used for artists such as Masaccio, Giorgione, and Raphael who died young.

FREE WILL

Moving away from specific types of history and, instead, considering the subject as a whole, any notion of development as both occurring and as not being foreordained, in other words any non-Providential account (Providence being treated here as a form of determinism), leaves a role for causal inference, and thus for counterfactuals. In one light, these counterfactuals can be seen as irreligious or blasphemous, which explains the tone of E. P. Thompson's criticism of them (see chapter 1). He was defending a secular form of religion. However, that response depends upon a narrow conception of Providential history, one in which options in the shape of free will do not exist.

Counterfactuals heighten the role of free will in the past, possibly to an excessive extent.[33] Moreover, in lessening the extent to which hindsight, and the stress on what actually happened, are allowed to close off lines of inquiry, counterfactuals emphasize free will in current discussion. Here the moral or ideological dimension to counterfactualism, with the possibility of a large if not infinite number of permutations, clashes with the intellectual and pedagogic principle that a minimal rewriting is the desirable norm in employing counterfactuals.[34] Yet, this clash is only a difference of emphasis in what is a critique of determinism. There are interesting parallels between this discussion and that about evolution.

Free will in current discussion is significant because historical interpretations change. To argue that the past happened, and, correspondingly, that counterfactualism is invalid because it proposes something that did not happen, is to propose too stark a dichotomy between what happened and what did not happen, because there are changing interpretations of what happened, and counterfactual speculation helps amplify this discussion. In my lifetime, for example, there have been major shifts in the assessment of the strength of Catholic devotion in the English Church on the eve of the Henrician Reformation, and of the early impact of Protestantism. These shifts, particularly the greater emphasis than in the past on Catholic devotion, clearly provide a different background for a discussion of the role of Henry VIII,[35] which leads to an uncertainty, if not indeterminacy, in our understanding of the context of sixteenth-century religiosity. The counterfactual of alternative expositions is readily presented.

There is also the more straightforward counterfactual of how far the situation might have been different had Henry VIII not followed the path of the beautiful Anne Boleyn and not decided to divorce his first wife, Katherine of Aragon. Henry's choice is apparently a classic instance of the French philosopher Pascal's adage about Cleopatra's nose: "Le nez de Cléopâtre: s'il eût été plus court, toute la face de la terre aurait changé" (Had Cleopatra's nose been shorter, the whole history of the world would have been different). Oft-cited, "Cleopatra's Nose" was also the title of a 1930 essay by J. B. Bury, the Gibbon specialist, on the importance of chance in history. The previous year, John Buchan had disagreed with Pascal's observation, writing that "Egypt, as the granary of the Roman world, was obviously a trump card for ambition to seize."

Josiah Ober argued in 2003 that Mark Antony's foolish infatuation with Cleopatra was not the cause of his defeat by Octavian (later Augustus Caesar) at Actium in 31 BC.[36]

A flippant aside on looks was Mao Zedong's reply when asked what would have happened if Nikita Khrushchev, the Soviet leader from 1953 to 1964, had been assassinated rather than President John F. Kennedy: "I don't think Aristotle Onassis would have married Mrs. Khrushchev," as the plutocrat did Jackie Kennedy in 1968. A more recent counterfactual would be to ask what if President Sarkozy of France had not remarried in 2007. This would probe the question of whether his personal life led to a loss of popularity and reputation that compromised his authority and affected his chances of reelection.

Obviously, Henry VIII did break with papal authority, but an understanding of his actions and options, however much they were affected by the looks of Anne Boleyn whom he married in 1533, has to rest on a dynamic relationship with assessments of developments in England in the period, because these assessments underline the constraints and opportunities he faced. Moreover, if the opportunities Henry faced are emphasized, this approach provides a greater validity for counterfactuals about his choice.

From a different direction, if the extent to which historians' interpretations have altered, and will continue to alter, for this and other episodes, is highlighted anew, this provides an additional context for counterfactualism. Returning to Pascal for a moment, counterfactualism amplifies, but also clarifies, an unknowingness to which he gave potent force in his remarks, "Le silence éternal de ces espaces infinis m'effraie" (The eternal silence of these infinite spaces terrifies me) and "Le coeur a ses raisons que la raison ne connait point" (The heart has its reasons which reason knows nothing of).[37] Counterfactuals thus testify both to the difficulty of accurate explanation and to the capacity and free will provided and underlined by the possibility of explication. Even though the explanations derived from counterfactual approaches may be unhelpful and inaccurate, if not frivolous, the range of possible explanations suggested by implicit or explicit counterfactuals can help clarify which is most plausible (possibly more than one), and can therefore be part of the rational project of analysis and exposition.

THE ROLE OF CHANCE

The need for historical expertise in assessing this range of possible explanations acts as a limitation on the wider (maybe wilder) possibilities that can be offered. Indeed, this expertise qualifies the perception of history (the past, rather than the profession) as a delicate network that develops very differently if a single strand is affected.[38] This perception of history looks toward the "chaos theory" of inherent unpredictability,[39] which was sometimes discussed in terms of the argument that a wave of the hand (Edgar Allan Poe), a match thrown from a train window (Sir Arthur Eddington), the death of a prehistoric butterfly (Ray Bradbury), or the flap of an animal's wings (Edward Lorenz) would affect the future. The emphasis was on small events or effects yielding large consequences.

This emphasis drew on the work of the noted French mathematician Henri Poincaré (1854–1912), professor in Paris from 1881, who came close to anticipating Einstein's theory of relativity. In reaction to the confidence of his age in prediction, Poincaré emphasized the role of nonlinearities, the small events or effects that had significant consequences, and argued that they put major limits on forecasting. Mathematics could be employed to demonstrate these limits. Poincaré argued that the error rate in prediction grows very rapidly with time, and that this means that near-precision is not possible because this error rate ensures that the past has to be understood with infinite precision. Poincaré's "three-body problem" demonstrated the impact, in a two-planet solar system, of a third small body on the hitherto predictable course of the two planets. Thus, a minor change had major consequences, and that irrespective of the role of humans with their free will.[40] Another French mathematician, Jacques Hadamard (1865–1963), contributed to developments in this field.

Working at the Massachusetts Institute of Technology from 1946, Edward Lorenz discovered Poincaré's results himself in the 1960s through his work on the computer simulation of weather dynamics. A minor change in inputs had major consequences for the results. In 1972, Lorenz, the leading American modeler of climate, gave a talk with a title proposed by a friend, Philip Meriless: "Predictability: Does the Flap of a Butterfly's Wings in Brazil Set Off a Tornado in Texas?" Indeed, in 2000, the French filmmaker Laurent Firode made a film called *Le battement d'ailes du papillon* (The beating of the butterfly's wings),[41] in which the emphasis is on the role of small events in changing lives. Lorenz's work played a part in the growing interest in the 1970s in irregular occurrences, for example the flow from a dripping tap and the shape of clouds. The resulting mathematics were developed as chaos theory by Mitchell Feigenbaum and others, and the theory was applied in a number of fields, including ecology, public health, and aerodynamics.[42]

The timetables proposed for the changes stemming from small events vary greatly, but in catastrophe theories the changes tend to be rapid. In practice, whatever the directions chaos theories and free will lead in, there are major constraints and significant probabilities affecting both the past and, indeed, the response from the historical profession. The latter, especially but not only in authoritarian cultures, generally has more rigidity and small-mindedness or conservatism than its self-image allows.

THE LITERARY APPROACH

Consideration of Henry VIII and the English Reformation highlights the extent to which the counterfactual approach does not "belong" to historians, as this issue has been a topic of literary discussion, notably with Kingsley Amis's novel *The Alteration* (1976), which provides an alternative history, present, and indeed future, located in the failure of an English Reformation. In the Amis novel, the papacy still wields supreme power. The role of personal commitment came into play as some of those who, over the centuries, considered this perspective were Catholics, and others critics of what they saw as the consequences of English Protestantism, notably the dissolution of the monasteries in the 1530s and the later bigotries of Puritanism. As a very different instance of the possible links in fiction between past and present, the successful detective writer John Dickson Carr located some of his stories in the early modern period, for example *The Devil in Velvet* (1951), with the detective moving through time from the present.

Much of the literary coverage, however, deals with more recent episodes, an emphasis particularly seen in the idea of a Nazi Britain, as with Noel Coward's play *Peace in Our Time* (1947), John Wall's novel *The Sound of His Horn* (1952), Len Deighton's novel *SS-GB* (1978),[43] and Owen Sheers's novel *Resistance* (2007); while a Nazi Europe is the background to Robert Harris's highly successful novel *Fatherland* (1992). The focus on the Nazis extends to television, for example *The Other Man* (1964) and *An Englishman's Castle* (1978), and to film, for example *It Happened Here* (1965), as well as to video games, such as *Turning Point: Fall of Liberty*. In his novel *Russian Hide-and-Seek* (1980), Kingsley Amis considered a Soviet takeover of Britain.

This fictional approach, locating stories in scenarios that did not occur but drawing on the possibility that in other circumstances they might have done, has become more common in recent decades. It is a product not of modernism, with its rejection of established narrative patterns, including, often, consistent characterization (let alone of magic realism or postmodernism, each of which are far more subversive), but rather of reader interest at the popular level. The prominence of this kind of, in effect, interactive history raises questions about the impact of the popularity of explicitly fictional counterfactualism on the reception of the nonfictional type of counterfactualism. A critic might suggest that they are part of the same process, but although it might be more helpful to think in terms of a continuum, there is a distinction between what is avowedly fictional and what is openly speculative.

The popularity of the fictional approach owes nothing to academic scholarship on counterfactualism, and probably nothing to postmodernist questioning about the basis and distinctiveness of the belief that truth can be ascertained.[44] Instead, as one aspect of counterfactualism, and providing another chapter in the long book of historical fiction, there has been much greater interest from the late twentieth century than earlier in time travel, both backward and forward, notably with the highly successful British television series *Doctor Who* (1963–89; 2005–) and its number of spin-off films. Although not all time-travel writing supports it, there is also interest in the idea that by going backward in time, it is possible to change the future, or, at least, that this is an issue that has to be addressed. Films such as *It's a Wonderful Life* (1946), *Back to the Future* (1985), *Peggy Sue Got Married* (1986), and *Twelve Monkeys* (1995) have outlined this theme, and it has been a staple of science fiction and other literature. Mark Twain's novel *A Connecticut Yankee in King Arthur's Court* (1889) and H. G. Wells's novel *The Time Machine* (1895) are prominent examples. In the first, the fictional Hank Morgan introduces nineteenth-century technology and ideology to Camelot, leading to a destructive civil war. As a further instance of the prominence of time travel and of the idea that it is possible to affect the past, computer games feature fantasy in historical settings a good deal.

REWRITING THE PAST AS RETHINKING IT

The impact of such time travel for the wider audience for historical writing is unclear, but the ethical and philosophical implications of changing the past have been fully ventilated, and this discussion is a key aspect of counterfactualism as entertainment. Yet, more than entertainment is involved in the fictional counterfactuals. The role of the past in the collective consciousness also emerges as an aspect of counterfactual history, and this role is encouraged, indeed greatly encouraged, by the fictional option. This role of the past can be probed to ascertain which alternative histories were/are particularly popular and, therefore, to at least some, desirable.[45] This approach may seem a dangerous instance of the role of counterfactualism in rewriting the past. However, the key point is different, as the intention is to help chart the development of collective memory, both chronologically and in terms of its changing content. Thus, counterfactualism is an aspect of the representation of the past and, also, of the ways in which this representation can be analyzed.

This emphasis on strategies of representation underlines the extent to which counterfactualism plays an explicit role in the use (and abuse) of the past in order to make political and other points. Groups seeking a justification of allegedly correct choices made in the past, and a condemnation of allegedly bad choices, create exemplary histories based on the idea that there was a choice, and that this choice entailed correct and incorrect options. For example, critics of Israel consider the implications of the Balfour Declaration of 1917 promising Zionists a national home in Palestine, and of the Holocaust, by arguing that, but for both, the Palestinians would be in a very different position. More generally, allegedly bad choices cannot be castigated by commentators, historians, and others without considering the alternatives.

This process of political conceptualization and utilization is one that joins past, present, and future. A classic instance is the frequent employment of the example of the appeasement of Nazi Germany in the late 1930s in order apparently to understand options in subsequent crises, such as Suez in 1956, Iraq in 2003, Syria and the East China Sea in 2013, Ukraine in 2014, or the response in the early 2010s to Iran's nuclear plans. In a speech to the Knesset (Israeli Parliament) in 2008, President George W. Bush made reference to "the false comfort of Appeasement" when criticizing the idea of negotiation with "terrorists and radicals." The implication was spelled out: had Britain and France been more robust in 1938, then Hitler would have been stopped, and the lesson from counterfactualism was that the past could be replayed in the present.[46] In the early 1960s, President John F. Kennedy made reference to appeasement, but he also saw the outbreak of World War I in 1914 as a warning about how a nuclear war with the Soviet Union that was sought by neither side could still break out, in part due to a failure of communication. He read Barbara Tuchman's *The Guns of August* (1962), a Pulitzer Prize–winning account of 1914 by an American popular writer, and was so impressed that he gave copies to Harold Macmillan, the British prime minister, and to the American envoy in Paris.[47]

George W. Bush kept a bust of Churchill in the Oval Office in the White House. As both inspiration and ostensible point of reference for his own campaign against Iraq (as well as offering public relations value), this bust, like the president's preference for reading history, reminded Bush that his reputation in standing up to dictators would be judged. An awareness of future judgment (as well as of future success or failure) plays a role in the counterfactuals of the present as choices are assessed. Churchill himself responded to the need to exculpate his failure over the unsuccessful Dardanelles/Gallipoli expedition in 1915 by discussing "the terrible ifs": conjunctures in which leadership, planning, and luck could have led to a more successful outcome. The value of these "ifs," however, is contentious, with the historian John Ramsden arguing that they "are more usefully seen as commentary on Churchill's mindset, his refusal to accept that the whole episode might always have been doomed, than they are an issue in historical evaluation."[48] As far as judging Churchill is concerned, it is apparent that the 1915 campaign suffered from inadequate preparation, specifically the lack of a relevant planning and command structure,[49] as well as from the poor implementation of an anyway flawed operational plan that was based on a problematic strategy. Moreover, Allied failure resulted in part from the Turkish defense being much stronger than they had anticipated.[50] These factors, however, do not demonstrate that the Allied operation was necessarily doomed. More generally, the margin between success and failure is generally close,[51] a point that counterfactuals can clarify, and although failure is usually readily explained, it is necessary to give due weight to the problems facing all operations. In turn, Churchill subsequently saw failure at the Dardanelles/Gallipoli as a basis for admonition, as in 1943 when discussing Anglo-American amphibious attacks on Italy.[52] Thus, the "what ifs?" of the past were still being brought into play in the contingencies of a later war.

Part of the potential problem with this focus on individuals such as Churchill, however, and a reason why counterfactualism appears more appropriate for political and military history than for other types, is that this focus is largely that of the short term. There is no inherent reason why counterfactual discussion of causes and consequences should not be long term, and indeed much of the literature relates to this. However, because of the multiple variables of possible change over time, counterfactualism can be regarded as less secure as a method of discussion, still less explanation, in the long than in the short term. Turned around, its value therefore depends in part on whether the question for analysis is seen as primarily to be understood in terms of short- or long-term causes.

Of course, the short-term moment can focus issues of long-term significance and interest, as in the discussion in chapter 6 of the Jacobite uprising of 1745–46. Another instance of such a focus is provided by John Gaddis's counterfactual account, in his history of the Cold War, of the American use of five atomic bombs against advancing Chinese forces in North Korea on December 2, 1950, followed, successively, by Soviet atomic reprisals in South Korea on December 4, American atomic strikes on Vladivostok and China, Soviet strikes on Frankfurt and Hamburg, and the collapse of NATO. This account served to enable Gaddis to underline the importance of the actual American decision not to use atomic weaponry in the Korean War (1950–53),[53] a choice that was to be repeated during the Vietnam War. Thus, the counterfactual demonstrates the importance of the choice that was made. This is an instance of the more general role of counterfactuals in debating choices.

Turning to the widest perspective, there is possibly a more profound sense in which history as a discipline is counterfactual, in that there are a number of possible ways to study the past. The use of one approach necessarily involves not only a decision not to employ another, but also, at least implicitly, a view that another choice would be inappropriate. An intellectual landscape based on these choices can then be charted, and it becomes a key aspect of the study of historiography. Historiographical choices themselves reflect cultural, ideological, and political themes, and their interaction with individuals in particular contexts. Moreover, the debates to which these choices give rise rest on explicit and implicit notions of best practice, and, thus, of the less desirable results of following alternative approaches. The criticism of these alternative approaches entails the supposition of a second-rate counterfactualism: "If you choose this approach you will fail to understand/explain the subject." This choice can then be seen as a counterfactualism based on the denial of history, or, at least, of how best it should be handled.

If history as an academic discipline can be approached in this fashion, then this is even more the case with popular history. There, the counterfactualism is often explicitly linked to marketing considerations, with authors, agents, publishers, and reviewers discussing how best to appeal to the public, and assessing the text, illustrations, title, cover illustration, and blurb in this light. This discussion is an aspect of history as entertainment in a commercial marketplace. That role has always been significant, but it has certainly become more apparent in recent decades, with publishers and authors searching for new opportunities within a context of the interpenetration of the visual world of television, film, and games, and that of books.

In respect to this search, counterfactualism appears as a form of entertainment. That factor explains part of the disdain it encounters in scholarly circles. Indeed, in some respects, discussion of counterfactuals by academics (including this book) is an aspect and product of this debate about the validity of counterfactualism, and finds it difficult to break free from the standard critique. The dominance of this critique within the academy owes much to a sense that historians in some respect own the past, or at least the interpretation of it, and that their conventions and priorities should guide the public in this interpretation, with other approaches necessarily being less valid and valuable. Linked to this is a particular anger directed toward academics who take part in counterfactual speculation, not least because they are challenging the authority of the professional system, as well as, allegedly, the distinctiveness of facts and scholarship.

The critique can, however, be reconceptualized, away from the academic dimension, by noting that most counterfactual work is popular history that is outside the academic world and in no way subject to its priorities. Indeed, the idea that popular history should conform to these priorities represents a failure to understand the wider culture and the related publishing. "One Document Might Have Prevented w w ii," the title of a newspaper article published in 2014 by Ben Macintyre, a prominent journalist with a strong interest in history,[54] was designed to attract readers in a way very different from an academic article. The subtitle was, "If President Hindenburg's will had been published the German people might never have given Hitler absolute power."

Insofar as there is an overlap in the case of counterfactualism between popular and academic history, it is reasonable to expect academics employing counterfactual speculations to do so in a responsible fashion that avoids the besetting problem of presentism, and even that takes note of the theoretical literature on the subject. Presentism is always a powerful element in the treatment of history, and not only in popular history; and it is this presentism that is responsible for much of the scholarly critique of counterfactualism. Yet, however valid this critique, it is clear that counterfactualism employed in a presentist fashion offers historians an opportunity not only to consider past developments, but also to assess an important aspect of the collective imagination at the time when they are writing. This approach provides a valuable insight into public culture, and notably into what seems possible, desirable, and to be feared, and into how these provide a comment on the situation at the time.

Thus, counterfactualism offers a way to consider memory and its presentation and politics. In one respect, counterfactualism, indeed, is a key element in the contest of memory. It thereby forms an aspect of the "history wars" that are so significant in contested public accounts of the past.[55] These "wars" are scarcely new. They were, for example, common in rivalries between religions. False autobiographies and biographies, and forged letters and documents, proved important in these contests.

The role of counterfactualism in the contest of memory helps explain the unhappiness of many scholars with the approach. It appears a challenge not only to the practice of their subject, but also to the autonomy of history—both of the past and of the study of the past. In particular, thanks in part to its role in "history wars," counterfactualism can appear to reject the concept of an apolitical academic world. This concept, however, is itself a historically and politically conditioned set of beliefs, and one that is more pertinent in certain countries and milieux, such as Britain (and then only to an extent), than in others.

The presentism that is central to the employment of counterfactualism in "history wars" is seen, in particular, in the use of counterfactual speculations to suggest different paths to a contrasting present. For example, dismayed by the nature of current European developments, notably the rise there of Islam, an issue for many American commentators, the influential American political scientist James Kurth asked in 2006 if there are "alternative European identities that could provide for a more promising, and a more vital, future." Having surveyed the possibility for a revived socialist or nationalist identity, he wrote, "What would have happened if Europe had adopted and practiced the precepts of Catholic social thought from the 1950s, including the precepts of the culture of life from the 1970s to the present?" Drawing on a discussion of Catholic social thought, Kurth argued that this would have led Europeans to address the problems of high unemployment as well as demographic decline, and thus to less of a need for Muslim immigration into the continent. For Kurth, past is linked to present and future, with a clear preference for changing all of them that may indeed justify Richard Evans's critique of support for counterfactualism as politically encoded: "In an alternative, counterfactual European history, the revival of Christian identity and adherence to the principles of Catholic social thought would have given Europe a sound religious basis on which to confront the challenges posed by . . . Islam. . . . The best way for Europe to regain its future is to reclaim its history. That means to return to the Christian faith that attended and vitalized Europe for almost two thousand years."[56]

The implications of this argument for debate about American identity are readily apparent. In the United States, much of the debate about developments in what has been termed the "culture wars" relates to the shaping of past, present, and future, with counterfactuals held out to warn of the likely consequences if rival interpretations succeed. These counterfactuals are not restricted to politics and war, but relate to wider cultural and social currents. Thus, in 1987, the prominent liberal senator Edward Kennedy, in a classic use of counterfactuals as part of political rhetoric, offered a nightmare vision of an America in which, as an alternative future, and thus a one-day alternative history, President Ronald Reagan's nomination of the conservative jurist Robert Bork to the Supreme Court succeeded: "a land in which women would be forced into back-alley abortions, blacks would sit at segregated lunch counters, rogue police could break down citizens' doors in midnight raids, children could not be taught about evolution."

On the Right, correspondingly, critics of immigration and multiculturalism, such as Victor Davis Hanson in *Mexifornia: A State of Becoming* (2003) and Samuel Huntington in *Who Are We? The Challenges to America's National Identity* (2004), provided a prospectus that was bleak unless a stop was made to immigration. Later in the decade, Tea Party commentators were to make similar predictions. On both Left and Right, future histories overlapped with accounts of past and present calling for different policies, with counterfactuals providing the options and also underlining past and present responsibility for the bite of the bleak future. This running together of past, present, and future is particularly the case with discussion of immigration.

In contrast, there is little interest, indeed almost none in the public treatment of counterfactual speculations, in suggesting that different developments in the past would have led to a present that would be similar, if not the same. In practice, although the paths to a contrasting present can be divided between optimistic and pessimistic, the relationship between, on the one hand, an improvable past or a past that could have been worse, and, on the other, the possibility of a better or worse present, is not automatic; and the same is true of the relationship with political sympathies, let alone politics. To suggest that the past could have been better does not automatically imply dissatisfaction with current circumstances (although it usually does). Conversely, offering the prospect of a worse past does not necessarily mean contentment with the current situation. Taking this distinction further, the former does not have to mean support for change, nor the latter a sense of conservative acceptance. Indeed, all, or any, counterfactual speculations can be inherently radical, in that they challenge the inevitability, indeed legitimacy, of the present situation, or inherently conservative in that they underline the hazards of change. As already indicated, all of these themes can be unhelpful, as political contexts vary by country while the counterfactual speculations can be motivated primarily by the drive for entertainment, or by the scholarly attempt to understand the past by clarifying the options that were available and the possibilities that could have occurred. Moreover, the counterfactuals in discussion may have been political at the time, and frequently intensely so, but their present consideration does not have to be.

INSTRUMENTALISM VERSUS COUNTERFACTUALISM

To return to the field of eighteenth-century international relations as an example, there were not only a number of diplomatic options, or apparent options, for each state to consider in an unclear international situation, but, in addition, their time scale, specifically the likely timing of particular crises, was also unknowable. This issue of timing is a key variable in many counterfactuals. For example, in the early 1750s, the crucial issue to Thomas, Duke of Newcastle, secretary of state for the Northern Department from 1748 to 1754 and the chief minister in the field of British foreign policy, was the Imperial Election Plan—the wish to avoid fresh instability in the Holy Roman Empire (essentially Germany and Austria) by securing the election, as king of the Romans (the heir to the emperor), of Archduke Joseph (later the Emperor Joseph II), the elder son of Emperor Francis I and Maria Theresa of Austria.[57]

However, the urgency of this as a means to stabilize international politics was by no means clear to contemporaries. In the event, Francis was not to die until 1765, by which time, after the Diplomatic Revolution of 1756, Anglo-Austrian relations were cool. Although less prominent, the Polish succession was also an issue in the early 1750s, one indeed that was widely seen by British ministers as likely to lead to war, but, in fact, Augustus III of Saxony-Poland was not to die until 1763. Moreover, in contrast with the death of his father and predecessor in 1733, this death did not lead to a full-scale European conflict. In part, this was because Europe was exhausted by the recent Seven Years' War (1756–63). Had the death occurred a decade earlier, then the situation might well have been very different. This counterfactual provides support for the earlier decision to devote diplomatic effort to the issue.

These were specific instances of a more general unknowable which affected eighteenth-century foreign policy. As the aspirations of foreign rulers, and their responses to developments, were unknown, so it was very difficult to assess likely changes. This difficulty made it hard to discuss policy options other than in hypothetical terms, but that did not accord with the desire of ministers to appear to be in command of events. This wish was encouraged in Britain by strident and frequent criticism from politicians and polemicists, and thus by the need for ministers to respond to the active public debate. Furthermore, the mental equipment of the period, more specifically the belief in mechanistic, rather than organic, theories of states and the state system, encouraged an approach to international relations that was instrumentalist: by means of adopting a specific policy, there would be assured outcomes.[58]

Correspondingly if the policy was changed, so also would be the outcomes, and again in a clear-cut fashion. Reflecting the sense of predictable interconnectedness, Robert, fourth Earl of Holdernesse, the secretary of state for the Northern Department and a former diplomat, wrote to the diplomat Joseph Yorke, in 1754, that the possibility of Britain settling differences between Russia and the Ottoman (Turkish) Empire would "naturally be productive of the happiest consequences, as His Majesty's [George II's] influence at the Ottoman Porte [court] will thereby be greatly increased, and the designs which the French may, at any time, have to create disturbances, between the Grand Signior [Sul-

tan] and either of the Empresses [Maria Theresa of Austria and Elizabeth of Russia] will be rendered more difficult for the future."[59]

The confidence in this instrumentalist approach can also be seen
as a product of what might be referred to as the Whig mind. It has to
be appreciated that this habit of thinking was not only associated with
Whigs. Nevertheless, there was a linkage that is worthy of comment. The
particular characteristics of this mind stemmed from a confidence that
rational calculation could be applied to understand and solve problems.
This confidence was born of the mathematization of experience and exposition of rules, and thus assured outcomes, in the prestigious "new
science" centered on Sir Isaac Newton's work, notably his mathematical
approach to physics.[60]

In some respects, the disdain for counterfactualism on the part of
some modern academics can be linked to this Whig mindset: counterfactualism can be related to an apparent unpredictability, in both
analysis and outcome, which is unwelcome to it. The merits of the two
approaches—to propose a dichotomy for what is, in reality, more often
a continuum—appear differently to both practitioners and observers.
These differences reflect intellectual convictions but also psychological
drives, while, in some contexts, political preference may also play a part.
If these comments may offer the basis for a critique of the counterfactual approach, they can also do the same for a criticism of those who are
unwilling to consider it. To adopt a more positive note, historians do
not simply record facts, but rather ask questions. In assessing history, we
need to consider the process as well as the record, and counterfactualism
can play an important role in so doing. It helps in considering cause and
effect, decisions and consequences; in focusing analysis; and in thinking
and explaining in terms of alternatives.

4

POWER AND THE STRUGGLE
FOR IMPERIAL MASTERY

Counterfactual speculations are most valid intellectually if considered like historical scholarship. As such, it is appropriate that these speculations engage explicitly with the problem of assessing both ideas and material factors, as well as conjunctures and structural factors, and treat each set of them as interdependent. The following three chapters relate, with a steadily sharper focus, to the struggle for imperial mastery that culminated in Britain becoming the leading world power. This chapter offers some theoretical points, the next considers the rise of the West, and chapter 6 assesses Britain's success in terms of "Which West?" They should be read as a sequence, but can also be considered separately. This sequence links specific counterfactuals to a wider global approach. Moreover, aside from the inherent significance of the eighteenth century, it is also favored because it is easier to establish and discuss the alternatives from a more distant perspective and without the controversies, notably political controversies, that more recent counterfactuals lead to.

MATERIAL AND CULTURAL POWER

The nature of power is a key issue and is also highly relevant for counterfactual speculations. In particular, the respective parts played by resources and ideas repay consideration. This is because, alongside the tendency in most counterfactual speculations to put an emphasis, possibly too strong an emphasis, on individuals, contingencies, and will, there is a contrary danger, as in other theories, that materialist explanations will prevail. In these explanations, the possibility of success for one or another counterfactual appears to lie in material factors. Key examples include the size of economies and the strength of armies,[1] or variants thereof such as improvements in military technology. Indeed, a conviction of the importance of this material strength can lead to a situation in which consequences are assumed to flow automatically, or even immediately, from a change in policy. This assumption represents a new, and misleading, form of determinism to which some counterfactual discussion is prone.

A number of caveats can be offered to these materialist explanations. For example, power and force are not identical, while success in conflict is not necessarily the product of economic resources, nor of a variant thereof. Wealth and other material determinants of power are important to success, but their importance depends on how they are applied. Organization, institutions, and leadership matter in this application. So also does culture, which cannot be reduced to being a variant on material factors.[2] All empires, for example, are not the same. Culture as a constituent of power covers a wide range of characteristics and attitudes,[3] a range which poses problems for counterfactuals. In part, this cultural constituent of power relates directly to the question of what power means in a given context. This point opens up the possibility of discussing the religious, intellectual, and cultural constituents of power status. This discussion directs attention to the issue of power as arising from nonmaterial considerations, or operating in a manner that is focused on them.

Religious power is a key instance, and there has been an interesting discussion of the consequences for the Roman Empire, not least in its subsequent reaction to Islam, of the counterfactual of treating Jesus as a prophet rather than the son of God.[4] To have done so would have made it easier to reach accommodations with other religions. To take another religious counterfactual, the absence or failure of the Protestant Reformation might well have stifled free thought; led to doctrinal orthodoxy that reduced the intellectual, and thus developmental, opportunities provided by religious pluralism; and also affected the rise of the West, discussed in the next two chapters. As an instance of cultural power, it is also instructive to consider Greek domination of Classical thought and language, a domination operating through Greek influence in the Roman Empire. This approach, which underlines the significance of the Roman conquest of Greece, would define power, and related counterfactuals, in part in terms of a capacity for the spread of attitudes and values. Cultural factors also greatly affect the material sphere. Indeed, any emphasis on material considerations needs to be contextualized with reference to the cultural issues involved in their understanding, use, and effectiveness.[5]

Moreover, the provision of resources in conflicts is not an automatic consequence of capability, but, instead, in part reflects the willingness to support goals. The parameters and nature of this willingness vary, which again opens the path for counterfactuals, but public opinion is a potent factor even in autocratic regimes.[6] This potency ensures that states (of whatever form, including empires and nation-states) have to be considered in large part in terms of their capacity to elicit consent and to avoid dissent. This approach, again, can limit the value of counterfactuals focused on different results for battles or campaigns (or indeed elections).

This capacity to elicit consent is a multilayered one. It embraces, for example, the agglomeration seen with composite states, a situation which is true of most empires. Furthermore, the practice of agglomeration may be different from the terms of the combination. This contrast can lead to a tension between competing interests and among varied goals, as with Charles V's Habsburg Empire in the early 1550s and also the Burgundian and Spanish cores of the empire of his son, Philip II, later in the decade.[7] The same is true of the tensions between Britain and the Dominions in the first half of the twentieth century. Such tensions provide a basis for counterfactuals.

As an extension of this point, it is necessary to see international coalitions in part in terms of the need to elicit consent and cooperation, with the obvious counterfactual that these may fail. Allies are not necessarily friends, and conflicting interests are with difficulty brought and held together by being persuaded of a common need. The course of World War II demonstrated the importance of alliance politics, with Churchill notably telling his private secretary, Jock Colville, with reference to the Soviet Union, that he would make positive reference to the Devil if the latter found himself at war with Hitler. (Churchill made this remark on June 21, 1941, the day before the news of Germany's invasion of the Soviet Union was revealed, but Churchill was certain it was coming.) If this focus on the importance of eliciting consent is extended to the combatants' domestic sphere, and the search for backing there when raising resources, then materialist conceptions of power change. Instead of offering a ready quantification which might seem to restrain counterfactuals, or at least contain their discussion within bounds set by the measurement of relevant criteria, these counterfactuals indeed take on some of the characteristics of political history. These characteristics notably include the extent to which political alliances involve issues of leadership and are molded through contingencies. The dynamics of the "Big Three" during their talks at Yalta in 1945 were instructive. Although Churchill and Roosevelt were the leaders of the West, Roosevelt snubbed Churchill in his attempt to woo Stalin.

Dealing in perceptions, rather than realities, also dents the materialist approach. The political history involved in counterfactuals, and notably with reference to alliances, moreover, has to be understood in the widest terms to include the political dynamics and consequences of social relations. The economic sphere also involves alliances, as management, government, consumers, investors, and labor all possess agency. Furthermore, they interact in a shifting fashion in which material considerations are not the sole factor.

Lastly, as far as alliances are concerned, it is important to note that this is also a case of cooperation, coordination, and consent within government, with all the contingencies and counterfactuals these factors imply. Looked at differently, the pursuit of goals and tasking requires cooperation between various branches of government. It is frequently difficult to secure this cooperation because there are no clear structural relationships or patterns of agreement between these branches. In the case of the military, this problem can be seen in the repeated deficiencies of joint planning, deficiencies which undercut some of the ready assumptions of counterfactuals in military history.

Moreover, clashes between army, navy, and air force views make the military dimension of the long-term assumptions described as strategic culture far more shifting and tentative than the term might suggest. We tend, for example, to view American policy as unitary when it was usually the outcome of complex internal struggles. The Pentagon was only established in 1943 as a much-needed (but by no means immediately successful) way of getting the service chiefs to work together. Mutual rivalry over funding, and conflicting strategic and tactical ideas, continued nonetheless—even after President Harry Truman created the National Security Council in 1947 to secure effective coordination.[8] The significance of cooperation can be taken further beyond the military, if other branches of government, such as finance and diplomacy, have to be included.

These caveats about government and policy are not points dependent on a particular stage in material "progress." Furthermore, an emphasis on consent within the varied alliance structures discussed above,[9] and on the practices that contribute to power, directs attention to the role of ideas and debate, and the issues these pose for counterfactualism. Here, a typology can be offered that is the opposite of materialist. Some states have an ideology in which obedience is owed to a leadership that is deistic or semideistic, while others accept a different situation, sometimes extending to recognizing the formal legitimacy of opposition. The former might today be treated as anachronistic, but twentieth-century ideologies and political practices, in fact, threw up similar situations, for example in Nazi Germany and in Communist North Korea, and future ones may continue to do so. More generally, it is not obvious how best to assess ready consent, or, at least, ostensible consent, as a constituent aspect of strength, but it is unclear why such consent should necessarily take a far smaller role than material factors. A similar point can be made about the openness of political systems to debate.

There are many past analyses of states in which commentators regarded domestic regeneration as entailing not solely improvements in material factors, but also processes of political, social, and ideological renewal; with again an obvious capacity for counterfactuals if this renewal did not occur. These analyses have been strident in the case of revolutionary regimes with messianic ideologies, such as the China of the Cultural Revolution in the 1960s, with its determination to purge the Communist Party and government. The same element is readily apparent in the content and vocabulary of democratic politics, for example in the early twentieth century, with tariff reform in Britain, progressivism in the United States, and anticlericalism in France. This stress on renewal is a reminder of the multiple perceptions of strength and weakness, and therefore of the number of possible narratives that can be followed in assessing the rise and fall of states.

Ideologies also play a more direct role in foreign policies in the shape of strategic cultures.[10] These strategic cultures vary with reference to a range of factors, but ideas, again, cannot be taken out of the equation. This point is particularly seen with the choice between "accommodationist" strategies and those that were more assertive. This is a choice that raises anew the prospect for counterfactualism. As a different point, the ideological framework of relations between state and society can also be regarded as crucial to the success and failure of states competing and warring across cultural divides, as with the success of the Christian states over their Muslim rivals in the *Reconquista* of Spain.[11] Again, this point ensures that counterfactuals, to be effective, need to deal with more than the specifics of political or military contingencies.

A SENSE OF POWER

As a reminder of the role of ideas, a belief in great-power status, traditionally expressed in terms of imperial identity and pretensions, provided a crucial means to strengthen the legitimacy of states. This strengthening was not simply a matter of anachronistic past values focused on dynasticism and sacral kingship, but was also the case with more "modern" recent great powers, such as, over the last century, Britain, the United States, the Soviet Union, and China, with the great-power status seen as serving idealist goals as well as realist needs, and these idealist goals proving crucial to legitimacy. France's determination to act as a great power after 1945 can in part be regarded in this light, as both the Fourth and the Fifth Republics sought legitimacy in these terms. It is also pertinent, in assessing counterfactual options, to underline the extent to which powers are great because they wish to be so and are ready to focus their efforts accordingly, not least by shelving or otherwise resolving internal disagreements. A sense of national exceptionalism and mission is part both of the sense of power and of thinking on an imperial scale, as with twentieth-century France. Such a sense is an important element that cannot be analyzed in materialist conceptions, nor discussed in counterfactual terms that are thus defined and limited.

An instance is offered by the strength of nationalism, for when nationalism is put under great strain, which is one interpretation of French divisiveness and political culture in the late 1930s, then it becomes harder to act as a major power. This analysis does not imply that France fell to German attack in 1940 because of internal crisis and moral weaknesses, as is sometimes argued, and that, if these had not pertained, it would not have been defeated. Such an interpretation dramatically underrates the military and international circumstances in 1940, not least the totally inappropriate French use of their army reserves.[12] However, the response to the success of the German offensive was greatly affected by a wider political malaise that fed through into a crisis of confidence incompatible with great-power status. Thus, a balance has to be struck in explaining France's defeat in 1940, however much this balance is expressed in counterfactual terms. Internal weaknesses certainly made France more vulnerable in defeat, not least widespread support for right-wing groups and for Pétain's image of country and traditional values, and a more general lack of commitment to the Third Republic.[13]

Belief in great-power status generally drew on a sense of exceptionalism that was presented in terms of alleged specific characteristics and also of a praiseworthy inheritance: for example, nineteenth-century Britain as the successor to Imperial Rome. This practice has been maintained by commentators who depict the United States and, before it, Britain and, sometimes, before that, the Dutch, in terms of a liberal tradition of effective maritime powers, whose success owed much to their liberalism. The explanation of success in terms of this liberalism leads to, or implies, a counterfactual based on what would have happened had this liberalism not been the case, an issue considered in chapter 6.

Conversely, decline can occur when societies lose the willingness to act as great powers, as, arguably, happened with the United Provinces (modern Netherlands) in the eighteenth century, with Britain from the late 1950s, and, as far as some (mostly American) critics are concerned, with a modern United States unwilling, notably as a result of a lack of confidence criticized as "declinism," to bear the burdens and costs of great-power status and aspirations. One aspect of this unwillingness in the case of Britain was a disenchantment with colonial rule. As a result, the end of the British Empire has very much attracted counterfactual speculation, of which some, but only some, is of the "If only" type. This disenchantment with colonial rule was a reflection of Europe's much-reduced status and strength after World War II. Therefore, the disenchantment is an indication of the extent to which attitudinal changes, both in individual states and in Europe as a whole, did not occur in a vacuum, which counterfactual approaches again have to note. Britain and France had weakened themselves and their material resource bases, trying to be great powers. However, a shift in attitudes toward empire was also crucial. In the case of Britain, a concern to spend far more money on social welfare in the metropole was combined with a changed view on the appropriateness of colonial rule.[14]

This shift in attitudes opens up counterfactuals based on Labour not winning the 1945 general election. Churchill, the Conservative leader, would probably have taken his reluctance to part with empire far further than Labour was to do. Churchill winning in 1945 opens up a counterfactual paralleling the more common one of his failure to become prime minister in 1940.[15] Disenchantment with colonial rule, however, was widespread in the West in this period; although not in Portugal, which if it had given up its large colonial territories would have been a very minor power without a mission, and which went on fighting to hold them until 1974. Thus, the role of ideas was crucial.

The emphasis on perception (by governing elites, domestic supporters, and foreign states) as a major factor in defining and determining the identity and strength of powers (X is a strong power because it sees itself and is seen as a strong power)[16] can be matched with reference to the means by which powers interact. Use of the language of norms and of a standard analytical model suggests a high degree of predictability in this interaction, an approach that limits the role for counterfactuals or limits their type to the on-off/yes-no switch. However, whatever the view of commentators, norms are, in practice, changeable and are very much molded by political actors. This molding is brutally obvious in revolutionary or dictatorial contexts, when existing norms can be publicly rejected. However, at other times also, there is a similar porosity about conventions of behavior, a porosity that affects the validity of explaining behavior (or indeed the perception of interests) in terms of predictable consequences. This is an issue both for conventional historical scholarship and for counterfactual approaches.

This porosity is especially pertinent for great powers because their range and commitments are likely to be most extensive. As a result, these powers are most likely to confront other interests whose views on norms are very different, just as their military practice may well be asymmetrical, each of which was the case for the United States in Vietnam and Afghanistan. These clashing views need to be taken into account both when assessing the goals of states and when seeking to vary them in counterfactual speculations. The perception held by, and of, the states involved, as well as their willingness to adapt to differing norms, were aspects of their power and effectiveness. Moreover, the capacity to understand the complexities of the strength and intentions of other states becomes necessary for countries, and is thus an aspect of power. It is a necessity not only to judge opponents, but also to consider allies. The assessment of the latter involves short-term factors, for example what could be contributed in a particular conflict, as well as long-term considerations, such as gratitude and the inculcation of a sense of empathy.

Perception is not simply a method of analysis, therefore, but is also an aspect of power. As such, perception is far less fixed and quantifiable than readily apparent material considerations, such as the number of troops or the production of pig iron. This role for perception helps undermine assessments of states based simply on such material considerations, and underlines the problem of analyzing power on a uniform basis and of treating counterfactuals as, in some fashion, predictable in their context and/or consequences. Counterfactuals profit if they can incorporate the variables presented by the strength and weakness of the process of perception. Looked at differently, an emphasis on perception offers a parallel to physicists' interest both in the dependence of reality on observation and in the concept of parallel universes.

Structuralist interpretations, which see situations in terms of systems, tend to underrate the role of perception, but the latter, instead, is emphasized in specific analyses, especially those based on archival sources that cover the views of those involved, although it is necessary to give due weight to the limited range of the archival material for some states. Contemporary commentators are also apt to stress the extent to which public moods affect both the assessment of options and policy, with these moods sometimes owing much to events, such as the terrorist attacks on the United States in 2001, which understandably greatly affected American public attitudes and American policy. Moods today similarly affect the degree of interest in particular historical counterfactuals, as well as the response to them.

At the same time, moods are, in varying and shifting proportions, shaped very much by the official reactions of opinion makers in government and the press. To employ a counterfactual, it is possible to imagine a very different national mood in the United States in the months following the terrorist attacks had the chief reactor been Al Gore instead of George W. Bush. This point requires only the counterfactual that the Supreme Court have ruled on different grounds in deciding the 2000 election. As another instance of the link between comparative and counterfactual history, it is possible to note the very different British reaction to the terrorist bombings in London in 2005 from the American reaction in 2001. The respective roles of governmental policy and national mood in driving America's reaction is thus a subject for discussion.

A ROLE FOR THE COUNTERFACTUAL

While the long- and short-term consequence of moods for policy formation and execution are a matter of debate, political history is formulated and acted out in the short term. This emphasis on the short term and on conjunctures is a point that counterfactual discussions are often very good at grasping, not least with their interest in turning points, as in Antonia Fraser's essay assuming success for the plotters in the Gunpowder Plot in 1605.[17] These discussions may appear far distant from the world of historical scholarship and its methods, but it is notable that counterfactual speculations are not necessarily alone in not employing these methods. For example, materialist interpretations, not least structuralist accounts of the operation of a world system with rising and falling hegemons, tend to emerge from those who do not use archival sources,[18] and particularly those of the political actors involved. In contrast, there is nothing to stop historians who focus on counterfactuals grounded in specific moments from looking at the records left by those prominent at the time. To conclude this chapter, the linkage between great-power status and economic and technological strength needs to be handled with care. Material characteristics do not define power itself, nor do they determine its use, or the effectiveness of this use. The organization of resources clearly matters, while technology has a cultural dimension: the same piece of hardware can be extremely useful in one society and of little use in another where there is no tradition of using and developing it.

Within and between states, consent and cooperation are important to strength, and they are subject to counterfactuals. A lack of visceral opposition might sometimes be confused with consent, but the extent to which imperial expansion drew on the military support of conquered peoples is notable and is relevant to the discussion in the next chapter. The role of consent and cooperation was also demonstrated within states, as by the case of France, which was Christian Europe's most populous state in 1650–1790, but which periodically was powerless and periodically had considerable power.[19] This variation poses a problem for structuralist interpretations, and also for counterfactual theses that assume predictable outcomes from initial changes. As a reminder, instead, of the role of uncertainty, political events in France in 1789 set in train an unexpected transformation within France by 1792, when the republic was declared. War began with both Austria and Prussia that year, and the events of 1789 thereby led unexpectedly to fundamental changes in international relations by 1795 when the United Provinces (the Netherlands) were conquered and both Prussia and Spain ended the war with France.

These changes affected other powers, such as Britain. They therefore serve to indicate, as is discussed in chapter 6, that offering one counterfactual speculation logically affects most others that can be advanced for this period. This element is not always adequately brought out, especially in popular work on counterfactuals. Yet, there is value in asking and explaining why and how one counterfactual should prevail over another, or how they can interact.

5

THE WEST AND THE REST

In 1730, London audiences could laugh at Politic, a London tradesman depicted in Henry Fielding's play *Rape upon Rape,* who is so convinced that the Ottoman Turks could advance to Britain that he does not notice the attempt on the virtue of his daughter: "Give us leave only to show you how it is possible for the Grand Signor [the Sultan] to find an ingress into Europe. Suppose, Sir, this spot I stand on to be Turkey—then here is Hungary—very well—here is France, and here is England—granted— then we will suppose he had possession of Hungary—What then remains but to conquer France, before we find him at our own coast" (act 2, scene 11).

Thus, nearly half a century after the Turkish failure to capture Vienna in 1683, this aspect of the "world question" could be an item for fun, an instance of the socially condescending theme that tradesmen should stick to their work and position, and not get involved in politics. Yet, there were also more profound issues at stake in that period, as the world was in part shaped—economically, politically, and intellectually—by and through this question.

The relationship between the West and the rest of the world is a central topic in global history, not least the issue of why the relative power of the West rose so rapidly during the great expansion and integration of the world economy in the eighteenth and nineteenth centuries. This is one of the major questions in history, and one that is fraught with difficulty because of its relationship with acute modern sensitivities and controversies about the imperial legacy, or rather legacies. Indeed, in a classic instance of the impact of the present on the past, it is possible to ask whether the character and content of the analysis would be different but for modern concerns. Thus, for example, "What if there were no modern Indian public myth and/or school of historiography to affect our understanding of the British conquest of, and rule in, India?"

THE RISE OF CHINA OR THE WEST?

Aside from such presentism, counterfactualism also comes into the analysis of the rise of the West, as it is necessary to abstract particular factors in order to discuss why the West succeeded. This abstraction for the purpose of consideration is a classic instance of the role of counterfactuals in analysis and also in narratives. A corollary of the decision to focus on one strand amongst the potential narratives is that other possible strands are downplayed or ignored. Turning to the rise of the West, how far, for example, was the ethos of the international system a key element, and what if China had been confronted by the same situation as the major European states? To explain the contrast on which the resulting counterfactual is based (and most counterfactuals are based on contrasts), China operated as a great power in a regional system without comparable rivals. This was a very different international context from the multipolar European system, and one that led to mutual incomprehension.

In Europe, the multipolarity of the states system, the anarchic nature of power politics, and the kaleidoscopic character of alliances all helped to account for the development of "realist" paradigms of international behavior, and thus of judging other states. These "realist" paradigms contrasted with the imperial psyche of China, in which geopolitical dominance, and a sense that invulnerability was normal, were linked to assumptions about the proper operation of international relations. Earlier, the Roman Empire was largely similar to China. With the exception of Sassanid Persia (Iran), it was not surrounded by competing powers, but faced opposing and resistant forces, which gave an edge to its possessive and acquisitive ethos.

How far these factors, and indeed similar factors in other cases, can be assessed, except by suggesting alternatives, is unclear. The situation is made more complex because of the need to consider the practicality of what did not occur, in order to establish whether a choice was possible. For example, there was no comparison between the transoceanic colonization and power projection of the Atlantic European powers (Portugal, Spain, England, France, the Dutch) and the more land-based character of non-European powers including those, such as China and the Ottoman Empire, with a lengthy coastline. Ming China had an important regional naval role in the sixteenth century, combining with the Koreans to defeat the Japanese off Korea in the 1590s, but the long-range Chinese power projection into the western Indian Ocean seen in the early fifteenth century was not repeated. Manchu China occupied Taiwan in 1683, but that was the extent of its amphibious operations.

This limitation of Chinese naval activity brings in the counterfactual dimension. By focusing on what did not happen, this dimension discusses factors that tend to be ignored. For example, in light, in particular, of their current economic links with Australasia, it is worth asking what might have happened had either China or Japan in the sixteenth and seventeenth centuries matched the long-distance Chinese naval expeditions of the early fifteenth century,[1] or launched voyages of exploration or created settlement colonies across the Pacific or around its rim. The latter possibly is not a helpful counterfactual: a seventeenth-century Chinese or Japanese California is scarcely worth discussing if space in a book is at a premium, as there was scant interest in such transoceanic activity. Yet, in considering the respective trajectories of East Asian and Western European developments, it is pertinent to assess the respective significance of their level of long-range maritime activity. Counterfactuals may well highlight these points.[2]

Such assessment is valuable because, without systematic study of the later medieval and early modern periods, the assessment of nineteenth-century change outside Europe, and of the reasons for eventual Chinese failure at the hands of Western imperialism, will remain precarious. Given that maritime power projection ensured that Western Europe was able to exploit the bullion resources of the New World, and thereby to acquire a comparative advantage, allowing the insertion of Western European maritime powers into the non-Western world, it is worth asking what would have happened had the Chinese or Japanese done so instead. The great silver mines at Potosi in modern Bolivia might have been more difficult for them to exploit as part of a transoceanic system than they were for the Spaniards, for the Pacific is a far larger ocean than the Atlantic, but there is room for a counterfactual. Exploration and colonization can seem like aspects of the battles approach to counterfactual history—but for that one day, it would all have been different—yet, as will be discussed in chapter 7, such events are more than the product of the moment. Indeed, exploration, colonization, and war all reflect characteristics and strengths of particular societies.

Moreover, in considering relative development, it is pertinent to assess wider issues of public culture, and to ask how far they could have varied. Thus, the formidable bureaucratic culture that was a legacy of the Chinese past maintained by the Manchu after they conquered Ming China in the 1640s–50s was not matched in Europe. The Eurocentric nature of much counterfactual analysis ensures that there is a focus on European characteristics and turning points when explaining relative success vis à vis China, but it is as viable to ask about Chinese counterparts. An obvious one is, "What if the Manchu conquest had led to a greater discontinuity in Chinese history, both in terms of their ethos and with regard to the destruction they wrought?" The general assumption discounts such possibilities because it emphasizes the capacity of sedentary societies to assimilate nomadic conquerors, and the willingness of nomads to be assimilated,[3] but there is room to pose counterfactuals on this account.

There are also broader questions, repeatedly, about whether the Chinese state would have continued, as opposed to Chinese states. The Mongols expanded, in the early thirteenth century, into a multistate environment. Without Chingghis, there would not have been this Mongol expansion. In turn, there is the question of what would have happened if Zhu Yuanzhang, who established the Ming dynasty in 1368, had not managed to create a new Chinese empire. If the multistate environment had obtained for longer, and even possibly achieved some level of equilibrium for an extended period of time, what would China's later imperial history have been like? In turn, the Manchus who invaded in the seventeenth century were a much more coherent group than the Mongols, with a broader strategy based upon more than one extraordinary leader.

Returning to the Europeans, they might have possessed a system comparable to that in China, had the fusion of church and state developed differently. A widespread disengagement of the church and clergy from state government took place in the early modern period, although church government remained an important aspect of administration. Without this disengagement of the church from state government, the impact of ideological (religious) goals on commercial practices and aspirations would have been fostered, and such a fusion of church and state might well have limited economic growth in Europe.

European states, however, had not yet developed the large, self-consciously meritocratic bureaucracies produced by public institutions that were to provide the manpower for the expansion of government, and its information support systems, in the nineteenth century. Moreover, these bureaucracies were to help direct public culture and social policy toward government-based solutions and to create strong vested interests in such solutions. In contrast, dependent earlier on relations with the landed orders, rulers delegated out many of the functions of government and had only a limited ability to execute policies for change. This situation provided opportunities for entrepreneurs seeking to benefit from overseas expansion. England and the Netherlands managed much of their colonial involvement through chartered companies such as their East India Companies.[4]

Moreover, as a reminder of the complexities that need to be borne in mind when considering counterfactual alternatives, which are too often presented in terms of a ready switching on and off of options, it is far from clear how far Chinese governments prior to the nineteenth century should be seen, as is generally the case, as radically different from those of Europe, a point that raises the subjectivity inherent in the judgment of radical difference. Indeed, there are signs that, alongside such impressive feats of Chinese government, and, specifically, administration, as the supply of the large forces that conquered Xianjiang in the 1750s, ending the steppe threat to China,[5] there were serious problems. These problems included widespread corruption, losses of tax revenue, and a deleterious role for tax farmers. As a result, from the 1720s, provincial officials were permitted to retain a percentage of taxes in order to support local administration: thus by providing reasonable salaries, corruption was cut. If the use of tax farming in China, as in much of Europe, is a valuable indication of the deficiencies of public administration, and of the openness of government to different systems of control, regulation, and revenue raising,[6] it also stands as a notice about the serious problems of distinguishing between China and Europe in order to use them as contrasting building blocks in a comparative, and thus counterfactual, analysis.

Looked at differently, comparisons of Chinese with Christian European government encourage the conclusion that it is unclear to what extent a particular type of state structure was necessary to economic growth. For example, governmental forms alone do not account for the lack of sustained large-scale coal mining in China (unlike Britain) or, more generally, for the absence there of the modernization seen as crucial in the West's ability to become central to global economic links, and thus to the process and profits of globalization.[7] This lack of clarity makes counterfactualism difficult. However, from another perspective, the lack of clarity also makes standard historical analysis problematic, and thus ensures that counterfactualism plays a role as an aspect of the process of discussion.

Such counterfactual discussion was certainly present for contemporaries with interest in the strength of different political systems and in discussion of the likely consequences of their adoption.[8] This discussion was scarcely unique to that period, but is a more general aspect of political commentary and of the gathering of information on other political systems, as was seen with Aristotle and Tocqueville. A modern institutional equivalent to such comparative assessment is provided by benchmarking, as in the EU's support for the open method of coordination.[9] More generally, lesson-drawing is seen as dependent on counterfactual reasoning, as that is the means of what is termed policy transfer. This reasoning is important because it is necessary, in order for borrowing to work in policy transfer, to establish causality carefully, and counterfactualism operates as a valuable control in this respect.[10] This control is the case whether the borrowing is from other countries or from the past.

The discussion of other political systems is frequently linked to the explicit or implicit question, "What if we adopted this system?" Sometimes this question is given a location by turning to the past and asking, "What if we had adopted this system?" These questions are not idle thinking, but, instead, prime ways to engage in constitutional debate. The historical dimension furthers the possibility of doing so by under- lining the possibility of different courses. In doing so, this dimension acts as a fundamental critique of notions of inevitable development and thus of national exceptionalism. This critique helps explain what can be an anti-Whiggish character to counterfactualism, its use in opposition to Whiggish/triumphalist narratives, and also why the counterfactual approach is unsettling to some commentators. Looked at differently, the approach contributes to humane skepticism toward overdetermined ac- counts of past, present, and future, a skepticism that can be regarded as central to liberal thought.

Returning to asking counterfactual questions about the relative development of the West and China, several focus on culture, specifi- cally the nature of Chinese science. There is the argument that, because Chinese education centered on preparing candidates for the imperial civil service, it was nonscientific and nonanalytical, a proposition in part challenged by Joseph Needham's *Science and Civilisation in China* (1954). These characteristics of the educational system are held to have caused a lack of relevant human capital, which fed through into a deficiency in en- gineering knowledge. In turn, this deficiency compromised possibilities for industrial development, and, indeed, helped make redundant the dis- cussion of such possibilities. Yet, this issue can be seen as a red herring, not least if a comparative approach is adopted. European governments were staffed by humanistically trained men with little or no technical knowledge. This is also true today. Thus, in the United States, Congress is filled with lawyers, not engineers or scientists. Moreover, there were plenty of handy Chinese workers around making all sorts of things, which poses problems for the cultural interpretation. Nevertheless, this interpretation has had a significant impact, as when Cliff Bekar and Richard Lipsey asked why, "if China had been on the verge of an Indus- trial Revolution in the XVIIIth century . . . there was no further progress over the final hundred years of imperial rule." Publishing this piece in the aptly named "Problems" section of the *Journal of European Economic History*, they went on to ask, "Why not in the Islamic countries?" and concluded, having considered the alternatives by posing the relevant counterfactuals, that "there was nothing capricious about the location and approximate timing of the Industrial Revolution."[11]

Yet, it is also possible to adopt a counterfactual perspective in which the Industrial Revolution itself is something of an exception, if not, in some senses, a bizarre counterfactual. That is, looking at the vast sweep of history up to 1750 and the general structure of traditional (preindustrial) civilizations, one's expectation, allowing for economic growth in parts of the world over the previous quarter millennium, would be continued nonindustrial continuity. Traditional societies were built to resist change (or at least assimilate it into existing power arrangements), and the fundamentals of industrialization inevitably and predictably undermined the position of traditional elites. From this perspective, no well-managed and coherent traditional society should have industrialized. Indeed, it took a very peculiar confluence of internal and external circumstances to push Britain onto an industrial path, notably the political, social, cultural, ideological, and religious changes contributing to and flowing from the Glorious Revolution of 1688–89 and the subsequent revolution settlement. The subsequent path of politics, with the unpredictabilities it entailed, such as German unification, can then be seen as necessary for Continental countries to follow. The Industrial Revolution can therefore be considered, as it were, as a counterfactual that actually happened, the key question being, "What had to go wrong to allow this to take place?" Such an approach has the advantage of at least treating the British, later Western, experience as not necessarily normal. And again, this example really gets at the point that counterfactuals are based on and reveal each historian's philosophy of history. The more nuanced and sophisticated that philosophy is, the more nuanced and complex the counterfactuals are. Simple "What ifs?" won't do.

As far as the West and China are concerned, there is also the issue of whether the crucial topic is the "tipping point,"[12] when China became weaker in comparative terms, or, instead, a longer-term situation of relative decline. The latter was certainly not readily apparent in the eighteenth century. From the late seventeenth century until the third quarter of the eighteenth, China could lay claim to being the most successful military power on land; and if this was no longer the case over the following half century, that was essentially because China was a satisfied power. By the end of the eighteenth century, China, which had the largest army in the world, was at peace with all its neighbors, and on China's terms—a situation that did not describe any of the European powers. In the 1680s, Russia had accepted its expulsion from the Amur valley by the Chinese, and in the eighteenth century the Russians took care not to anger China. In 1792, the British East India Company was unwilling to heed Nepalese requests for assistance against China. In the event, a Chinese force reached Kathmandu and reduced Nepal to obedience.

In contrast, the geopolitical revolution was to be readily apparent in 1860 when Anglo-French forces occupied Beijing and the Russians founded the port of Vladivostok as a Pacific base, and in 1904 when an invading British-Indian force under Francis Younghusband reached Lhasa, the capital of Tibet, in order to enforce British influence. Yet, it is possible to pose a different question—not "Why did the West conquer much of Asia?" but "Why did Chinese and Western historians, writers, and politicians all read the First Opium War (1839–42) and subsequent events as evidence of Western power?" After all, despite a series of defeats, China, unlike most of Asia and Africa, was, while exploited for economic reasons, not really colonized, and also maintained its own culture. It was only when the Japanese invaded in 1931 and, more widely, from 1937 that the Chinese suffered the widespread effects of territorial imperialism. And the Japanese attempts at conquest had already run into the impasse of an intractable struggle that Japan could not win before Japan attacked the United States in 1941.

Nevertheless, the growth of world trade in the nineteenth century gave Western maritime powers a particular advantage in terms of relations with China, and it is significant that it was Britain, the leading European economic power, that defeated China in the First Opium War (1839–42), which was the first victory over China by a Western power. Industrial technology (rather than technology specifically for military ends) provided the Western powers with a strong comparative advantage in the world economy, and this advantage enabled them to change existing economic relationships in the nineteenth century.[13]

What, though, if China had been internally stable or if a vigorous and successful ruler like the Kangxi emperor (r. 1661–1722), who overcame the large-scale Revolt of the Three Feudatories (1674–81) and, in the 1690s, defeated the Zunghars of Xinjiang, had been in charge during the First Opium War? He would probably have rejected British approaches and would have settled in for a long war that the British could not have won, because, despite significant support from their colonies in India, they lacked the willingness to commit large-scale resources over the long term. A problem the Manchu dynasty faced in the nineteenth century was extremely bad leadership at the very top. Moreover, aside from other serious political problems,[14] such as insufficient central control over the provincial viceroys, problems which also had economic consequences, the crisis of the longstanding Taiping rebellion, which began in 1851, was as significant as Western pressure, and possibly more so.

But a "What if?" focused on Chinese politics can only go so far because, to take the valuable comparative perspective, the situation of Western relative advantage and the process of Western pressure were more general. The course and consequences of this pressure might be different, for example in China or Japan, Malaya or Siam, Persia or the Ottoman (Turkish) Empire, but, alongside the maintenance of independence in most cases, the fact of this pressure was a constant.

Indeed, instead of focusing on Chinese politics, Kenneth Pomeranz, employing a subdued counterfactual (no question is formally posed), emphasized the nature of Western economic development: "Europe's impact on the colonised societies would have been very different had these conquerors—like so many others in the past—brought with them some significant technological advantages concentrated in a few militarily significant sectors (such as iron and steel) rather than a generally transformed economy supporting a much higher standard of living and radically different patterns of work and resting on very large differences in per capita supplies of energy and other primary products."[15] Thus, European development triggered the tipping point as far as relations with the non-West were concerned.

INDIA

As a reminder that the "world question" does not solely relate to China, the prominent Indian scholar Sanjay Subrahmanyam drew attention to the uncertainty and importance of developments in India. Without dominance there from the 1810s the British would have been militarily weaker in Asia, for it was thanks in large part to Indian resources and troops that the British were able to exert and sustain influence in China, Southeast Asia, the Gulf, and East Africa, and, during World War I, the Middle East.

Subrahmanyam therefore asked what would have happened had the aggressive Nadir Shah of Persia chosen to remain in Delhi after he conquered the capital of the Mughal Emperors in 1739 following his victory at Karnal.[16] In some respects, this question is a reprise of the speculations that focus on Alexander the Great marching further east, although Nadir Shah, who was more successful in India than Alexander, was faced by incessant problems on a number of frontiers that made it difficult for him to focus on India, as Alexander wished to do once he reached it. Thus, in 1740, rather than mounting renewed efforts in India, Nadir Shah attacked the Uzbeks, capturing the cities of Bukhara and Khiva, while, in 1743, war with the Ottomans was unsuccessfully revived.[17]

This example serves as a reminder that counterfactuals have to be assessed within an unstable, not fixed, contemporary context, as indeed also with the questions, "What if Nadir Shah had died (as he nearly did) in an assassination attempt in 1741, and his able son, Reza Qoli Mirza, had succeeded him?" and "What if Nadir Shah had not been assassinated in 1747, leading to the splitting of his empire?" In the case of Subrahmanyam's counterfactual, the context was of a series of imperial crises and expanding polities in South and East Asia. Indeed, the conquest of Delhi made manifest the weakness of the Mughal Empire, and the opportunities for other powers. This series of imperial crises and expanding polities continued into the early nineteenth century.[18] The relationship between this series of crises and the growth of European power is unclear, a point worth considering when discussing how best to assess, or indeed map, Indian history.

In considering the rise of the West in the case of India, it is pertinent to focus, alongside systemic European strengths, on particular factors, not least in the shape of the degree to which the British were fortunate between 1790 and 1850 that they were able to fight Mysore, the Marathas, the Gurkhas, and the Sikhs in sequence, rather than simultaneously. The obvious counterfactual raises the possibility of simultaneous challenges, and this parallels questions relating to the role of internal instability alongside foreign challenges for China in the nineteenth century and the 1930s. Another counterfactual suggests that, despite the obvious contrasts, notably the lack of unity in India, there was no inherent reason why there should not have been a challenge in India comparable in seriousness (within the different contexts) to that the British faced in North America in 1775–83. Moreover, specific counterfactuals arise, for example, the possibility that the use of the Mysore navy in 1769 could have brought about the total defeat of British forces in southern India in the First Mysore War.[19] Moreover, the victory over the Marathas at Assaye on September 23, 1803, was a very hard-fought battle, with the Maratha artillery proving particularly effective,[20] which therefore prompts the question, "What if the British commander, Wellington, had been killed?" It is certainly worth considering how far this would have made a difference in the Peninsular War, and at Waterloo, more particularly testing Wellington's view that his presence at the latter was decisive.[21]

A discussion of British success in India in terms of war may seem to risk a return to the militarization of counterfactual history that can be so often observed. That process is understandable, however, not only because war is particularly subject to discussion in these terms, but also because conflict pulls together a range of factors, including financial strength, economic capability, and demographic weight. These, in turn, can be subject to counterfactuals, for example the last bringing in the role of resistance to disease. The rise of the West can be located with reference to each factor. Financial strength was in part a product of access to New World silver,[22] while Western economic capability reflected technological, intellectual, and organizational developments, for example in building warships equipped with cannons and capable of transoceanic navigation. The use of compasses and maps was particularly helpful in this regard, as it made it possible to establish and record locations and routes, and thus to plan repeat journeys. Moreover, the West benefited in the New World from a positive disease gradient: Western settlers, though very vulnerable, as in Virginia and the West Indies, were less so than the native people to the diseases exchanged through contact, unlike the situation in sub-Saharan Africa, for example for the Portuguese in Mozambique and the British in West Africa.[23] Each of the factors discussed in this paragraph is subject to counterfactuals, but isolating one alone is misleading if doing so is based on the supposition that it is the key factor. In reality, the process and causes of Western success were more multifaceted.

This multifaceted character poses problems for counterfactuals as they are more readily advanced, at least in popular writing, in terms of single factors. This situation is another reason for scholarly unhappiness with counterfactualism, but making that criticism of the approach underplays the extent to which the simplification of the past is a characteristic of much historical writing. Indeed, in criticizing counterfactuals we need to be honest about the limits of much conventional writing. There is no inherent reason why counterfactuals should be simpler than other historical approaches. In one respect, counterfactuals offer greater complexity because their effect presupposes knowing what happened and yet also being able to offer a contrasting narrative and a different analysis.

Indeed, the impact on the reader of this narrative and analysis in large part depends upon knowledge of the standard approach. Arguably, the complexity of this task encourages the simplification displayed in many counterfactual expositions, but, again, this simplification is not too different from much presentation of the past. To point out that to single out counterfactual analyses as limited in scope is to ignore the limits also of much conventional writing ensures that this criticism does not provide the knock-down argument for rejecting counterfactuals that critics might think. Instead, our assessment of the method should be made against the background of honesty about the actual state of historical writing. Moreover, counterfactualism is an approach that operates at different levels and with varied success. Therefore, to discuss the counterfactual approach in terms of simple judgments is unhelpful as it assumes some inherent characteristics that reflect credit or criticism on the entire process. This approach neglects the extent to which a given method can be useful or not in particular contexts, while, in its use, skill can be displayed to a different extent.

A discussion of the rise of the West exemplifies these points. There is no inherent reason why counterfactuals should not be employed in tackling this question. Indeed, they are of particular value in helping discuss why specific developments did not occur. This is a subject that needs to be explained in terms of more than "nothing happened." This is the case for example of why China did not experience comparable growth to the West, or why Britain avoided major war between 1815 and 1914. Yet, it is possible to produce work of very varied quality in employing counterfactuals. In particular, in this case, it is necessary to understand the variety of both the West and the non-West, the complexities of their relationships,[24] and the drawback in assuming that there was an obvious linear pattern in which a tipping point toward Western success can be readily identified. Instead, counterfactuals that offer complexity and indeterminacy are more accurate. However, as with noncounterfactual history, they do not respond to the popular and, indeed, scholarly demand for answers and thus the pressure to presume more knowledge of the past and more certainty in our analysis than is appropriate.

6

BRITAIN AND FRANCE, 1688–1815

CONTESTING THE WEST

The struggle between Britain and France from 1688 to 1815 enables one to amplify and reconsider the discussion of the rise of the West, by offering a very different perspective from that provided in the last chapter. The rise of the West is one of the metanarratives of world history over the last half millennium, but more attention has been devoted, not least in counterfactual discussion, to the linked questions of "When/How/Why rise?" rather than to "Which West?" Yet, the latter question can be profitably reexamined. It is important in its own right and also needs to be addressed as a second-order counterfactual. In short, "Would the rise of the West have occurred at all, or possibly followed another path, and with other consequences, had there been a different West?" At the outset, instead of posing the question of whether, once Western dominance had been established, it had to take the forms it did, it is more pertinent to link with the last chapter by asking if a variety of possible courses of Western development existed that might have precluded such a dominance. This issue is a variant of the questions in chapter 5 about Chinese weaknesses and how far they helped lead to a tipping point toward Western success. This chapter focuses on the struggle between Britain and France in 1688–1815, although that is not the sole possible counterfactual in terms of "Which West?"

For example, aside from the possibility in 1688, when William III of Orange successfully invaded England, that there could still have been, at least in some fashion, a Dutch West, it is also worth noting that the contingent events of 1776, 1914, 1917, 1940, and 1941,[1] and the issues that each focused, greatly altered the relationships between Britain, France, the United States, Germany, Russia, and the rest of the West. The events of each year therefore greatly changed the character of the West. As a result, they have attracted counterfactual speculations, for example Robert Cowley's consideration of Britain winning the American War of Independence, Norman Stone on Archduke Franz Ferdinand surviving attack in Sarajevo in 1914,[2] and Andrew Roberts on Lenin being assassinated at the Finland Station in St. Petersburg in 1917.[3] The late Alan Clark used to ask what would have happened had Britain negotiated peace with Hitler in 1940, although, in his case, that of a far-right maverick, there was a degree of the "If only" that justifies some of the criticism of counterfactualism.

More generally, it is possible to stress a number of different courses, and related points of indeterminacy, all of which would have altered the character of the West and, definitely, probably, or possibly, its impact in the wider world. Some courses are implausible or unhelpful other than as an aid to thinking, as with the question I was asked in May 2008: "What if Protestants had settled what became Latin America? Would it have been more successful?" As there was no chance of Protestants successfully doing so, this question is of value only to direct attention to the role of religion in the ideology and culture of Latin America. French, Dutch, and British attempts to conquer parts of Latin America had only limited success.

As it was the struggle for rivalry between Britain and France that was most important to the course of Western overseas expansion in the lengthy period 1680–1900, it is on this struggle that it is most appropriate to focus, as this, as was appreciated at the time, was the "tipping period" in relations between the West and Asia, Africa and Australasia. Moreover, other rivalries can be subsumed into this Anglo-French struggle. This is especially so for that between Britain and Spain, as the latter was ruled by a branch of the House of Bourbon, the ruling French dynasty, from 1700, and France and Spain were allied for much, but not all, of the period 1700–90. Britain was the leading naval power from the 1690s to the 1940s, and France was the second naval power for most of this period, particularly the eighteenth century, during which Spain was the third naval power.

Compared to the protracted struggle of Britain and France, the rivalry between Britain and Russia from the 1710s to the 1900s was less significant, which itself opens up a counterfactual, designed to highlight why that was the case, namely, "What would have happened had the rivalry with Russia been the most important one for Britain?" It is instructive to consider periods when this rivalry was indeed foremost—1716–17, 1720–21, 1791, 1854–56, 1877–78 and 1885—not least in order to raise questions about the significance of the Anglo-French rivalry. Such a consideration also permits the testing of structural interpretations of international relations, such as that of a necessary rivalry between the Eurasian "heartland" great power of Russia and the maritime "peripheral" great power of the British Empire.[4] This is an approach taken further with the argument that this was a Cold War before the term is usually applied.[5]

In large part as a consequence of the struggle between Britain and France, the West was left in 1815 without a hegemonic power, and notably so as far as Europe was concerned. Russia led there militarily, but dominance was part of a wide-ranging conservative political alignment. The absence of a single hegemonic power in Europe was a British objective, while Britain, conversely, enjoyed this status on the oceans and outside Europe. The political settlement at the close of the Napoleonic Wars, in particular at the Congress of Vienna (1814–15), ensured that much of Europe was stable, insofar as territorial boundaries were concerned, with both Britain and Russia free to pursue expansionist interests elsewhere in the world. Yet, this resolution of the struggle in the Western "core" was far from inevitable and was not seen as inevitable by contemporaries.[6] The eventual resolution was very important to the subsequent century of European territorial expansion, not least by helping ensure that Britain could concentrate on imperial growth.

In focusing on Britain and France, five counterfactuals are linked. Firstly, the question just suggested, namely, "Would a different course and result to that struggle have affected the relationship between the 'West and the rest,' both then and thereafter?" Secondly, "Did Britain have to win?" Thirdly, "Could Britain have developed differently in this period?" This can relate to industrial development, a topic mentioned in the last chapter, or to political developments, which can be seen as a vital precondition for economic change. Fourthly, "Could the Jacobites, the supporters of the exiled Stuarts, have won?" This is one of the more obvious instances of the third counterfactual, although not the only one. In addition, a counterfactual could be devised in terms of radicals being more successful in Britain, for example in 1779–81, the 1790s, the 1800s, and the 1810s, all periods of radical activity; and this consideration could be further extended by focusing on possible developments in British radicalism and by probing contrasts between Britain and Ireland. Lastly, "Could the British have won the American War of Independence and suppressed the American Revolution?"

These questions are very different in character and scale, but they are all important, and all invite valid counterfactuals, although they are also selective and many other counterfactuals could be considered. In particular, there are counterfactuals of the *deus ex machina* type, for example, "What if William III (r. 1689–1702) and Mary (r. 1689–94) had had children," creating a closer Anglo-Dutch link and a more powerful British monarchy, and ensuring that there was no Hanoverian succession in 1714? Or, "What if the French fleet had been sunk in a storm before reaching the Chesapeake in 1781," so that the British could have retreated from Yorktown, avoiding military defeat in the American War of Independence, thus ensuring a different political outcome?

Furthermore, the questions cited in the paragraph before last are all linked, indeed closely linked, which itself poses major problems in terms of actual and implied relationship and causality, and also of prioritization. This is a more general problem in the discussion of counterfactuals. As effects percolate and ramify through the system,[7] so positive and negative feedback loops greatly complicate causal and counterfactual inference in history. Particularly important are questions about whether variations in preconditions make given outcomes more likely.

At the same time, it is all too easy to assert links that are, at best, without much supporting evidence and, at worst, questionable. This practice is a besetting problem with counterfactual speculations, and one that invites criticism; although this point can be made equally forcefully about conventional scholarship. Most notably, in the case of the latter, the argument by assertion, or "truth by declaration,"[8] that characterizes much historical writing frequently rests on an assurance of academic authority that does not, in practice, demonstrate the accuracy of the analysis offered. Moreover, links that are misleading can be advanced, whether or not they are employed for counterfactual arguments. To take, for example, a link that I have not seen suggested, and another that is more commonly advanced, there is no evidence to support the claim that the successful suppression of the Jacobite rebellions led to complacency in Britain's policy toward her North American colonies, however plausible that might seem. Furthermore, it is mistaken to argue that the financial crisis caused in France by intervention in the War of American Independence led directly to the French Revolution. Nor, and linked to this, is there any way to prove that attempts in France to improve financial administration and/or to produce a political solution were, or were not, foredoomed.[9]

Before, however, counterfactuals and links are addressed, it is necessary to offer the context, and to explain why the character of the "West" was indeed important. This explanation, which depends on the question "How and why did the West triumph?" will lead directly into the first of the counterfactuals. Amplifying the last two chapters, many answers have been given to this question, which is one that evades empirical constraints. In the nineteenth century, answers to the question, which very much addressed a "here and now," focused on issues of supposed cultural and religious superiority or providential protection, and the technological advances of the Western world were seen as indicators of strong and superior cultural norms. This thesis is a concept that has been revisited in a different form in the scholarship of the late twentieth and early twenty-first centuries. For several decades, accounts of the rise of the West have primarily focused on technological explanations. At one level, this approach has concentrated on particular devices and their development, which has led to important work on the so-called Gunpowder Revolution. This work seeks to explain why, although gunpowder was first developed in China and was widely used across Asia, it was applied most effectively, on land and sea, by Western European powers, providing a key force multiplier.[10] There have also been comparable studies of Western European advances in maritime technology.

More generally, technology has been seen as relating not only to devices but also to their use, as part of a culture of organization in which analysis, planning, and informed prediction came to play a major role. This approach involved aspects of the cultural argument, with superior education required for technological advance. In short, technology was the opposite of fatalism; it was an earned providence that was then used to construct rationality and a scientific worldview, in which and through which dominance by the West was both natural and attainable. This view, which was an aspect of nineteenth-century Western confidence, survived, furthermore, to affect subsequent analysis. The character of this analysis is a key element that needs to be considered, and not only when discussing developments, but also when ascertaining the possibility of counterfactuals. Many explanations of the rise of the West get trapped in teleology—"The West industrialized, so the developments in the West that preceded industrialization must have led to it." Counterfactuals play a key role in combating such teleological interpretations and, indeed, the teleological view of history.

The West was not only more varied than teleological notions, and other descriptive and/or analytical attempts to lump it together, might suggest. There was also greater complexity in what might be termed the cultural politics of conquest, or, more bluntly, the "Why?" question; and this question in part can be related back to the issue of the inherent variety of the West, in short the problematic character of regarding it as a unit. This issue can be addressed by looking at European development as a whole (and seeing it in terms of a complex narrative in which our own assessment appears as a counterfactual), and then by turning to specifics.

First, a different time frame from the dominant one in much of the literature can be offered. The argument here is for a time frame that provides a context for multiple indeterminacies, and thus for counterfactual approaches. Indeed, the standard notion of a modernizing (and thus successful) early-modern European world as a prelude to a modern Western world (with the consequence that counterfactuals about the rise of the West have to focus on the former) can be presented as an artificial and misleading construct. It can be argued that this standard notion exaggerates aspects of modernity in early modern Europe, gives them a false causal power, and underrates conservative social/cultural/intellectual patterns in Europe in the sixteenth and seventeenth centuries. In doing so, a false antithesis to the rest of the world is presented, and this is generally given causal power in terms of the rise of the West.

Moreover, to take forward chronologically the theme of modernizing change in Europe, although it was the case that established beliefs and practices were affected in the eighteenth century by what was subsequently termed the "Enlightenment," it was also far from inevitable that the new ideas and governmental practices of the period would do more than shore up existing structures, as they did in Turkey. Indeed, the interactions of reform, change, revolution, and novelty in the eighteenth century were not fixed; and the results in terms of Western development were far from clear-cut, let alone inevitable. Arguably, the consequences of the eighteenth-century European Enlightenment in terms of the intellectual mindset of modernity were not fixed until the utilitarian hegemony and self-consciously rationalizing drive of the mid-nineteenth century, although that description underrates the still potent aspects of conservative thought and practice then, not least the Catholic and Protestant religious revivals of the period.

Counterfactualism therefore can be directed not only to battles and ministers—the approach to the varied outcomes of the sieges of Quebec taken in the next chapter—but also to the varieties of cultural politics and intellectual mindsets. The latter should be done in terms that would make sense to contemporaries. For example, in place of a simple account and use of the Enlightenment, it is only if the complex cultural and intellectual context of the eighteenth century, and the extent to which it did not simply prefigure the nineteenth, let alone the current age, is grasped that it is possible to avoid ahistorical theorizing,[11] which is perhaps the most obvious temptation of the counterfactualist. Indeed, the need to avoid such ahistorical theorizing is a significant challenge to counterfactualism, as each can be seen as an example of the other. Instead, it is necessary to be explicit about the problems posed by ahistorical theorizing, and that, indeed, is similar to the situation as far as conventional scholarship is concerned.

It is important to understand the past cultural and racial ideas of the peoples of Christian Europe, and of other societies, in order to apply counterfactual perspectives to the notion of a drive for ascendancy and the trajectory toward an appropriating psyche. For example, the utilitarian/mercantile conception of territorialization, of land that should, and could, be profitably seized, even if not then settled, although already formed in the New World, developed late in other spheres of European activity, certainly insofar as European attitudes toward South and East Asia and most of Africa were concerned, and thus was not simply inevitable. In short, European dominance did not have to take the forms it did. In many respects, a distinctive form (or forms) did not arise until quite late. More generally, the cultural and intellectual mindsets of Christian Europe were important to its global role, and were far from fixed in content or application.

One counterfactual perspective can be provided by disaggregating Europe, and, instead, comparing and contrasting the Atlantic West and the Continental powers, a process which reveals the differences between the two. Indeed, Continental expansion by Austria and especially Russia was not so dissimilar from expansion by non-European empires, particularly once the initial "mercantile" (Cossack) phase of the Russian conquest of Siberia, which had begun in the 1580s, ended in the mid-seventeenth century. Russian cities in Siberia in the eighteenth century were similar to the new Chinese bases in Xinjiang. Thus, a model of Euro-Asian landward conquest can be provided;[12] and it can be suggested that it was different from maritime expansion, as in, "What would have happened to Western expansion had it followed the Russian pattern?"

This suggestion of alternative methods and periods of expansion can be given historical depth by looking back to Crusader expansion. The latter, in turn, invites counterfactuals, particularly in two respects: first, "Was the kingdom of Jerusalem progressing to a genuine fusion of East and West, in other words, what would have happened had it lasted longer?" and second, "Was the military failure of the Crusaders in the Middle East inevitable?" Denying the latter and treating the efforts made as heroic and necessary were, for long, an approach that encouraged renewed attempts against the Islamic world.

Even for the early modern period, a model of European landward conquest to the east has to be employed with care. For, far from being uniform, continental European powers drew on different societies and cultures, as a comparison of Austria and Russia readily indicates. This lack of uniformity extended to significant contrasts, which, in turn, provide opportunities for counterfactuals, for example, "What if Habsburg rule of Hungary had collapsed in the face of such rebellions as those that took place in the 1610s, 1700s, and 1780s? What if Hungary had been the key player in Balkan expansion at the expense of the Turks?"

Aside from enabling us to indicate important contrasts within the West, a focus on the difference between maritime and continental Europe provides another sphere for counterfactual analysis. It is possible that different political developments within Europe would have affected the balance between maritime and Continental expansion. These developments might have included the suppression of the Dutch Revolt against rule by Philip II of Spain in the late sixteenth century, a suppression that appeared possible on a number of occasions, as well as the struggle between Britain and France in 1688–1815. It is also necessary to consider whether domestic developments within individual European states would have made a major difference. These developments might have included, for example, different political trajectories within France, such as the triumph of the Huguenots (Protestants) in 1560–1600 or their ability to avoid defeat in the 1620s. In England, the possibility that there were no Wars of the Roses in the late fifteenth century can be linked to the idea that England might have experienced the Renaissance earlier, and might have become involved in trans-Atlantic exploration earlier also. In Britain, a Stuart victory in the Civil Wars of the 1640s, or in the conflict with William of Orange in 1688–91, repays consideration. In Germany the earlier adoption of primogeniture, which would have avoided the patchwork of tiny states, is worth probing.

Domestic and international developments were linked, and such links can therefore be offered for counterfactuals, which, indeed, was a large part of their importance for contemporaries. Had the Huguenots seen off royal forces in 1626–29, defeating the attempt to besiege their major stronghold, La Rochelle, which had not after all fallen when besieged in the late sixteenth century, then French politics and policies might well have been very different. Cardinal Richelieu, the leading minister, who was very much associated with the siege, might have fallen from favor, and Louis XIII, following the advice of *dévot* ministers, might have continued his policy of noninvolvement in the Thirty

Years' War (1618–48), despite the fact that the Habsburg rulers of Austria and Spain had enjoyed a run of victories from 1621.[13] Under Richelieu, France fought the Habsburgs, first in the War of the Mantuan Succession of 1628–31 and then from 1635, while Sweden was encouraged and subsidized to enter the struggle against Austria in 1631.

Had these French actions not taken place, then it is possible that the Habsburgs would have succeeded in extending and securing their dominance of Christian Europe.[14] As a reminder of other possible outcomes in this period, Stuart victory in 1643 in the English Civil War is the topic of a counterfactual essay by John Adamson,[15] although he does not assess the overseas consequences of such a victory. The primogeniture question in Germany provides a good instance of the extent to which counterfactuals do not have to focus on war, but can include sociocultural issues.

There is not the space to address all these possibilities. Mentioning them, however, both highlights the number and range of indeterminacies and underlines the role of authorial choice in selecting a focus, a point that should be made explicit in scholarship. Unfortunately, instead, there is all too often a content and a tone based on the certainty that only one answer is possible. This certainty, the craving for the supposedly definitive answer, is a conflation of a hierarchical approach to knowledge, with, all too often, the exigencies of individual career advancement and the assertion stemming from personal arrogance. Other features also play a role in suggesting that only one answer is possible. These include publishing practices (publishers and the academic readers they tend to employ dislike ambiguity and complexity, the former because of the impact on sales and the latter because they seem to believe that study brings definitive clarity) as well as institutional cultures which encourage arrogance. In contrast, counterfactual works underline the place of authorial choice, as indeed does detailed historiographical scholarship.

The focus in this chapter on the Anglo-French struggle, and on related conflicts within the British world, the major counterfactual discussed in this book, reflects a belief that the period was of particular importance to world history and, specifically, but not only, to the rise of the West, and that options on the global scale had not been foreclosed by the earlier rise of the Iberian powers (Portugal and Spain) and, subsequently, the Dutch; but clearly this focus is also an authorial choice. This choice rests in large part on my own research and invites the counterfactual, "If Black's prime topic of research was different would he come to a contrasting conclusion? Or, indeed, would he have focused on a different question?" This is a reasonable point which needs to be borne in mind when reading what follows, as does my personal conviction that ambiguity and uncertainty have a positive part to play in historical practice.[16]

Following from the last two chapters, the argument here is that different developments within particular European states would have affected the cultural suppositions that molded the use and choices of power. Thus, an understanding of the fluidity of Europe's development, and of the Anglo-French struggle as a key part of the fluidity, can be perceived as crucial to any counterfactual analysis of European expansion. This fluidity has to be seen in relations between *and* within European states, and both can be regarded as important in terms of structures, priorities, and ideas. Firstly, the forms of government and the structures of politics and administration that enabled societies to mobilize and control resources, both for relations with the non-West and more generally, were not fixed, indeed far from it, and in Britain they changed radically.

Secondly, the priorities for the use of resources were not set in stone. The concept of strategic culture has been advanced from the 1970s in part in order to suggest or imply otherwise, but, in practice, strategic culture was a sphere for contention, not an agreed outcome, and the emphasis ought to be on competing strategic cultures within individual states, including Britain and France. An instance of this contention is provided in chapter 9.

Thirdly, the ideas that influenced relations with the non-West were culturally conditioned and affected by developments within Western societies and by the struggles between them. The fluidity already referred to extended to cultural norms, as a consideration of the Counter-Reformation and the Enlightenment would suggest. In twentieth-century Europe, this fluidity in norms can be seen with the rise of extreme movements on both left and right, followed by the mainstream rejection of empire.

What does this all mean? To indicate the role of shifting priorities in the case of Britain, the deployment of regular troops from the 1750s to assist the East India Company in India, for example, involved choice and reflected particular priorities and ideas that had not been present twenty years earlier. Counterfactuals in India were established by the debate between expansionists and those who adopted a more cautious stance, for example in reaction against the viceroy Richard Wellesley's, expansive and expensive policy at the expense of the Maratha Confederation in the 1800s.[17] Similarly as an instance of shifting priorities, but here within the transoceanic European world, the unsuccessful attempt in 1763–75 to increase the contribution of Britain's American colonies to imperial resources was very different from an earlier stance characterized as salutary neglect.[18] These attitudes and ideas can be seen as more important than the mechanics and techniques of force, and, also, as necessarily open to counterfactual speculation. Indeed, such speculation helped drive the British and American critique of the ministry's North American policy, both at the time and subsequently. Much discussion was of the form, "What if the British government followed/had followed other policies?" with an "If only" very much part of the discussion.

It was unclear which power would prevail in North America until the failure of the French attempt to regain Quebec from Britain in 1760, on which see the next chapter. In 1750, in contrast, France was not only taking the initiative in the interior of North America, as it continued to do successfully until 1757, albeit not without contest, but was also more powerful than Britain in India. For much of the century, France also put as much effort as Britain into Pacific exploration, and it was also energetic in trying to develop links in Southeast Asia, Persia, the Turkish Empire, and West Africa. Allied with Spain, the third-most-powerful naval power, France, the second most powerful, was able to challenge the most powerful, Britain, on a number of occasions, notably in 1779 when a joint invasion was prepared against Britain, although delay and disease prevented it from being brought to fruition,[19] and in 1805 with both France and Spain defeated at Trafalgar.

On many occasions, French victory appeared possible, and if France had beaten Britain during their protracted conflict for much of the period 1688–1815, then this would have greatly affected the struggle of the

West versus the Rest. Why? France, after all, had oceanic and transoce-anic interests and ambitions of her own. Furthermore, after 1815, France again took a path of transoceanic expansion, and successfully so, first in North and West Africa, and then, as that expansion continued, in Indochina (Southeast Asia) and Madagascar, and finally as part of the World War I settlement, in the Middle East and in West Africa. Thus, had France beaten Britain, it is at first glimpse unclear why this should have made a difference to the extension of European power; although the nature of that power would not have been the same, and, as already sug-gested, that might have been very important to the rationale and process, as well as the consequences, of conquest. A French-dominated transoce-anic world would have looked to Catholicism, civil law, French culture and language, and a different notion of representative government and politics from that of Britain, or, rather, of Britain as it turned out.[20]

Furthermore, after the French Revolution (had that not been pre-vented by French predominance and mercantile success), there might have been a contrasting racial politics. The options here are several. The abolitionism of Revolutionary France in the 1790s, with slavery abol-ished by the National Convention in 1794, might have been the key theme, but Napoleon's reversal of these policies in 1802, and the delay (compared to Britain) in ending, finally, first the slave trade (1815) and subsequently slavery (1848), might be more indicative of what would have occurred had France been the leading power and not been exposed to British abolitionist admonition. As a reminder of the degree to which large counterfactuals can enfold others, French overseas predominance would not necessarily have prevented the slave revolution in the largest French plantation economy, St. Domingue (modern Haiti), nor neces-sarily have ensured its suppression. Both of these were important to the chronology and, in part, content of French policy toward slaves in the 1790s and early 1800s; and this opens up the larger question of how far French abolitionism was driven by metropolitan ideas or by events in the West Indies. Counterfactualism plays a useful role in the discussion of this issue.

Had France beaten Britain, the transoceanic situation would also have been very different in other ways. This difference would have been due to geopolitics, priorities, and assumptions about the international system. The geopolitics were that France was both a maritime and a European continental power, and far more so than Britain, even when the latter was ruled by the electors (later kings) of Hanover, as it was from 1714 to 1837.[21] French geopolitics led to conflicting priorities, for example in 1741, when France could have helped Spain against Britain in the Caribbean, rather than attacking Austria, as it did; in 1756–57 when it could have focused on overseas war with Britain rather than invading Hanover and attacking Prussia, as it did; or 1778, when France could have intervened in the Austro-Prussian War of the Bavarian Succession, rather than the War of American Independence, as it did.

Priorities and prioritization, of course, are choices and processes that immediately invite counterfactual speculation, as they did for contemporaries. Moreover, in some cases, contemporary speculation probably affected decisions even if the choices made by the other power proved a surprise. Thus, in 1756 and 1805, the British feared that the French would invade England or Ireland; instead, the French turned elsewhere, to attack Minorca and Austria, respectively and successfully. The French also pursued Continental goals with most of their forces when some of their invasion attempts were mounted on the British Isles, for example in 1708 and 1796–98, although the situation was different in 1779. British survival thus had something to do with the fact that Britain was not the first priority for French policymakers for much of the period; and this at once invites a counterfactual. A similar point can be made about America and British policymakers in the 1840s–60s, and this point helps explain Britain's accommodating position to the United States on a number of occasions including during the Civil War.[22]

Priorities owed something to resources and a sense of the possible, especially in the case of invasion plans. They also reflected ideas, in this case the dominance of Continental conceptions in French geopolitical thought. More specifically, this dominance sustained French concern with dynastic and landward aggrandizement until the mid-eighteenth century (and, territorially, also from the 1790s). Anxiety about the impact in Europe of the rise of other land powers, the Habsburgs from the early sixteenth century, and Russia and Prussia, in addition, from the early eighteenth century, was also very significant. In part, this anxiety reflected French commitments to Sweden, Poland, and the Turkish

(Ottoman) Empire. These commitments can be presented in pruden-
tial terms, notably with reference to a *barrière de l'est* capable of helping France against Austria, but values also played a role, especially a
normative sense of the form and character of the European system. In
particular, this normative sense led to hostility toward Russian expansionism at the expense of Sweden, Poland, and the Turks.

Contrasting priorities in part reflected the extent to which French
society was less dominated than its main maritime rival, Britain, by an
ethos of commercial strength and maritime destiny. This ethos was the
prelude to territorial ambitions in South Asia, Africa, and the Pacific,
and to the necessary power projection, notably in the face of alternative commitments on the Continent. It is worth noting, however, that
there were several competing views in Britain, especially in the critical
period after 1650 when it was establishing the infrastructure for expansion. Linked to this, and a key point that challenges patterns of causality, whether or not they are counterfactual, the ethos of commercial
and maritime strength may have been the result of overseas expansion,
rather than the cause. Alternatively, the strengthening of this ethos as a
result of expansion may have been a factor, which itself raises the question of how much of an emphasis to place on this factor. As a consequence, varying this expansion in a counterfactual, by assuming British
defeats or the alternative use of resources, most obviously in civil conflict or in war on the Continent, can lead to changes in the ethos. As an
instance of such a counterfactual, "What if Britain had faced protracted
civil war after the Glorious Revolution or the Jacobite rising of 1745?
Would this have led to a failure to focus on transoceanic interests and
opportunities?"

The spatial composition of French power was largely that of inland
France,[23] and, compared to Britain, France was introspective and internally focused. The landed nobility was crucial in Valois and Bourbon
France, and the role of the land in elite identity was underlined under
Napoleon by his reliance on a new service aristocracy who were provided with estates. The nobility were far more interested in the army
than in the navy, and in the land rather than in trade or empire. The
social, cultural, and economic focus on land affected military and political policy, not least because these values permeated French society as

a whole. The French loss of Canada to Britain in 1760, and of Louisiana to Spain in 1763, was criticized in mercantile circles in the Atlantic ports, but had only limited impact elsewhere, as the ceded territories were seen in fashionable circles as barren and profitless. Aristocratic families had scant presence in French North America, and, if this was also true of their British counterparts, the latter were less significant in policymaking. Indeed, the values of aristocratic power were very important to French policymaking and diplomacy, and, despite the efforts of Colbert, in effect Louis XIV's chief financial advisor from 1661 to 1683, trade was not the most resonant symbol of French national identity.

The role of individuals, moreover, is generally a key element in counterfactual history, and the character of individual rulers was certainly crucial to policy in seventeenth- and eighteenth-century Europe. The French royal family has been presented as committed "to continentalism's political program which viewed colonialism as a form of adventurism leading to a weaker France."[24] Louis XIV of France (r. 1643–1715) was no Peter the Great of Russia, keen to develop and sustain a navy and to move the capital to the coast in his new city of St. Petersburg. Louis XIV also yielded French colonies to Britain as part of the Peace of Utrecht of 1713, as well as accepted Britain's gain of benefits in Spain's colonial empire. Louis XV (r. 1715–74) lacked the emperor (ruler of Austria) Charles VI's ostentatious commitment to overseas trading companies. Louis XVI (r. 1774–92) failed to match Charles III of Spain's interest in the colonies and trade. There were also choices in French foreign policy. Policymakers repeatedly put Europe first, and were able to establish the Bourbon dynasty in Spain, Naples, and Parma, and to maintain France's leading position in Western Europe. However, they could not gain a comparable position in the expanding European world, nor indeed sustain France's allies in Eastern Europe.

Had France achieved greater success overseas, then it is likely that the resources of the transoceanic world would have been employed to further its European ambitions, rather as Spain had used the bullion of her New World conquests to pursue European objectives, instead of seeking fresh transoceanic conquests. For example, France's long-standing interest in European allies, such as Bavaria, Poland, Sweden, and Turkey, might have resulted in a more sustained intervention in

Central and Eastern Europe. The attempt in 1741 to reorder Central Europe totally at the expense of Austria, an attempt that led French troops to St. Polten (near Vienna) and Prague, might have been given greater force. So also with the attack on Prussia in 1757, an attack that, in the event, was heavily and humiliatingly defeated by Frederick the Great at Rossbach:[25] Napoleon was to suggest that the loss of prestige this defeat entailed for the Bourbon dynasty made the French Revolution more likely, which offers the basis for a counterfactual. Further east, the small and unsuccessful French expeditionary force sent to Danzig in 1734 and the squadron dispatched to the Baltic in 1739 could have been part of a stronger French effort to help Poland and Sweden against Russia, while France could have taken a more prominent role against Russia in the Baltic crisis of 1749.

As an important indication of interests that again invites counterfactuals, when, in 1783, Vergennes, the experienced French foreign minister, negotiated peace with Britain, it was not in order to pursue expansionist plans outside Europe, for example in India, but, rather, better to oppose Russian aggrandizement in the Crimea.[26] In contrast, from the perspective of a late nineteenth-century empire builder, the best-case scenario for France, instead, would have been first to dismember the British empire in 1778–83, then, partly through the acquisition of British commerce, to avoid revolution herself, and, finally, to compete with Britain for empire overseas from a new and equal, if not better, starting point. All this was feasible. A France that was militarily and economically stronger as well as better governed could have avoided revolution. Munro Price has argued that "the disasters of late 1787 might well have been avoided had he [Vergennes] been master of his own foreign policy."[27] This argument invites a variant on the Rossbach and revolution counterfactual, this time one focused on the Dutch crisis, in which France was seriously humiliated by Prussia and Britain when her Dutch protégés were overthrown in 1787 by a Prussian invasion backed by British naval preparations, leading to the imposition of an Orange order. In contrast, greater success for France could have encouraged obedience and respect for the political system and monarch.[28] As a reminder, however, of the difficulty of drawing out consequences, that outcome would not necessarily have left France freer to pursue international ambitions outside Europe.

Instead, it might have encouraged a more assertive, even hegemonic, stance within Europe, and this outcome could have resulted in a weaker commitment to overseas expansion.

This counterfactual is important, because the period 1789–1842 was very much the tipping point in South and East Asia. During that period, the Turks, Persians, Marathas, Gurkhas, Burmese, Chinese, and Mysore were all defeated, as was the Egyptian fleet: the first two by Russia, all the others by Britain. European territorial gains included Singapore, Aden, Karachi, and Hong Kong, all acquired by Britain. Promising political and military developments in the defeated powers, developments that might have led to problems for Britain, for example by Egypt under Mehmed Ali, were cut short or seriously curtailed.

To suggest that in some way there would have been no European overseas expansion had France, and not Britain, been the leading European power is implausible. The British bombarded Algiers in 1816 into submitting to demands for an end to attacks on British trade and for the return of Christian slaves. However, the French occupied the city in 1830 (against British wishes) and went on to devote a major, sustained, and eventually successful effort to conquering its hinterland. They also established themselves in the Marquesas and Tahiti in the Pacific in 1842 and in Gabon in West Africa in 1844.

Nevertheless, the pace and extent of European overseas expansion would probably have been less had France, rather than Britain, been the prime European power, whether it had had a revolution or not. As it was, France intervened in Spain, Belgium, and Italy between 1820 and 1860. The overseas focus would probably have been different also if France was the leading power, not least if the price of beating Britain had included cooperation with non-Western powers such as Mysore and Egypt. A French-dominated Western expansion would probably have been weaker in South Asia than the British-dominated system and therefore would have placed less of an emphasis on southern Africa— the route to the Indian Ocean prior to the building of the Suez Canal. Instead, the stress would have been on North Africa, maybe including Egypt primarily in that light, and possibly, also, on supporting Spanish attempts to regain control of Spanish America, a course that might have taken France into serious opposition to the United States.

The race to gain colonies heated up with the fear of the "closing door" in Africa, Southeast Asia, and the Pacific after 1880, but there might have been no such anxiety driving forward expansion had there been one dominant European power in the shape of France. More specifically, French dominance in Europe might have prevented German colonialism by thwarting the precursor stage of German unification under Prussian control. A slower pace of European overseas expansion from circa 1790 to the end of the nineteenth century could well have given non-European powers, including China and Egypt, a vital opportunity to consolidate politically, to develop militarily, and to acquire Western industrial technology by trade and investment, rather as Latin America,[29] and later Japan, indeed did.

Did then Britain have to win? For geographical, cultural, and political reasons, France was different from Britain as an economy, a society, and a state. When the two powers were allied and François-Marie, duc de Broglie, arrived in London as French ambassador in 1724, he was astonished by the apparently innumerable ships on the River Thames.[30] The British economy indeed enjoyed particular institutional advantages over other European powers, as well as those derived, with the large-scale use of coal, from the move away from an exclusively organic economy.[31]

Structural limitations indeed played a major role in France's failure, not least because, as discussed above, the character of French political culture affected the perception of options. Rulers living in the great palace at Versailles, with its symbolic demands,[32] were much less exposed to the dynamic forces of European economic life and overseas activities than a government and Parliament located in London, the growing center of world trade and finance. The concentration of both politics and trade in London was not matched in Paris; but, taken together, the various French ports were extremely active, and each a significant center of trade and maritime activity. Even the River Loire in the eighteenth century was alive with sails, and vast quantities of goods were traded along it. Trade and expertise were not lacking in France, but political awareness and commitment were less than in London, where the commercial lobby was so prominent, and trade so very visible.

These French structural limitations, however, affected, *but did not determine,* policy choices, resource availability, and international responses. Indeed, part of the value of counterfactual scenario-building is that it can tell us a lot about how government cultures can change, what forces resist change, and how much, and in what ways, such changes matter. Louis XIV could have devoted more resources to transoceanic activity in the 1660s and 1670s,[33] and could have sought to prevent Anglo-Dutch cooperation in 1689–1713, either by making more of an effort earlier to retain Dutch support, or by thwarting William III of Orange's invasion of England in 1688 (not least by sending his troops toward the United Provinces rather than east to capture the Rhineland fortress of Philippsburg), or by providing more assistance thereafter to the Jacobites, particularly those resisting William in Ireland in 1689–92.

Moreover, greater effort could have been put into sustaining and strengthening the promising French positions in India and North America in the early 1750s, for example by supporting the governor of French India, Joseph François Marquis de Dupleix, who was the key proponent of expansion in India. Possibly the promise for France of 1783–86—expanding transoceanic trade, as well as alliance with Spain, Austria, and the Dutch; better relations with Russia; an isolated Britain; and moves toward peaceful reform internally—could have been realized, not least if, in 1787, the Assembly of Notables had provided the last and Prussia not intervened in the Dutch crisis. Maybe, despite his aggressiveness, Napoleon could have maintained the Tilsit agreement with Russia of 1807, successfully incorporated Iberia (Spain and Portugal), peaceably or by conquest, into his system, and then forced an isolated Britain to terms. There were impressive French ministers during the seventeenth and eighteenth centuries, for example Colbert, Maurepas, and Sartine, who wanted to devote more effort to commercial and colonial goals, and to building up the navy, while cooperation with Spain enhanced possibilities for naval and overseas conflict with Britain. France's failure, and thus Britain's success, therefore, was as much the consequence of political, diplomatic, and military contingencies and decisions, as of structural and socioeconomic factors.

If, in 1815, Britain was the strongest state in the world, the situation had been very different seventy years earlier, as Jacobite forces under Charles Edward Stuart (Bonnie Prince Charlie), the elder son of "James III and VIII," the Jacobite claimant on the British throne, advanced on Derby. He outmaneuvered the armies sent to defeat him, and the British government correctly feared a supporting French invasion of southern England, for one was ready. Similarly by 1815, Britain was the dominant military power in India. However, in 1746, the British East India Company had lost Madras, its base in Southeast India, to the French; in the early 1780s the British position in southern India was very much under pressure from France (especially from a fleet commanded by Suffren) and its ally, the sultanate of Mysore; and in the mid-1780s,[34] and again in the late 1790s, British politicians had worried about France's global and Middle East ambitions, especially in the Indian Ocean but also in Ireland, Egypt, and even Vietnam. There had been fears that the French would overthrow the British in India, as they had earlier done in North America. Such varieties of circumstance underline the role for counterfactuals.

Was it the French victory at Minden in 1759, or in the Mediterranean in 1798, or Napoleon's triumphant entry into London in 1805, that put an end to the idea that France's geopolitical position was such that she could be the dominant power on the landmass of Western Europe, but would fail to be the leading European colonial and maritime power? To buy peace in each case, Britain had to return colonial gains. She had already done so in 1748, at the close of the War of the Austrian Succession, when she returned the major fortress and naval base of Louisbourg on Cape Breton Island, which had been captured three years earlier. In each of the scenarios outlined, for 1759, 1798, and 1805, France was able to assert her position in the world, both in her own right and in conjunction with her allies, especially Spain. The claims of domestic and foreign critics, most prominently the *philosophes,* such as Voltaire, that particular aspects of French society and the French state made them less likely to prevail over more mercantile, tolerant, populist, and attractive Britain now seemed redundant.

These events of course did not occur, but the fancy outlined above directs attention to the question of whether France's failure was inherent or the product of contingency and chance. Those who are inclined to emphasize resources and their mobilization will tend to see failure as inherent, while the proponents of choice and policy will be more cautious. There is much for the proponents of choice and policy to stress.

In particular, Napoleon's exploitative and insensitive treatment of his allies compromised France's position within and outside Europe. Reflecting both Napoleon's personality and the extent to which, under his rule, France was not a satisfied power,[35] this treatment, and its consequences, contrasted with the greater success of French policymakers in 1713–86 in creating and sustaining alliances, and in stabilizing France's position.

More generally, focusing on diplomatic failures makes sense of the contrast between long-term "structural" characteristics and the very varied short-term fates of Britain and France as great powers. Counterfactual speculations are more useful if they make clear which level is being addressed, and how far the consequences are seen only, or mostly, at that level. If a counterfactual focused on a short-term factor is advanced, are the consequences only to be seen in terms of such elements, factors, and results? If not, how are the causal links between the short and the long term to be established?

The counterfactuals in this chapter about British versus French imperialisms raise questions about the predictability of chaotically contingent paths. Some counterfactual turning points seem to point toward outcomes that, though different from what actually happened, flow within the same broad structural constraints. Such changes appear more predictable, therefore, because their hypothetical paths follow channels actually carved by events. But some counterfactuals—and this chapter suggests a French-dominated European expansion is one of them— involve turning points from which a reconstruction of the broad constraints themselves flows. In such cases, once one gets past the point where it is clear that broad constraints would have changed, subsequent paths become much more unpredictable. The writer is reduced to saying, "And that would have changed all sorts of things," without being able to specify with any reliability how things would have changed. This is in the nature of a chaotic system. However, such a system does describe the way in which present and future were (and are) often viewed.

Metaphorically, the first type of counterfactual turning point generates a short-term weather forecast which is likely to be largely correct, while the second type generates something more like a long-term weather forecast, where, despite recent advances in mathematical mod-

throughout the period from the 1530s to the Napoleonic Wars. There was a sense of precariousness about religious, ecclesiastical, dynastic, institutional, and political settlements, not only within England, but also in the other parts of the British Isles and with reference to the relations between these parts.

Furthermore, these disputes did not take place in isolation. Instead, foreign intervention, especially French, Spanish, and Dutch, was frequent, as had been true for centuries. The French had sent troops to England in 1216 in the crisis following Magna Carta and a French prince claimed the throne before French and allied forces were defeated off Dover and at Lincoln. France had also subsequently supported Scottish opposition to English rule from the 1290s to the 1560s, and thereafter on occasion the Stuarts until the unsuccessful 1759 invasion attempt. Spanish forces had been sent to Ireland to help the resistance to conquest by Elizabeth I and to Scotland in 1719 to assist the Jacobites.

As a result of such interventions, developments within Britain were played out in a wider international context and, thus, had consequences for European power politics and for the position of Britain and other countries in the global system. This dimension tends to be underplayed in the public (as opposed to scholarly) discussion of British history. This context also ensured that many British rulers, politicians, and commentators believed it necessary to intervene in Continental power politics, although the need for, and terms of, engagement were bitterly contested within British politics, on which see chapter 9.

Comparisons provide fruitful insights when discussing Britain's development, and they overlap with counterfactuals. A comparison between Britain and Poland is instructive, not least because both were linked in personal unions with German principalities: Britain with Hanover from 1714 until 1837, and Poland with Saxony from 1697 until 1763. Comparisons can also be drawn earlier, with the British Union of the Crowns of England and Scotland in 1603 compared to the Polish-Lithuanian one of 1569. George I's accession in Britain in 1714 was followed by civil strife in 1715–16, as those of James II and VII (1685) and William III (1689) had been; while, in Poland, the Saxon rulers, Augustus II and Augustus III, gained the throne through violence, with a Russian invasion on behalf of Augustus III proving crucial in 1733.

Yet, the civil wars in Britain after 1637–51 ended swiftly, especially in England (for example in 1660, 1685, 1688, and 1715). Moreover, although England and Britain were bitterly divided in the 1640s and 1680s, Britain acted like a major power in the 1650s and 1690s. Defeats were avoided in the wars of these periods, whereas, in contrast, for Saxony-Poland, the Great Northern War of 1700–21 proved disastrous, with Charles XII of Sweden overthrowing Augustus II, who was only restored to Poland as a result of Russian intervention following Peter the Great's victory over Charles at Poltava in 1709. Given Charles's earlier victory over larger Russian forces at Narva in 1700, the overthrow of the Swedish empire did not seem as likely to contemporaries as to modern commentators more mindful of Swedish overstretch. As a concept, indeed, overstretch had less salience in the eighteenth century than it does today, which is instructive.[42]

There was no crisis for William III, Anne, and the Hanoverians to compare with those that faced Poland or Sweden. There was an elective character to the Williamite position and the Act of Settlement (1701), as there was to Polish kingship, but Poland did not develop a strong government comparable to that in Britain. Possibly the important difference was that, in Britain, the Jacobites were not able to prevent William III and the Hanoverians, both of whom also represented the hereditary principle, from winning parliamentary support, whereas, in Poland, the political and constitutional system did not work to the benefit of the Saxons. Indeed, Jacobitism in Britain helped to preserve a measure of both Whig unity and Whig-royal cohesion. In the Age of Liberty in Sweden that followed the death of Charles XII in 1718 ("What if he had not been shot?") and that lasted until the coup by Gustavus III in 1772 ("What if he had not been assassinated in 1792?"), it did not prove possible to develop an effective limited monarchy comparable to that in Britain, which invites a "What if?"

JACOBITES AND AMERICANS, 1745, 1776

Earlier, war had had different consequences when Britain parted from a more general European trajectory because its monarchs were defeated in civil wars in the late 1630s, 1640s, and 1688–91. These defeats obliged their successful opponents to consider new political, constitutional, ecclesiastical, and dynastic arrangements. Yet, none of these defeats were inevitable, and all were reversible, as was to be shown by the restoration of the Stuart dynasty (and much, but by no means all, else) in 1660. The Stuart cause had seemed hopeless after Charles II's total defeat by Oliver Cromwell at Worcester in 1651 and Charles's subsequent flight into exile, and later conspiracies failed; but the cause triumphed easily in 1660.

In turn, 1688 showed that even the Restoration was reversible, while the unwillingness of many in England to fight for an unpopular regime, that of James II, in 1688 could have been repeated in the 1740s at the cost of the Hanoverians. Moreover, 1688 revealed a role for personality that indicated the place of chance. In 1688, James, an experienced soldier, lost his nerve, possibly suffering a mental breakdown, and did not put up a fight,[43] which offers another more general theme for counterfactuals: had the mental condition of certain individuals been their normal state on significant occasions, then outcomes might have been different. James II could have been more robust in 1688, while George II, another former soldier and a distant relative, could, under pressure in 1745, have behaved in a similar fashion to how James actually did. Had George, born in 1683, died before that crisis, his eldest son, Frederick, Prince of Wales, offered no indication of resolution.

A second Stuart restoration after 1688, at the behest and with the help of France, however, would have left an unpopular Catholic dynasty and its political supporters dependent on France. Was such a second restoration possible? That question can be addressed by looking at the closest chance, the Jacobite invasion and rising of 1745,[44] although this episode does not exhaust the question. Again, there are the two dimensions of counterfactualism, to adopt a simple typology: first, the specific, in this case military, dimension, in which the possibility of different developments is constrained by the context of a particular conjuncture, much of which can be recovered and assessed within the prime Western tradition of historical research, namely, empirical positivism. For this reason, it is possible to dwell on this example at some length. Sources for all the major players are readily available, which is significant as sources for defeated movements are not always so. There is also the specific dimension of diplomacy. A belief that the Jacobites might succeed led to a slowing down of diplomatic negotiations in 1745–46 as governments waited to see what would happen. This is a reminder that counterfactualism is crucial not just for Jacobite studies in general but also for the wider resonances of Jacobitism. Returning to the point about the relationship between counterfactualism and political preference discussed in chapter 1, this crucial importance is the case whether or not the scholarship on Jacobitism is revisionist in character, and, linked to the latter, really or allegedly sympathetic to Jacobitism.

This, however, is not the sole context. Indeed, Jacobitism becomes an important instance of the role of counterfactualism in Scottish history. That relates in part to the idea of a destiny separate from that of England. Thus, regnal union with France in the 1560s linked to longer life for Francis II (r. 1559–60), the French husband of Mary, Queen of Scots (r. 1542–67), offered a different prospect from what happened. There are also different outcomes linked to debates over the Act of Union of 1707 that united England and Scotland.

There is also the wider context—that of possibilities stemming from a conjuncture that in fact worked out differently. In this case, they relate most interestingly to the possibility that a new political settlement in 1745 would have altered Britain's position in the world, and thus the West, thereby returning us to the question raised at the outset of this chapter. Significantly, this possibility of a different Britain is not only the case with regard to geopolitical alignments but also with reference to the nature of public culture, economic interests, and social dynamics. In turn, changes or the prospect of changes in these factors would have encouraged other counterfactuals.

Turning to the military angle, the Jacobite invasion of Scotland under Charles Edward Stuart in 1745 quickly succeeded, with a total victory at Prestonpans on September 21. After Prestonpans, Charles Edward consolidated his position around Edinburgh, while his opponents assembled an army under the experienced but elderly field marshal George Wade (1673–1748) at Newcastle, the key blocking point for any advance, south or north, to the east of the Pennines. Wade was familiar with northern Britain, but his combat experience was on the Continent, most recently in 1744 against the French in Belgium, where position warfare and sieges predominated, and he proved far too slow-moving to cope with Charles Edward. The latter avoided Wade by invading England to the west of the Pennines via Carlisle, which fell after a short siege (November 10–15). The defenses were not impressive, but, even had they been, the defending force was insufficient in number and it lacked civilian support. Wade's slow attempt to march via Hexham to Carlisle's relief was hampered by the winter weather, leading to a "non-battle." As in this case, non-battles are a basic building block in counterfactual studies, and one that is generally underplayed in military history.

Instead of fighting Wade, the Jacobites advanced unopposed through Penrith, Lancaster, Preston, and Manchester, en route toward London. Their advance west of the Pennines followed, at least initially, the course of the invading Scots in the Second Civil War in 1648 and that of the Jacobites in 1715. Both of these armies had been decisively defeated at Preston; but, in contrast to each of the former occasions, the advancing force in 1745 outmarched its opponents. The ability of armies to respond differently to similar operational and strategic parameters, and the role of their leadership in doing so, were amply demonstrated in these three advances; again this invites counterfactuals, and for 1648 and 1715 as well as for 1745.

Aside from that under Wade, another regular army was assembled to confront the Jacobites. The government was not short of money: substantial sums were voted by Parliament in November 1745. Built up in the West Midlands, and commanded by George II's younger son, William, Duke of Cumberland, this force, however, was outmaneuvered, in large part because it was misled by deliberately circulated reports that the Jacobites intended to advance on Chester and North Wales in order to recruit support there. Cumberland moved to block such an advance, and therefore failed to stop a Jacobite advance, past him, on Derby, which Charles Edward entered unopposed on December 4.

What if the Jacobites had marched on, as they planned to do? It is a subject that has often been discussed. At that point, the Jacobites held the operational and strategic initiatives and were also in a central position while the opposing forces were divided. Wade's army was still in Yorkshire and Cumberland's was exhausted by its marches. The government was assembling a new army on Finchley Common to protect London, but it was a relatively small force. Unlike the Scots, the English population had little access to arms. Even the militia, who did obtain arms in 1745, would not fight, perhaps less because they would not uphold the Hanoverian succession than because they did not regard themselves as soldiers.

Nevertheless, the Highland chiefs were disappointed by the lack of the backing promised them by Charles Edward: both assistance from English Jacobites and the absence of a supporting French landing in southern England. After bitter debates, the chiefs forced Charles Edward to turn back, and he began his retreat on December 6. A loss of nerve had been a characteristic of the Jacobites in the 1690s, 1714, and 1715–16, so possibly this should not be surprising, but it was far from inevitable and justifiably attracts counterfactual attention, as indeed do earlier Jacobite episodes.

Having retreated to Scotland and defeated a government army at Falkirk on January 17, 1746, the outnumbered and outgunned Jacobites were to be crushed at Culloden on April 16. Was this defeat inevitable? Is it valid to ask, "What if they had won?" Culloden can certainly be seen as a defeat for an army emphasizing speed, mobility, and primal shock power by a force reliant on the concentrated firepower of disciplined infantry and their supporting artillery. That, indeed, is how the battle has been depicted; and visual force is lent by the contrast between disciplined rows of British troops, with their standard weaponry, and the more fluid, but also archaic, individualism of their opponents, who are generally, but misleadingly, presented as without guns.

The mental picture created is somewhat similar to the film *Zulu* (1964), an account of the failure of the Zulu attack on the British-held position of Rorke's Drift in 1879. It is made clear that the two sides are starkly different and that one represents order and other characteristics commonly associated with military activity and progress. Indeed, although the Zulu charge was at times effective, most conspicuously at Islandhlwana in 1879, it was only so at the cost of heavy casualties, and British firepower generally defeated it, and proved particularly decisive at Ulundi that year.[45] Thus, the Jacobites can be seen as representatives of an earlier form of warfare, one that was bound to fail because it was redundant for tactical and technological reasons. This form of warfare can be compared to those of other eighteenth-century forces using non-Western tactics, for example the Cossacks and the Crimean Tatars. They can be treated as examples of barbarian warfare, rather as Edward Gibbon presented the Tatars when asking if European civilization could be overthrown anew. Alternatively, these forces can be regarded, at the very least, as dated by the March of Modernity, as an Ossianic fragment of times past, primitive virtue, and prowess, that might be impressive at the level of the individual warrior, but that was unsuccessful as an organized, i.e., social, means of waging war.[46]

Another dimension in considering the Jacobites can be added by noting the success of the British state in dealing with its military opponents in the British Isles from the 1640s. The New Model Army was highly successful under Oliver Cromwell, against both Irish and Scots, so that, from the early 1650s, for the first time, all of the British Isles was under effective control from London. The failure of this to occur earlier indicates the questionable nature of what might be termed geopolitical determinism: the ready transference of geography into results. Moreover, in 1685, James II defeated the rising by his illegitimate nephew, James, Duke of Monmouth, while, in 1688, he would probably have destroyed any domestic risings had it not been for the invasion of a Dutch regular army under William of Orange, who became William III in 1689. However, an interesting speculation is whether Monmouth would have succeeded had he delayed his challenge until 1688: he certainly would have done better in recruiting support than in 1685. William's forces, in turn, suppressed Jacobite opposition in both Scotland and Ireland, while Jacobite risings in 1715–16, 1719, and 1745–46 were defeated, and, in 1798, the Irish rising was crushed.

Within the British world, only the American colonists were successful in rebelling, but the War of American Independence (1775–83) is commonly seen as different, and treated in both its military and its political aspects as a harbinger of a new world, and as an aspect of the modernity of the period.[47] The apparent differences between the American war and the Jacobite risings thus help to underline the necessary failure of the latter. Such an approach can, however, be challenged from a number of directions. As far as the contrast with the United States is concerned, the assessment as progressive depends in part on whether the American republic is understood as inherently a weak, libertarian state, in contrast to the more authoritarian monarchy aimed at by the Jacobites. It is conventional to do so, but, allowing for the contrast between a presidential and a dynastic monarch, an alternative view can be considered.

As far as the military dimension is concerned, the challenge comes from adopting a counterfactual approach toward Jacobite failure. In proposing this, and in the subsequent discussion, it can be suggested both that Jacobite warfare was not anachronistic and that the Jacobites came near to success in 1745. As a result, an entire set of assumptions underlying the supposed context and chronology of military modernity can be queried, at least insofar as Britain is concerned. Detailed consideration and contextualization of the warfare of the period provides an empirical underpinning for the counterfactual argument. Large-scale irregular warfare was atypical in Europe in the middle of the eighteenth century. However, refusing to follow suit in the rigorous orders that were imposed on warfare under the auspices of linear tactics was not specific to the Jacobites, but, instead, a general aspect of the "little war" at the time.[48] Furthermore, later in the century, there was to be a major breach in the rules pertaining to linear tactics with the formation of columns.[49] Thus, far from being a reactionary anachronism, the Jacobites, ironically, can be seen as anticipating the kinds of warfare that were to become more prominent toward the end of the eighteenth century, and to play a role in the tactical success of the French Revolutionary forces from 1792.

The Jacobites were also helped by the unfortified nature of most of Britain. The major fortified British positions were in Ireland, or naval dockyards, or overseas bases, such as Gibraltar and Fort St. Philip on Minorca. Berwick, a prominent exception, was not part of a defensive network, and there was no system of citadels in England protecting major domestic centers of government. Not only did this ensure that the Jacobites did not have to fight their way through a series of positions, losing time and manpower as they did so, but it also meant that the British army lacked a network of bases that could provide shelter and replenish supplies. After Charles Edward captured poorly fortified Carlisle, he faced no fortified positions on his chosen route to London, and had he instead chosen to invade North Wales, as was feared for a while, he would have been able to bypass Chester. Thus, the determinism apparently offered by discussion of fortification, and its ability to focus and express hierarchies of capability based on resources and applied science (commonly seen as indicators of military capability),[50] can again be subverted by an empirical understanding that opens the way for a positive response to the specific counterfactual argument.

The Jacobites were of course different from the British military in several major respects, each of which invites counterfactuals. They lacked a navy and were, therefore, unable to challenge the maritime strength of the British state. This strength was crucial in a number of respects in the '45, especially because it covered the movement of British troops back from opposing the French in the Low Countries in 1745, as well as the supply of advancing British forces on the eastern seaboard of Scotland in 1746, while also being a factor affecting French invasion preparations.[51] The Jacobite army was also a volunteer and nonregular force, with nonbureaucratic supply and recruitment systems, and this situation necessarily affected its modus operandi, not least in matters of control and command, and logistics.

Government action against Catholics and suspected Jacobites in England limited the popular support the rising might otherwise have received in England, as did widespread anti-Catholicism. There was no Jacobite rising in England, but then there had been no decisive popular rebellion when William III invaded in 1688.[52] A measure of English support was shown by a marked lack of resistance, especially at Carlisle where the aldermen presented the keys to the city to Charles Edward on bended knees. Rather than arguing that the stance of the English Jacobites demonstrated that there was scant possibility of establishing and grounding a new political settlement, their leaders were waiting for the French to land and had not agreed to rise until then.[53] They seemed congenitally timorous or sensibly prudent on each occasion when opportunity presented itself.

The Jacobite forces, indeed Celtic warfare in general, was recognizably different in type from contemporary and subsequent concepts of military modernity, but the '45 raised a question mark against the thesis about social change and military effectiveness that Edward Gibbon was to propound three decades later. The more "advanced" society in conventional terms was nearly overthrown, and its eventual victory was far from inevitable. The Jacobites won two of the three battles they fought in 1745–46, and the projected night attack on Cumberland's forces at Culloden might also have been successful. Indeed, to propose a counterfactual, it is arguable that the Jacobites should have pressed on in their night attack at Culloden even when their advance had become disordered and they had lost the element of surprise. Poor visibility would certainly have affected British fire discipline and morale. If, in 1685, Monmouth's night attack with irregular forces at Sedgemoor had been defeated, that does not provide a reliable predictor for what might have happened in 1746.

The Jacobites not only won at Prestonpans and Falkirk, but they also managed to advance through Scotland and into the heart of England, creating a military crisis that, for example, was greater than any faced by France during the century. The nearest comparison is probably the Prussian advance on Paris in 1792. However, at Valmy, the Revolutionary French were able to field a substantial (indeed larger) undefeated force to block this advance and, after applying limited pressure without success, the Prussians pulled back. The Jacobite challenge in Britain was more serious in 1745. Possibly the nearest equivalent was the Franco-Bavarian advance toward Vienna in 1741, an advance that, in the event, was diverted by its commanders to Prague.

The Jacobites had another advantage in 1745. Unlike in 1715, when it had been neutral, France was then at war with Britain and planned to assist the Jacobites, and had indeed already attempted an invasion in 1744. France provided much that the Jacobites lacked militarily. It was the second-leading naval power in the world after Britain and, in 1745–46, the French navy was still undefeated. It was thus a potent force in being, a situation that lasted until the two defeats it suffered at Britain's hands off Cape Finisterre in 1747. This poses the question, "What would an earlier French naval defeat have meant for Jacobite chances in 1745?" Until 1747, the British lacked a clear margin of naval superiority, and the French fleet in Brest retained the strategic initiative because the port could not be blockaded effectively. Indeed, in the summer of 1746, the Duc d'Anville's Brest fleet was able to sail in an attempt to regain Cape Breton. As on other occasions, when confronted with French (and other) fleets, and notably so in 1798 and 1805, the British were unsure of the French destination. They had feared that the fleet would mount a landing on the west coast of Scotland. Furthermore, D'Anville's fleet was thwarted by disease and the weather, suffering many casualties as a consequence,[54] and was not defeated by the Royal Navy in 1746. Again, this throws light on the extent to which British naval strength should not be used as a reason to close down counterfactuals about possible French invasion chances.

The French also had an effective army, much of which was stationed near a series of ports from which they could sail to Britain: Boulogne, Calais, Dunkirk, and, once it was captured from an Anglo-Dutch-Austrian garrison in the summer of 1745, Ostend. Charles Edward asked the Duc of Richelieu, commander of the projected French invasion in 1745–46, to make a junction with him near London. Richelieu himself was to mount a successful amphibious attack on British-held Minorca in 1756, which was an important display of French capability. French battlefield superiority over British and allied forces was shown in the Low Countries at Fontenoy (1745), Roucoux (1746), and Lawfeldt (1747). Cumberland, the victor at Culloden in 1746, was the defeated commander at the first and the last, and was, at the head of Hanoverian and allied forces, to be defeated again by the French, this time under Richelieu, at Hastenbeck in 1757. That battle was followed by the overrunning of the Electorate of Hanover and the capitulation of Cumberland's army at Klosterzeven. This campaign provided an interesting indication of the possibility of achieving total victory, overthrowing a state, and forcing a Hanoverian capitulation. This point again has to be taken into account when considering a counterfactual about the chance of French success in 1745.

In 1745, the French had the advantage of making the British government believe that preparations for the expedition were being made at Dunkirk, as they had been in 1708 and 1744, whereas, in fact, they were at Calais and Boulogne. This was important from the perspective of the British blockade. In 1744, however, the French abandoned the projected smaller expedition to Scotland, much to the anger of Lord Marischal and the Scots, and, in 1745, they tried initially to help with some forces and money in Scotland, but were not prepared to send substantial forces under their best general, Marshal Saxe, the victor at Fontenoy. In the event, their invasion plans for southern England came too late and were seriously compromised by the winter weather.[55]

The potential role and consequences of French intervention in 1744–46 highlight the positive importance for Britain's security of relatively good Anglo-French relations in 1713–14 and 1716–31, and of the Walpole government's refusal to fulfill treaty commitments and help Austria against France in the War of the Polish Succession (1733–35).[56] This refusal again underlines the extent to which wars that did not take place are important in counterfactual discussion, a point that was to be relevant in Anglo-Bourbon relations throughout the eighteenth century, for example, with the avoidance of conflict in the Falkland Islands crisis of 1770 and during the Dutch crisis of 1787.

The prospect of French intervention in support of the Jacobites also raises the comparison of the '45 and the American War of Independence. In the latter, the British lost control of the sea, most obviously and importantly off the Chesapeake in 1781, the background to Cornwallis's surrender of his blockaded army at Yorktown; but also (briefly) off New York in 1778 and Savannah in 1779.[57] There was no such comparable loss of control of the sea during the '45, but no necessary reason for this difference. During the American war, the French had no military commitments except for war with Britain. Crucially, despite its Austrian alliance, France did not get involved in the War of the Bavarian Succession of 1778–79. In contrast, in 1745, France was also at war with Austria and the Kingdom of Sardinia (Savoy-Piedmont) and fighting the Dutch. However, this situation did not weaken France appreciably at sea, and did not prevent the French from planning invasions of southern England, both in 1744 and in the winter of 1745–46, nor indeed from overrunning the Austrian Netherlands (Belgium).

Even without French intervention, the British military had been badly handicapped in 1745 and 1775–83 by other factors that do not relate to the issue of whether the Americans had a progressive, and the Jacobites a regressive, military system. The Jacobites were more of a threat than the distant Americans were to be, because they could readily threaten the centers of British power. Equally, relative propinquity in Scotland (compared to America) ensured that the Jacobites could easily be attacked by the British military. This situation interacted with the issue of time, one of the central factors in counterfactual arguments. The British failure to crush the American rebellion in 1775 gave the Americans time to organize themselves politically and militarily, to extend the rebellion greatly, and to weaken the Loyalists. The Jacobites lacked this margin, just as they lacked the wealth of the American economy. Both were arguably more important than the location of each movement in terms of military modernization, and counterfactuals can play a role in the discussion of these contrasts. A wider perspective, both comparative and counterfactual, casts light on the different results of the two conflicts, but does not ensure that the question of whether the Jacobites could have won should be answered in the negative. As so often, moreover, a study of a conflict from both sides, which is an important aspect of successful counterfactual exercises of this type, reveals the danger of making its course or result appear inevitable.

The gravity of the Jacobite threat should therefore be underlined, and mistaken notions of military modernity and its apparent consequences challenged. A rewriting of the mid-eighteenth-century British crisis can thus be offered. The union with Scotland in 1707 nearly had as serious consequences for England in the mid-1740s as, in a very different fashion, that with Ireland was to do for English politics in the nineteenth and early twentieth centuries. Each raises possibilities for counterfactuals, as does the question, "What if Charles Edward had landed in Ireland?"

"What if Charles Edward marched south on December 6, 1745?" is a counterfactual that is superficially not too different from a number of hypotheticals in the American War of Independence. These include, "What if the British general Sir William Howe had advanced on Philadelphia overland in December 1776?" as he indeed suggested, or, "What if he had moved north from New York in 1777, reducing the pressure on General Burgoyne's army in the Hudson Valley?" or "What if there had been more British ships off the Chesapeake in 1781, preventing the French from blockading the British at Yorktown?" None of these are implausible, no more so than the British fleet moving into the East River to block George Washington's retreat from Long Island to Manhattan in 1776 in the face of victorious British troops,[58] or, indeed, the Americans following the military strategy outlined by Charles Lee rather than that of Washington. Lee proposed a kind of irregular warfare and guerrilla strategy, avoiding large-scale battles with the British. France's not entering the war, either in 1778 or on any occasion, also poses an important counterfactual, not least because France's move to war with Britain in this case was hesitant, affected by the course of the conflict in North America, by European power politics, and by the state of French preparations.

Counterfactuals therefore help direct attention to the extent to which the American War of Independence was a series of highly contingent events, and thus should undermine notions of inevitable American victory. Even the American folklore of the conflict, with its stress on the heroic character of the American resistance at Bunker Hill in 1775, still more George Washington's hazardous crossing of the Delaware River at Trenton in December 1776, and the privations and training at Valley Forge in the winter of 1777–78, affirms contingency, which is appropriate. A close reading of American military correspondence, for example the extensive and published papers of George Washington and Nathanael Greene, scarcely suggests a confident sense of victory, even as late as 1781. Instead, there is a reiterated stress on acute deficiencies in resources, particularly manpower, money, and munitions.

There was also a need to respond to British initiatives that could not readily be countered successfully, particularly because of the strength of the British navy until 1778 (and indeed still after French entry into the war that year), and the extent to which, from 1776, New York City and Canada were safe bases from which the British could mount offensives. As late as 1781, given the weak state of the armies of Washington and Greene, and French concern with the West Indies, it is probable that Clinton and Cornwallis could have preserved their positions and waited on the defensive while Britain pursued its maritime war against France and Spain. This strategy would not have brought victory, but might have resulted in negotiations with the Bourbons and the consequent collapse of the anti-British coalition. Such a scenario was a threat to the Americans, and one of which they were aware. Conversely, although a different balance of naval power and advantage would have led to a successful British withdrawal from Yorktown in 1781, this would not have resulted in British victory. Having fought their way to impasse in the Middle

Colonies and the South, the British would have had to evacuate Virginia as well. Instead, rather like the Prussian arrival at Waterloo for the British in 1815, French intervention in the war turned one important type of American success (avoiding being defeated) into another very different type of success (defeating Britain). In 1781, Britain's opponents saw an opportunity and grasped it. Franco-American cooperation, especially between Jean, Count of Rochambeau, and Washington, was crucial to the British failure, as was the insufficient and belated response of the British navy.

The political dimension is also an important sphere for counterfactuals, as well as a varied one. Different British policies in 1763–75 offer a prospect that was debated by contemporaries.[59] Moreover, because America became independent, it is too readily assumed that Loyalism could only be a failed option for Americans. As a consequence, the political counterfactuals of the struggle are not adequately probed, not least the possibility that it might have resulted in a different political solution, one in which negotiations led to a conclusion short of full independence.[60]

Furthermore, the issue of timing does not attract sufficient attention. In the Seven Years'/French and Indian War, it was crucial to British success that the war did not end in late 1757 or early 1758, or even in October 1759, when William Pitt the Elder, then the key secretary of state, told the Prussian envoy that he was ready for a peace that did not involve retaining Louisbourg, which had been taken in 1758, or Quebec if it was captured.[61] In the American War of Independence, it is not clear whether a longer conflict might not have led to a different result, one more favorable to Britain, especially if France had made peace after its naval defeat at the hands of Admiral Rodney at the Saintes in 1782. By then, France had made valuable gains in the West Indies, and the British were under serious pressure, but peace also offered France attractions. Britain could have fought on against the Americans. After all, in the French Revolutionary and Napoleonic Wars, Britain was to make a greater and more sustained war effort than it did between 1775 and 1783.

The historical purchase of counterfactual approaches such as those outlined in this chapter is weak, however, for they do not correspond to the Whiggish teleology that is so powerfully established in Western public culture and intellectual life.[62] This lack of correspondence is especially the case with any argument that the Jacobites could have won or the Americans lost. The suggestion that counterfactual approaches throw light on situations by returning us to the uncertainty of the past is of scant interest to those in the present who lack such uncertainty, as it challenges not only powerful academic constituencies but also a major social role of history as the assertion and support of public myth. This attitude is seen both with eighteenth-century Britain and with American independence.

The argument that Britain could have become Jacobite or that American independence was not inevitable, or might have been compromised—with, for example, South Carolina, Georgia, and the Floridas remaining under the Crown, as Canada did, or with the Old Northwest remaining in British hands—are fundamental challenges to powerful suppositions about British and American history.[63] Yet, each was possible, and both would have interacted with, indeed were episodes in, the struggle between Britain and France. Thus they contributed to the character and strength of the leading power of the West, with all the possibilities that this entailed for changing which state would be the leading power, and thus the relationship of the West with the non-West. In the specific case of the War of American Independence, a different outcome, at least for the Old Northwest beyond the Appalachians, would have left the Native Americans far better protected against expansion by settlers. The value of this counterfactual may be questioned, but it helps explain the eagerness of the American War "Hawks" of 1812, such as Henry Clay, the Speaker of the House of Representatives, for war with Britain, and for the conquest of Canada as the means to solve the future of the Native Americans.

It may seem a long way from Derby on December 5, 1745, to the East River on the night of August 29, 1776, let alone to British troops storming the Mysore capital at Seringapatam on May 4, 1799. Yet maybe the distance and difference between Derby and the other occasions mentioned earlier in this chapter were not that great, a point that can be brought out by counterfactuals. Had the Jacobites succeeded, then it is unclear whether the imperial relationship with the Protestant American colonies would not have been sundered in 1746 (or earlier in 1689), and more rapidly than was to be the case in the 1770s when there was considerable hesitation before declaring independence. If the link had not been sundered, then it is still likely that suspicion of and hostility to British rule would have been greater and that the American Revolution would have occurred earlier than it did; although, conversely, the Stuart breach with the Church of England under James II *might* have been less unpopular in North America than in Britain, and not only with Catholics in Maryland. After all, James II awarded Pennsylvania to William Penn and the Quakers.

Sir Charles Petrie was to present the argument that a Stuart Britain would have been a great imperial power in the late nineteenth century, a counter-counterfactual in that the same end result was assumed. However, as far as the eighteenth century was concerned, a Jacobite British state overshadowed by France might not have been able to mount an effective counterthrust to such an American revolution in North America, although so much would have depended on French attitudes, not least because the French would still have been in control of Canada and Louisiana, and their Spanish allies of Florida.

Had the French acted in 1746, or subsequently, to impose Stuart control on British North America, then another counterfactual offers, one that is of major importance for American history. French-backed Stuart control might have led to a much more arduous independence struggle for America, and one that was far more revolutionary in character, because it would have been necessary to mobilize national resources and energies to a greater extent than was done in 1775–83. The obvious comparison here is with the radicalizing mobilization of France in the French Revolutionary Wars. Had the Americans rebelled against a French-backed Stuart regime, they, thanks to the Franco-Spanish alliance, would have been resisting the remainder of the Atlantic world, rather than being able to benefit from rivalries within it as they did during the War of Independence.

French-supported Stuart success in Britain in 1745–46 might therefore have made the struggle for American independence relatively easy then, but, more likely, would have made it a more difficult process whenever it occurred. Thus the British 1745 counterfactual, "What if Charles Edward had marched south and triumphed?" leads to an American counterfactual: "What if independence had had to be won against French-backed Stuart rule?" The latter counterfactual challenges the benign exceptionalism that reigns in American public culture. Rather than seeing an independent America as necessarily a society with a federal state, weak government, a balanced political system, and a relatively tolerant public culture, it is possible to envisage a process of radicalism and authoritarianism under the pressure of struggle and war akin to that which occurred in France in the 1790s.

The burden of the independence struggle could also have been similar to that of Spanish America in its independence war against Spain, and this burden left Spanish America segmented, impoverished, and with a divided public politics that contained many features of instability. Comparison with the United States[64] indeed leads to the counterfactual, "What if the United States had followed the same path as Spanish America?'

Had it done so, this would have affected the character of what might still have been the greatest twentieth-century power. A more radical, authoritarian, and centralized United States, like France, and later Communist Russia, might have devoted more effort to exporting the revolutionary struggle. In particular, support from France and its ally Spain for Jacobite British rule of America could have led an independent America, in response, to sponsor revolution in French and Spanish colonies on the Gulf of Mexico, and in Florida, the West Indies, and Latin America. This sponsorship might have been a cooperative process, with assistance provided to local allies. However, as with French sponsoring of revolution in Europe in the 1790s and 1800s, the result of such activity could as easily have been conquest and expropriation. Thus, a more authoritarian America might have become even more obviously an imperial power in its own hemisphere, *possibly* further accentuating its domestic authoritarianism, not least an authoritarianism within conquered areas.

More generally, the dynamics of the struggle could have led to a very different America geographically. Newfoundland might have joined a revolution against Stuart rule in 1746, and Nova Scotia might have joined one had it been held after 1763, although the revolution would not have been supported by a Quebec assuaged by tolerant British treatment of the Catholic Church and repelled by the Puritanism of New England.[65] There might also have been more energy devoted to extending the revolution to the British colonies in the West Indies and even to the British Isles, especially linking with the Protestants in Ireland. A commonwealth or federation of formerly British possessions now led by the United States could have been a possibility.

Aside from the consequences for America, such a struggle, a bitter civil war *within* the British Empire, and thus the West, might well have left fewer resources and less drive for the projection of British power at the expense of non-Westerners elsewhere, especially in India and to Australia. The notion that there was a "turn to the east" in British imperialism as a consequence of the loss of America is controversial,[66] but not without value. Had this loss been more incapacitating, then the "turn" might not have been possible, or at least not to the same extent.

Alternatively, a Jacobite Britain could be seen as more likely to lead to cooperation with France, and thus to diminishing rivalry within the West, which might have increased the force available to a French-led alliance for the pursuit of policies either in Europe, for example against the powers partitioning Poland, as the French wanted in 1772–73, and against an expansionist Russia in the Balkans; or against non-Western powers. As already suggested, the net effect could have been a more assertive France within Europe and/or outside Europe, with Britain offering support in either scenario.

Yet, as a reminder of the hazards of this type of approach, and specifically of trying to "fix" or program the consequences, having unfixed the event, a Jacobite Britain might not have been a French client state or pro-French for long. In 1678, after all, Charles II had turned against Louis XIV, despite his having signed the Secret Treaty of Dover with France in 1670 to further their shared Catholicism, especially at the expense of the Dutch.[67] Charles made this turn as a result of his supple response to English circumstances, while James II, "James III," and Charles Edward Stuart lacked his suppleness. Nevertheless, aside from his poor relations with the papacy, James II was neither the ally nor the client of Louis in 1688,[68] although he admired aspects of his rule. While in exile at St. Germain, James became a French client, but, if restored to Britain, he would not necessarily have remained compliant. Claude de Mesmes, Comte d'Avaux, the French envoy to James, and the French in general, frequently remarked that his heart was "too English." Further-more, James's grandson, Charles Edward, kept up an independent atti-tude toward the French which worried them, and he would have been no tool of France.

After all, to note other comparisons, the American colonists owed their independence to help from France, but did not become clients of France; far from it.[69] Indeed, the two powers came close to war in the late 1790s during the "Quasi War": on the Atlantic they were in effect at war from 1797 to 1800. Conversely, the Catholicism and autocracy of France, and past hostilities, did not lead to lasting hostilities; instead, George I and II, who had opposed France until 1714 (George II, as a Hanoverian prince, had fought the French at the battle of Oudenaarde in 1708), were allied to France in 1716–31, and were accused by critics of being overly pro-French.

To take the counterfactual further, and, again, indicate the crucial interaction between international and domestic developments, a Jaco-bite Britain, with its stress on legitimism, Catholicism, and conservatism (although also *maybe* religious pluralism and Scots and Irish separate-ness), would presumably have been bitterly opposed to a Revolutionary and Napoleonic France. There are, of course, obvious problems with deriving such a conclusion for the 1790s from events in the 1740s, let alone the 1680s. Nevertheless, adopting this scenario, revolutionary change in France in the 1780s and 1790s would have sundered the link between (Jacobite) Britain and (Bourbon) France, but done so when Britain was relatively less powerful in the world and less united than was in fact the case for Britain in 1793. An alternative, Jacobite condition for Britain might have made a revolutionary France's intervention there in support of radical options, such as Irish independence or politicosocial revolution in England, Scotland, and Wales, more attractive and, partly for that reason, likely to succeed. Conversely, there might have been no revolution in France but, instead, one against the Stuarts in Britain after their restoration in 1745–46. As with an American revolution against restored Stuart rule, such an event might have led in Britain to a more violent and radical period of transformation, specifically one in which politics and society became more authoritarian, while ideology and cul-ture were radicalized.

As a reminder of continued possibilities, thereafter, for different outcomes in British history, had George Canning, the Tory prime minister,
not died in 1827, the Tories might have held power longer, leading to some
sort of reform act, but not the Whig Reform Act of 1832. Moreover, in
the 1890s, it seemed possible that British socialism, instead of wrapping
itself, via the Independent Labour Party, in the clothes of the Noncon-
formist liberal and internationalist tradition, could have gone for a more
nationalist form of socialism and one which appealed to popular culture
and the drinking classes. The big weakness of the Labour Party was that
this course was not taken and many workers were to see the party as
unpatriotic, and were willing, instead, to support the Conservatives.

For the period 1688–1815, the global implications of the discussion can
be crudely enumerated:

Option 1	Radical France and Radical Britain.
Option 2	Conservative France and Conservative Britain.
Option 3	Conservative France and Radical Britain.
Option 4	Radical France and Conservative Britain.

This summary may confirm that, once you move a certain distance
from the event, the variables and possibilities become so many that the
counterfactual enterprise is hazardous, and even runs out of steam,
as the cause-effect line is drawn out beyond the immediate historical
situation,[70] and that this assessment is particularly valid if insufficient
allowance is made for variable outcomes.[71] Conversely, the counterfactuals are useful for forcing to the surface a realization of the contingency
about what did take place.

Returning to the list, terms such as conservative and radical of
course conceal many differences and numerous tensions. Furthermore,
the history of the period 1500–1945 reveals conflicts between conservative powers, and also (for example, the First Anglo-Dutch War of 1652–
54) between relatively radical counterparts. Nevertheless, it is possible
to see a mutual need for support in the case of options 1 and 2, especially
option 2, with a Stuart regime dependent on French backing. As already
suggested, the energies of such a league might well have been concentrated on ambitions and anxieties in the European or, alternatively, in the

wider Western world. In North America, the British and French devoted more energy to conflict with each other than with the Native American population (or the Spaniards); but these choices were not inevitable and were not seen as such. Indeed, a Stuart Britain, whether or not allied with France, might have needed to devote part of its resources to controlling dissidence in North America.

In teasing out different global trajectories, it is pertinent to ask several questions. Would an alliance of Britain and France as conservative or radical powers have made a major difference, and, if so, more or less so had they been conservative or radical? What is the relationship between interest and ideology? What if the cooperation they were to display against the Turks in 1827, in support of Greek independence, most dramatically at the battle of Cape Navarino, or against Russia in the Crimean War of 1854–56, or in China in 1860, when the two powers occupied Beijing near the close of the Arrow or Second Opium War, had been seen earlier and been more sustained? The Anglo-French alliance of 1716–31 had had scant global impact because both powers were then focused on European enmities, while their joint war against Spain in 1719–20 was short and small-scale, in large part because the French government did not wish to see a major defeat of Philip V of Spain, a grandson of Louis XIV, for the benefit of Britain. In 1727 and 1729, the Fleury government was even more reluctant to help Britain against Spain. The situation thereafter, however, could well have been very different had the two powers cooperated, not only because of the opportunities presented by expansion in India and the Pacific, but also because of the greater resources made available for European powers by sustained demographic and economic expansion from the 1740s.

The most exciting counterfactual, at least for most modern readers, is that of two radical states, both benefiting from early industrialization, setting out to expand their power, but possibly doing so with what were, at least in terms of the age, more progressive ideas. In 1792–93, republican French politicians toyed with the idea of winning British cooperation by proposing joint action against the Spanish empire,[72] a reversal of the situation in 1790 when Bourbon France had ordered a naval mobilization to support that of Bourbon Spain in the Nootka Sound crisis with Britain over the Pacific coastline of Northwest America.

As a reminder of the range of possible scenarios considered at the time, and thus of counterfactuals, the latter crisis itself led to informal British discussions with Alexander Hamilton about the possibility of joint action against Spanish America, more specifically New Orleans.[73] What if that had been pursued? Could the two states have cooperated, could they have sustained this cooperation, and with what consequences? Would an Anglo-American alignment have made the Federalists stronger, and would it have led the Jeffersonians to turn more openly to France? In short, does this "What if?" entail an even greater internationalization of American politics than in fact occurred? Such an internationalization would have gone further had Britain heeded Aaron Burr's request in 1805 that Britain back an independent Louisiana, a prospect seen as likely to lead to further separatism in America.[74]

Adopting a different approach, Anglo-French cooperation might have led, not to the stress on territorial control and landed values discerned by Christopher Bayly in his account of British expansion from 1780 to 1830,[75] and by Geoffrey Plank for the mid-eighteenth century,[76] but, rather, to a stronger emphasis on commercial growth, and even possibly a set of liberal values including free trade and opposition to slavery. In 1794, the French National Convention was informed that France would gain influence in India if it stood for justice and liberty.[77] This prospectus was, in part, an aspect of the naiveté of French radical thought, as well as a response to British naval power. The prospectus was also a looking ahead to different strategies for influence in the nineteenth-century world, and indeed to a distinctive form of informal empire, such as was to be seen with the British in Latin America. It may be difficult to feel confident about possibilities for such French informal empire, not least because developments in India by 1806 demonstrated the consequences of British power, rather than the possibilities for French cooperation with local rulers. Moreover, France under the Third Republic (1871–1940) was scarcely a benign imperial power, whatever that ahistorical concept is held to mean. Nevertheless, the prospect of a very different character to the imperialism of the two leading Western maritime powers is worth considering.

The attempt by American politicians and commentators to argue that their imperialism and power were/are distinctive takes this awareness of contrasts within the West a stage further. These contrasts are not secondary to the rise of the West, no more than those within the non-West are immaterial to the cause and process of this rise. Indeed, the contrasts within the West were to become more pronounced in the twentieth century when, in the 1930s, they included the Soviet Union, Nazi Germany, Fascist Italy, Britain, the world's leading empire, and the very different empire of the United States. Scholars analyze the respective strength of these states during World War II, just as, for earlier, contrasting types of Western empire have attracted much attention.

Thus, the question "Which West?" sits as part of a far longer discussion about differences between the Western states, one, indeed, that can be traced back to contemporary comments on that point. One aspect of counterfactual speculation assumes the ready interchangeability of types of government in varying the success or failure of particular states. This discussion can be mocked, as in the "What if Germany had been like Russia?" approach, but this chapter seeks to show that, if located carefully in an understanding of particular contingencies, the counterfactual method is not without value. Moreover, the method, employed in this chapter, throws considerable light on the possibility of linking short- and long-term counterfactuals so long as they are both anchored in an understanding of the specifics of the situation. As with conventional scholarship, there is a need to beware of understanding complexity in one's own subject for study, for example a particular country, while underrating it in that of others, but this point underlines the extent to which there are overlaps between conventional and counterfactual approaches. The notion of national exceptionalism can be considered in this context, and comparative imperial history is simply an extension of this issue.

Thus, the question posed at the outset of this chapter—"Would the rise of the West have occurred at all, or possibly followed another path, and with other consequences, had there been a different West?"—can be answered, as this lengthy case study has argued, in a number of ways. The differences between Western empires, and the possibility of varied outcomes, also refocus attention on the "why" questions. "Why should the West wish to extend its power?" and "What did power mean in this context?" are both worth considering. Neither was fixed, not least because, as our counterfactuals suggest, it was unclear which state would emerge as dominant. We are also, in answering these questions, in the realms of cultural construction, but those also are as open to counterfactual scenarios and analysis as the strategic decisions and military outcomes that more usually attract counterfactual attention.

Looked at in this light, the question posed at the outset can be answered by arguing that the rise of the West was not inevitable and that, in addition, it could have taken another path. The two are linked. Indeed, partly because Western political dominance did not have to take the forms it did, it was always changeable, even reversible, and *was* reversed after 1918. Counterfactual scenarios lend support to the need for better explanations of the rise of Western dominance than Whiggish *apriorism,* and also demand an improved narrative altogether about Western hegemony.

This conclusion indeed is one of the great values of the counterfactual approach. It both indicates the need for an improved narrative and suggests a way to ask questions that will help decide what this narrative should cover. It would be unrealistic to assume that counterfactuals would play as large a role in such a narrative as they do in this chapter, but there is room for them to take a part, both in order to understand contemporary views and as an analytical tool.

7

COUNTERFACTUALISM IN MILITARY HISTORY

Quebec was besieged three times within sixteen years: French-held, it was besieged by the British in 1759; British-held, by the French in 1760; and British-held, by the Americans in 1775–76. These sieges readily provide opportunities for counterfactuals, not least what would have happened had the British success of 1759 been repeated by the besiegers in 1760 and/or 1775–76. "What needed to happen" in order for this "What if?" to be achieved is also a question of considerable interest. It leads to a focus on naval superiority in the St. Lawrence River, which was vital to the British capture of the city in 1759 and to its relief by British amphibious forces in 1760 and 1776, and to the subsequent success of those forces: the advance on Montreal in 1760 and the expulsion of American forces from Canada in 1776. This amphibious capability highlights the importance of British naval victories in 1759, and the failure of American naval forces to act to strategic effect by challenging the British command of the St. Lawrence estuary, either in 1775–76 or during the War of 1812.

A second scenario poses the question of whether the British conquest of New France (Canada) in 1758–60 was a necessary prelude to the American Revolution, while a third considers the likely future of the United States had it included Canada. This counterfactual, which was reawakened by the prospect of American success in the War of 1812, is based on the idea that, although conquered, Canada would eventually have enjoyed a share in power once divided up into states within the United States. To modern readers, this implies a more liberal United

States, which might indeed have been the case, but, in the shorter term, a key counterfactual might have been, "What if the United States had included an assertive Catholic state in the shape of Quebec?"

Each of the three counterfactuals indicates the extent to which military counterfactuals can probe larger questions, in this case the extent to which the North American question, in the shape of its geopolitics, was uncertain. Furthermore, it was intertwined with the wider geopolitics of the Western world. Thus, "What if Napoleon had avoided defeat by Russia in 1812?" (either by not invading or by securing a negotiated peace) is of direct relevance to the course of the Anglo-American War of 1812.[1]

Indeed, the North American question was only really settled in 1861–71, a decade which saw not only the defeat of Southern separatism (alongside the basis for the reentry of the South into national politics, which was completed in 1877), but also the absence of Anglo-French intervention on behalf of the Confederacy, the failure of France to establish a client state in Mexico, the Russian sale of Alaska to the United States, Canadian Confederation, and Britain's decision to withdraw most of its garrisons from Canada. Each of these developments was subject to counterfactuals, and the combined effect reminds us of the uncertainty about power politics in North America until the end of this period, an uncertainty that is undervalued in accounts that assume that the topic was fundamentally settled by 1783.[2]

Military history is particularly prone to counterfactualism, which reflects both the inherent issues in the subject and the extent to which it is open to commercially attractive attention. As far as the first are concerned, the key topic is that of victory, and thus the question repeatedly arises as to whether the result could have been different. Given the amount of space devoted to the subject of victory in battle, it might seem surprising, but, in fact, it is more difficult to assess what happened on a battlefield than is generally appreciated. When several sources exist, the need to reconcile them suggests the problems (of omission) facing scholars when they have only one source upon which to rely. For the battle of Poitiers in 732 (see chapter 1), indeed, even the place and year of the battle are contested, while the numbers on both sides are unknown and the course of the struggle is unclear.

Source issues affect the possibility of accurate discussion of what happened and why, and thus of counterfactuals. Even allowing for this, there is still uncertainty. For example, one of the standard "What ifs?" relates to the question of whether the Mongols could have conquered Europe. While it is generally agreed that the Mongols pulled out of Hungary because their ruler Ogodei died in 1241,[3] there is dissension on this point. Moreover, there are historians of medieval Europe who claim that the Mongols could never have conquered Europe because of its fortresses and forests, and the lack of pasture for Mongol cavalry. This argument ignores how the Mongols conquered China, as well as the degree to which the Mongols often made opposing fortresses operationally unimportant. Moreover, the Mongols were able to make allies, and Europe, unlike Jin or Song China, was definitely not united. Indeed, even as Pope Innocent IV and the Holy Roman emperor Frederick II called for crusades against the Mongols, they each accused the other of supporting the Mongols or hampering the crusade, while both were criticized for carrying on their petty feud in the face of a grave threat.

There are serious issues with sources and analysis not only in ancient and medieval history. For example, a postwar paper on the tank strength of German armored divisions in 1942–43, produced for the official British history of World War II, argued that casualties and fluctuating replenishment priorities were important factors in variations, and commented, "It shows how misleading formal establishments can be compared with the actual—and fluctuating—establishment of a division, and illustrates the importance of keeping this factor in mind. It doubtless applies to all armies at one time or another in their war careers."[4]

Brigadier C. J. C. Molony noted, "I am apt to turn a rather jaundiced eye on strength returns—perhaps because of vague memories of conjuring rabbits out of hats, as an adjutant a long time ago!"[5] Tank numbers were important enough for contemporaries to seek to distort them, as with Operation Magic in which the British faked tank track marks in order to mislead German aerial reconnaissance in 1941–42. Tank strength was also a particular issue for subsequent analysis because, as the military thinker and tank specialist Basil Liddell Hart pointed out, "To deduce correct issues it is necessary, above all, to determine the tank strengths on either side in any important operations." Reconciling sources involved addressing issues such as how best to distinguish those tanks that were fit for action, and also the treatment of light tanks that were only appropriate for reconnaissance duties.[6] It was important to know tanks' numbers in order to study effectiveness through quantitative historical analysis, a method employed by British specialists in operational research.[7]

This example offers one particular detail of the more general problem of assessing military strength, which is a very important issue due to the tendency to ascribe success to superior resources. Whether or not the language employed is deterministic, explanation in such terms is a key approach to the study of war. Indeed, it is an aspect of the extent to which this study is located in terms of material culture, as, for example, with the focus on technological developments, specifically in weaponry. However, as also discussed in chapter 4 in terms of the power of states, success in battle and in war is not necessarily the product of military or economic resources. An explanation of success in terms of resources has several flaws, including, for wars, underrating the potential dynamic between events and goals, and thus the extent to which the latter can change during the course of a conflict. Instead, a resource-based approach is apt to downplay the role of goals or, in military terms, tasks, and to treat conflict simply, or largely, as an elemental struggle for total victory.

THE AMERICAN CIVIL WAR

This approach is misleading and fails to capture the complexity of warfare and indeed the extent to which goals could alter, with everything that entailed for counterfactuals, notably the impact of the course of the conflict so far. For example, in the American Civil War (1861–65), the war goals of the Union (North) were up for debate, especially, but not only, in 1864, and as contemporaries were aware, had Abraham Lincoln been defeated by the former commander George McClellan, the Democratic candidate, in the presidential election of that year, then the Union might have been willing to offer the Confederacy (South) more moderate terms. An entirely separate counterfactual centers on the possibility of Lincoln not winning the previous presidential election, ensuring that the Civil War did not occur, or did not occur in the 1860s, an issue probed by Robert Fogel. The possibility of a triumph for the Democrats in the congressional elections of 1862,[8] and of a McClellan victory in 1864, provided the South with a viable military goal—trying to create among Union public opinion a sense that the war was going badly. This strategy had operational consequences which might seem foolish if the emphasis is on a resource-centered interpretation with the stress on preserving resources. Instead, the Confederate goal encouraged offensives into the Union in 1862 and 1863, which were designed to suggest to a war-weary Northern public that the Union could not win and that the Confederacy retained the initiative.

In the event, in 1864, in large part because of Sherman's success near Atlanta, the Confederate strategy failed, while, by then, Lee was locked into the defense of the Confederate capital, Richmond, so that he could not advance north in strength again. This failure of Confederate strategy does not, however, invalidate counterfactuals centering on the issue of whether it could have succeeded. Indeed, the Confederate strategy was not made unviable by superior Union resources, as might be assumed if the emphasis is on the marked disparity in resources in favor of the Union. Other things being equal, the Union had a higher probability of winning, and the South had serious disadvantages from the outset, but to argue that that situation made the eventual outcome likely ignores the political dimension as well as the role of contingency.[9]

More generally, the resource approach limits counterfactual options, but the latter are opened up by a number of other perspectives. These include underlining the extent to which the availability of resources in conflicts was not an automatic consequence of capability but, instead, in part, reflected the willingness to support goals, which varied and was a matter of support from not only within states but also within international coalitions. Moreover, it is all too easy to assume that because a battle or war was lost it was bound to be lost. Assessments about the strength of armies that point in this direction are retrospective, and need to take note of the views of contemporary experts who, for example, thought the Austrians stronger than the Prussians in 1866, and the French stronger than the Germans in 1866 and 1870. In each case, the experts were wrong.

WORLD WAR I

Resources are frequently brought into play when discussing the two world wars, as is appropriate, especially in the attritional later stages. At the same time, it is necessary to consider how resources were used, not least by making qualitative assessments about military effectiveness and the creation and management of alliance systems. As an instance of the appropriate use of resources, in World War I (1914–18) the constraints of trench warfare were overcome, especially by the Western Allies by 1918, in large part because they had devised effective tactical and operational means to do so. Their success is a reminder of the need to consider not so much resources as their transformation into the successful conduct of operations, which was a process that, in part, was a learning one in which such variables as planning, strategy, tactics, command skills and systems, and morale all played a major role.

Resources, moreover, were shaped by, as well as responded to, new technologies. The scale of resources was important in this context, and concern to deny or gain them led to such policies as the Allied naval blockade of Germany, and also to German determination to seize resources in Eastern Europe. Yet the variables mentioned above were also significant, as was the combination and interaction of warmaking with political determination and dissent, most dramatically so with the revolution in Russia in 1917. This combination and interaction serve as a reminder of the role for counterfactualism, not only in the conventional form of, for example, "What would have happened in World War I had there been no Russian Revolution?" or, indeed, if Britain had not entered the war,[10] but also because there is no clear way to compare such factors as those already mentioned. This problem leaves room for different approaches. Looked at in one respect, these approaches constitute counterfactuals, while, in another, counterfactuals provide the way to assess the different approaches. As Christopher Duggan has succinctly pointed out, "In all big 'why?' questions, historians have to decide whether to privilege long- or short-term explanations and what weight, if any, to attach to over-arching and inherently-deterministic theories of change."[11] These choices entail considering alternatives.

Thus, in the case of Allied victory in 1918, it is also necessary to give due weight to a range of operational factors, including Erich Ludendorff's poor generalship in the German offensives on the western front that year, notably his unwillingness to maintain the axis of attack and his preference, instead, for attacking on different sectors of the front, as well as the extent to which the German army suffered more seriously from the influenza epidemic than its British and French opponents. More generally, should the weight be on the extent to which the German army was outfought on the western front or on the attritional pressures on the German war economy arising from superior Allied resources? The latter leads to the counterfactual, "What if the United States had not intervened on the Allied side?" The contentiousness of these issues is indicated by the extent to which an emphasis on the "home front," in the shape of the acute strains on German society and Germany's economy, and on resulting discontent, rather than on operational factors, can elide into "stab in the back" myths, as was the case with arguments from the right in Germany after 1918. It was claimed that the German army could have avoided defeat, indeed won, but for weaknesses in Germany caused by a lack of loyalty on the Left. This example showed that counterfactuals can enter the public consciousness rapidly, and also suggested the importance of counterfactualism and how "natural," even unavoidable, counterfactual thinking is. Moreover, to assess and/or contest such interpretations, it was necessary for scholars to discuss the counterfactuals.

INTERWAR YEARS AND WORLD WAR II

Turning to World War II (1939–45), the resource-based approach to war seems less pertinent for the early stages, when the competing sides were still not fixed, than it does for 1943–45. Even so, then it was still the case that far more than resources were at stake in the Allied victory. The United States and the Soviet Union were, it is true, wedded to concepts of operations that were founded upon a significant advantage in resources and industrial capability, as (eventually) with the use of American aircraft carriers in the Pacific, and the Allies came to display a deliberate use of superior resources in the sure knowledge of victory.

At the same time, Soviet operational art and, even more, American war-making also reflected a determination not to be limited to attritional methods. This characteristic of Soviet operational art was very much displayed with the total success of the campaign against the Japanese in Manchuria in 1945, a campaign in which the Soviets took forward the methods of rapid advance they had successfully displayed against the Germans in 1944.

Moving away from a resource-focused explanation of World War II, with the determinism that implies or can imply, leads to a recovery of prewar and wartime uncertainties, with the room for choice, and coun-terfactuals, that this entails. This room for choice was particularly the case with interwar (1918–39) military developments. Indeed, the variety of tasks that militaries might have had to face in the 1930s, as well as looking forward from the perspective of the 1930s to World War II, is a re-minder that the quantity of military resources, as well as transformation, in the shape of new capability, which is the dominant theme in accounts of revolutions in military affairs, have to be understood in interaction with tasking: the goals set and envisaged. These goals were neither pre-dictable nor readily quantifiable, while the interaction was a two-way process, in that capability can help shape tasking and, moreover, affect the assumptions referred to as strategic culture. The crucial, and related, issues and processes of procurement and prioritization indicate that, far from capability flowing automatically, or semiautomatically, from new developments, it is necessary to understand that, at any one time, there was, and is, a range of military options available for fresh and continuing investment. At sea, in the 1930s, for example, it was possible to emphasize the role of gunnery in future ship-to-ship clashes, or of air power, or am-phibious capability, or submarines, and the likely tactical, operational, and strategic relations between them was unclear, and a matter for debate and counterfactual speculation. From hindsight, the battleship seems re-dundant, but this was not how it appeared to contemporaries. Instead, it was believed that battleships could be protected against air attack, while aircraft carriers appeared vulnerable to gunnery, and World War I had showed that submarine campaigns could be beaten.[12]

Another good example would be the writings of Charles de Gaulle in the early 1930s, especially *Le fil de l'épee* (The edge of the sword, 1932) and *Vers l'armée de métier* (1934), published in English as *The Army of the Future* (1940). These were later much touted, by himself, as prescient for his recognition of the need for a professional army of movement, relying on a large and mobile armored corps; but he altogether failed to see the significance of air power, either in a military support role or as an independent arm. Mostly de Gaulle just wanted a much bigger professional army, and foresaw a rerun, on more mobile lines, of World War I. The possibility for enhanced capabilities that stemmed from technological developments, such as submarines, aircraft, and tanks, made procurement and prioritization more difficult, because the range of possibilities grew at the same time that real costs rose.[13] As a cause of further difficulty, the option of interchangeable usage among weapons, and indeed personnel, diminished in this period, in large part as it was a product of the need for specialization, in both weapons specification and training, in order to obtain cutting-edge advantage. For example, aircraft became far more specialized in function than had been the case in the late 1910s, especially with the development of different types of fighter and bomber. These developments, and the problems they posed, both ensured the need for greater claims for proficiency on behalf of particular options, in order for them to justify support, and led to a related need to rank options, whether weapons systems, organizational models, doctrines, or tactical and operational methods. This need emphasizes the requirement for military coordination, under political control. Rethinking the strategic and intelligence framework is a lot harder, and rarer, than agreeing on some new weapon or design.

This competition between options for procurement and doctrine was (and is) one of the contexts for discussions about military change. Claims about the potential for change offered a prospectus that combined futurology with counterfactuals and threat environments. These claims became a key aspect in bidding wars. In these, the military-industrial complex in each major state was not a monolith, but rather a sphere of competing interests, each advancing its case through bold claims.[14] Thus, procurement and strategy, far from being determined by strategic culture, were contested through different interpretations both of this culture and of how best to implement it. In Britain and, to a lesser extent, the United States, classic instances were provided by arguments about the respective values of the indirect approach, focusing on amphibious attacks and on not engaging the main army of the opponent, as opposed to seeking such an engagement.

The same is seen with procurement politics today, most obviously in Britain with discussion of eventualities in which nuclear weaponry or the two "supercarriers" being built in the 2010s would be required. "What if Russia employs its advantages in natural resources and military strength in order to pressure Europe?"—as in 2014 in the Ukraine crisis—is an instance of the type of counterfactual raised in these discussions. There is often a failure, particularly in public discussion, to give due weight to similar issues in the past, and, not least, to appreciate the politicized nature of the counterfactuals involved. This politicized nature was the case with past planning for, and discussion of, nuclear war, especially because there had been no conflict between nuclear powers that could serve as the basis for the discussion of possibilities.

However, it is possible to use a more specific counterfactual in order to assess the likely impact of not having canceled in 1966 the CVA-01, the planned British supercarrier of its day. This counterfactual could play a role in the debate about whether the current supercarriers should have been canceled, notably after the coalition government came to power in 2010. In his autobiography, Denis Healey, the Labour defense secretary in 1966, made clear that discussing possible threats, in a "What if?" fashion, played an important role in his decision to cancel the carrier: "I asked the navy to invent a plausible scenario in which the carrier would be essential. The only one they could conceive was a prolonged naval battle in the straits in Sumatra, in which the enemy had Russian MIGs [fighters] on the adjoining coast, but we had given up our bases in the area."[15]

Linked to this was, and is, the issue of prioritization. If there had been a supercarrier in 1982, then it would have been easier to secure air cover over the British naval task force sent to recapture the Falklands from the Argentinians, and to attack the islands from the air. However, assuming the same expenditure level, there would have been fewer British military resources for other tasks. The focus of naval planning at that stage was on NATO goals centered on the protection of North Atlantic shipping lanes from possible Soviet attack. The British naval force structure was organized accordingly, not least with carriers designed to carry antisubmarine VSTOL short-range Harrier planes, rather than larger, and more expensive, through-deck carriers. In the event, a totally unexpected "What if?" occurred, in the shape of Argentinian attack, an attack that also had major consequences for both Argentinian and British politics, leading, as it did, to the fall of the Argentinian *junta* and contributing to Margaret Thatcher's victory in the 1983 general election.

These issues can also be seen in the interwar period. Thus, for example, in 1936–37, it might have appeared necessary in Britain to invest in tanks in order to confront the possibility of a Continental war with Germany. However, as far as the threat environment was concerned for Britain, there was also the prospect of naval action against Italy in the Mediterranean arising from the Abyssinian crisis and against Japan in the Far East, as a consequence of the Japanese invasion of China. Furthermore, there were large-scale current military obligations in the British Empire, particularly in the shape of the Arab rising in Palestine and the Waziristan campaigns against the Faqir of Ipi on the North-West Frontier of India. Thus, the Appeasement of Germany, Italy, and Japan has to be understood at least in part in terms of competing tasks, and the related issue of prioritization. This understanding should illuminate the discussion of the counterfactuals that are so readily raised about the run-up to World War II.

Even if the colonial dimension were neglected—and for Britain, France, and Italy this was not feasible—there were serious choices. Should France focus on defense against Germany, or should it also assume Italian antipathy, which, because of the buildup of the Italian navy, challenged the maritime routes from France to North Africa and Lebanon/Syria, and would require more investment on the part of the French navy? In the event, Italy only declared war in June 1940, when France was already being defeated on land by Germany, and thus, as also in the Franco-Prussian War of 1870–71, there was insufficient time for sustained naval conflict. In turn, what happened in 1940 cannot be used to settle counterfactuals that may be raised about the earlier situation, not least the issues of Appeasement, as what occurred did not foreclose earlier options.

In the case of the United States, there was the question in the 1930s of whether there should be an emphasis on intervention in Latin

America, or on military expansion (and if so to what extent) to cope with the challenge from German and Japanese militarism. If there was to be war with both, on which should the Americans focus? From 1935, the Army War College's exercises assumed Germany. Looking ahead, however, what if the American navy's concern about the prospect of war with Japan had led to different overall priorities? Yet, the navy itself had differing priorities, with many scenarios focused on the Atlantic theater, and much naval construction and bases aimed at such a deployment.

A key element of military training, war games accept the fluidity of outcomes and the influence of the contingent, but they also prepare options, using counterarguments in order to refine and defend analyses.[16] In 1927, Lieutenant-Commander Tagaki Sokichi planned an attack by two aircraft carriers on Pearl Harbor as part of his graduation exercises at the Japanese Naval War College, but was held to have suffered heavy losses. The different plans subsequently devised for such an attack lead to speculation about the possible consequences had another plan been followed in 1941. The Americans played war games with model ships on the floor of a lecture theater. In one 1933 exercise, Captain Ernest King chose a northern attack route on Japan via Hawaii-Midway-Wake and the Mariannas, while the president of the college, Rear Admiral Laning, preferred a southern route beginning with Micronesia, and criticized King's plans as the worst possible. A decade later, King, commander in chief of the fleet from March 1942 to December 1945, put his plan into action with success.[17]

More generally, there were the questions of how far any interwar revolution in military affairs should focus on offensive or defensive capabilities, and how far weapons systems suited to one capability were appropriate for the other. Furthermore, what would be the social implications of modern warfare, and could they be successfully managed? And what if a lengthy war posed issues of labor mobilization and civilian morale that could not be readily confronted? Such issues and choices did not end with the outbreak of World War II in 1939. Instead, they changed and became more serious, while, separately, a lack of clarity about allies and enemies made it difficult to produce effective strategic plans.

Few could prepare adequately for what was to happen, which underlines the problem with assuming that the situation can be varied to permit one counterfactual, and that this variation can then be pursued in a predictable pattern, as happens in some of the discussion of Appeasement. To do so underplays both the general environment of uncertainty, if not chaos, and, conversely, the extent to which learning was occurring. As Jeffrey Gunsburg noted when considering the death, while rock climbing, of King Albert of Belgium in 1934 and his replacement by the inexperienced Leopold, "How different the course of events would have been had Albert continued to reign, no man can say."[18]

As another aspect of uncertainty, its relationship with the process of learning varied, not least as it was unclear what other powers had learned or would learn. Learning could enhance the uncertainty of developments, but could also limit it by delivering an answer that set a pattern. For example, the Germans in 1938, and even in 1939, were not really prepared,[19] or indeed preparing, for the *blitzkrieg* (lightning war) with which they were to be associated and, instead, learned what could be achieved with their armed forces from their successful war of maneuver in Poland in 1939. This learning was linked to another aspect of uncertainty, that of command, with Hitler feeling emboldened after this success, to advance particular generals. As an instance, both of the ability to learn lessons and of contingency, the rapid defeat of France in 1940 reflected German strengths at the tactical and operational levels that had been enhanced by the experience of the Polish campaign. Yet, this defeat also owed much to the serious deficiencies of French planning, particularly the use of reserves, which were concentrated on the extreme left of the French line, and thus not available to repel the German breakthrough in the Ardennes. Counterfactuals, like scholarly research, have to take note of both sides of the hill. As far as the benefit from the experience of attacking Poland is concerned, the Germans would probably have been less successful had they attacked the French in 1938, which underlines a key counterfactual, that of timing. Furthermore, in 1938–39, they gained the benefit of taking over Czech industry and military *matériel*.

Turning to the other side, a more successful Anglo-French defense against German attack in 1940 might have repeated the 1914 situation. It is important to remember that a key element is that of understanding the present of our past, in other words, both how we today appreciate the past and, more particularly, how it was perceived by contemporaries in terms of the past of that present, in short our past in terms of its past. Thus, there is a need to consider and analyze history forward, in terms of learning from experience, and not backward in terms of those in the past supposedly learning from their future. A German offensive could have been held in 1940, as in 1914, 1916, and 1918, and this defensive success would have enabled the Western allies to make more effective use of their superior economic resources and of their geopolitical position, specifically on the oceans and their ability to thwart access to them by the Continental powers. This ability would have contributed to the attritional economic strategy the British intended to pursue[20] (and the one advocated by the Royal Navy before and during World War I), and would have posed serious problems for Nazi Germany. That this strategy was not pursued successfully does not make it necessarily unviable. As World War I had shown, French defensive strength was, thus, a crucial adjunct to British power, and therefore an important aspect of a world in which American economic power was not yet matched by political and military primacy. A relevant issue for consideration, therefore, is how far France's defeat in 1940 was a necessary prelude and/or precondition for American primacy, at least with regard to Western Europe and the Atlantic world. Phrased as a counterfactual, this becomes, "What if France had not been defeated in 1940?"

Further uncertainties related to the tasks the militaries had to face. The German *Luftwaffe* (air force), which was designed essentially for operational and tactical purposes, was unexpectedly called upon to play a strategic role against Britain in 1940–41, and lacked the necessary doctrine, leadership, and industrial capability to do so. These deficiencies lead to the counterfactual "What if the Germans had put greater effort in the 1930s into developing long-range bombers and a related doctrine and infrastructure?" which is not adequately answered by pointing out that the Germans had a weak aeroengine industry, as more effort could have been devoted to confronting constraints. More generally, prewar force capabilities were developed for particular goals, and then it was discovered that they had to be, and sometimes could be, used in other contexts.[21] For example, prewar navies, the Japanese providing a particularly good example, conceived of carriers and submarines as a subordinate part of fleets that emphasized battleships, only to find in World War II that carriers were more useful.[22]

Resources, an element often deployed to argue against counterfactuals, were important to the course of the war, but the tangled web of diplomacy in its early stages indicates the degree to which political factors played a major role in developing the configuration of the conflict. These factors repeatedly involved choice (as Ian Kershaw has shown[23]), which enhances the role for counterfactualism. Stalin, for example, could have chosen to move to an anti-German policy in 1939, as Britain and France did. He did not, instead allying with Hitler against Poland, and nor were there any Soviet guarantees to Yugoslavia and Greece in 1941 as an equivalent to the British guarantees of Poland and Romania in 1939.

Eastern Europe provides some pointed counterfactuals, not least those posed by the German concept and practice of race war, which played a central role in Hitler's quest for power there and more generally. It is possible to ask what would have happened if Hitler had not launched the Holocaust,[24] and also taken such a harsh position toward conquered Slavs, and whether, as a result, he could have constructed a stronger anti-Communist coalition, notably by including the Poles. Yet, the value of this question is unclear because, to Hitler, war with Jews and Slavs was a racial conflict, and, as such, an existential struggle in which the Germans would earn their right to survive and triumph, creating a Europe that they would dominate. Moreover, there is, at least to a degree, a strong politicized presentism in such speculations as they focus, at least implicitly, on the idea of an acceptable Germany resisting the Soviet Union, which, in fact, was not a possibility while Germany was a Nazi state. This issue therefore risks becoming an instance of the aspect of counterfactualism particularly decried by Evans.

More viable counterfactuals are provided by Operation Barbarossa, the attack on the Soviet Union. "What if Hitler had not launched it, or had done so earlier in 1941?" are well-established questions, the latter linked to the fortuitous basis for the German invasion of Yugoslavia and Greece that April. Moreover, Stalin had a nervous collapse of will on June 28–30, 1941, when the advancing Germans reached Minsk, and there was possibly consideration on his part of a settlement with Germany, similar to the Treaty of Brest-Litovsk accepted by Lenin in 1918.

Indeed, this treaty might have been used to vindicate such an agreement. Reference to Brest-Litovsk serves as a reminder of the degree to which the past creates options that help define and explain later choices. As a result, the range of possibilities that can be defended with reference to history increases, but there is also a process of limitation, because the lessons of past episodes can be held up to criticize options and to condemn choices.

As another turning point, there was also a panic in Moscow in mid-October 1941, but Stalin decided not to flee, and the ruthless N K V D secret police were used to prevent anarchy and restore order. Conversely, in a counterfactual, Holger Herwig has Stalin decide to flee, only to die in an explosion in his dacha arranged by Larrenti Beria, the head of the secret police, and the Red Army, lacking leadership, thereafter ceases to offer effective resistance. Relying on the United States, Herwig goes on to suggest that the Germans still would not have won the war, while Michael Burleigh's counterfactual of German success suggests that Hitler, victorious against the Soviet Union, would have pursued ambitions for world conquest.[25] In contrast, in another counterfactual, Simon Sebag Montefiore has Stalin's flight lead to his overthrow by the Politburo (led by Beria), and to his replacement by Vyacheslav Molotov, the foreign minister. Under the leadership of the latter, the Red Army regains Moscow.[26]

The contrast between the Herwig and Montefiore essays can be seen as challenging the value of counterfactualism, but it is more pertinent to argue that the contrast indicates the ability of such works not only to suggest possibilities, but also to expand the imaginative range and, in so doing, return us to the uncertainty of the past. Montefiore's piece ably recaptures the atmosphere of the relationship between the leading Politburo figures, and this provides an insight into one of the major values of counterfactualism: knowingly fictional, the counterfactual approach can help give history some of the strengths of fiction because, especially at the popular level, it lacks the need for the tone and methods of empiricism. Conversely, such empiricism can be pertinent and can greatly enhance counterfactual discussion. Counterfactualism therefore offers a range of methods, with varied strengths and weaknesses, as is noted throughout this book.

The fictional approach was taken a stage further in the Flashman novels by George McDonald Fraser, in that his invented Victorian adventurer and eventual general purportedly leaves memoirs which can serve to provide a simulacrum of empiricism, in the shape of footnotes, while in fact being largely fictional. Real characters, such as Queen Victoria, Bismarck, Lincoln, and Palmerston, appear, but the novels focus on their fictional antihero. At the same time there is a central counterfactual in the shape of, "What if nineteenth-century history, and, in particular, such leading episodes as the Charge of the Light Brigade, John Brown's raid on Harper's Ferry, and Custer's last stand, in all of which Flashman took part, were written from that perspective?" This question might seem to take the fictional dimension of counterfactualism too far, but, instead, it underlines the extent to which fact and fiction can be mutually supporting, at least in engaging interest in each other.

Returning to 1941, the issue of the stability of the Soviet regime was more significant than the usual Barbarossa counterfactuals which, instead, focus on the German strategic and operational failures, more specifically the question of good strategy badly executed or simply a bad strategy. Overconfident of the prospects for a swift offensive, and completely failing to appreciate Soviet strength, the Germans suffered from a lack of consistency, with goals shifting over the emphasis between seizing territory and defeating Soviet forces, and also over the question of which axes of advance to concentrate on. This lack of consistency led to a delay in the central thrust on Moscow in September 1941, while forces, instead, were sent south to overrun Ukraine and to destroy the Soviet forces there. Both these goals were accomplished, but the delay in the advance on Moscow hindered the Germans when they resumed it, and the Red Army, more effective in defense than is frequently appreciated, was able both to hold the assault eventually and to mount a major counterattack in December 1941.

The standard military counterfactual for this campaign is that of the Germans pressing on earlier against Moscow, which, however, assumes that the seizure of Moscow would have been decisive. Leaving aside the historical comparison with Napoleon's capture of the city in 1812, which, in fact, turned out to be the prelude to a Russian refusal to negotiate and to his worst defeat,[27] this approach makes the classic mistake of assuming that output, in the shape of battlefield success, leads automatically to outcome, in the form of victory. Victory, however, requires the defeated accepting that they have lost, as both the Germans and the Japanese did in 1945, rather than attempting to fight on, and there was scant sign of such an acceptance in the case of the Soviet Union in 1941–42. Although the Soviet government was evacuated to Kuibyshev on the Volga, there was no military or political collapse comparable to that in France in 1940, no more than there had been with Alexander I in 1812.

Hitler did not offer the Soviet Union terms likely to open the way to a compromise peace, the way in which most nineteenth-century European state-to-state conflicts ended and the way in which France accepted peace in 1940. In the eighteenth century, moreover, battle was usually an attempt to force the situation for diplomacy. For Hitler, in contrast, war with the Soviet Union, which he saw as a land of Slavs and Jews, was an end, not a means, and, indeed, a metahistorical and existential struggle without finish. If this invites the counterfactual of how far the situation would have been different without Hitler (not, as above, Hitler with contrasting policies), there is much validity to it. World War I also indicated that the German military leadership, at least then, was unprepared to end an apparently intractable struggle by negotiations in which they paid serious heed to their opponents' views, but Hitler's racial paranoia and prospectus gave German policy in World War II a distinctive character and helped ensure that Germany did not negotiate an end to the war after defeat in 1944 as it had done in 1918. The importance of his views lends interest to counterfactuals about the success of attempts to assassinate and/or overthrow Hitler, although their consequences would have depended on contingency: the situation in July 1944, the time of the unsuccessful Bomb Plot, was very different from that four years earlier.

The possibility that the Bomb Plot might have succeeded was important in West Germany after World War II, for it emphasized the role of a German resistance. Counterfactuals do not tend to play a central role in public myth, but they can be strongly linked to an account, in such myth, of unfair treatment, as with such Polish "What ifs?" as "What if Britain and France had launched a major attack on Germany in 1939, taking the pressure off Poland?" or "What if the Red Army had come to the assistance of the Warsaw Rising in 1944?" As an instance of the role of popular choice in what to cover, another counterfactual located in Poland, but not playing a role in the Polish public myth, is, "What if the Allies had bombed Auschwitz and, more particularly, its rail lines?"[28]

If the outbreak and early progress of the war between Germany and the Soviet Union left room for counterfactuals, the same was true of Japanese policy. The bid for power by Japan was, in part, an attempt to take advantage of the unexpected, in the shape of the opportunities provided by French and Dutch defeat by Germany in 1940, as well as the extreme pressure Britain was under, but there was also a concern about the apparently intractable nature of the Japanese commitment to war in China, and a wish to close down possible international means of supporting resistance there. As an indication, however, of the opportunity for counterfactuals, there were differing views in Japan on the desirability or need for conflict with individual powers, including the Soviet Union and the United States, as well as the institutional priorities of particular army and navy lobbies, including the powerful Kwantung army in Manchuria. These views and priorities all amounted to a range of possible tasks, and thus a lack of clarity as to the military-industrial capability that would be necessary for Japan to fulfill its goals. For Japan, there was also the more profound uncertainty, seen repeatedly with major powers, as to whether it was necessary to act in order to retain and secure great-power status, or whether such action might actually jeopardize it.[29] Counterfactuals have been discussed. Conrad Black has considered what would have happened had the Japanese not attacked Pearl Harbor, concluding that President Roosevelt would have gone to war with Germany.[30] Counterfactuals about the likely consequence of the Americans not dropping the atomic bombs in 1945[31] relate to military and academic discussion to the same end.[32]

COLD WAR

The Cold War was a very different conflict, and again there are a host of counterfactuals that are employed, not least different results for the Chinese Civil War (1946–49) and the Cuban missile crisis (1962).[33] Some counterfactuals, such as that by Victor Davis Hanson, reflect continuing

American anger about defeat in Vietnam, but these tend to suffer from the output/outcome contrast already discussed. More military pressure on North Vietnam, notably in the shape of heavier bombing or even a ground offensive, would not necessarily have led to a settlement on American terms. They might also have led to serious pressure on American interests elsewhere, notably in South Korea, the Middle East, and Western Europe.

There are also central counterfactuals concerning the end of the Cold War, and, in particular, the major contrast between the Soviet position at the close of the 1970s and that a decade later. Ironically, the end of the Soviet bloc could be seen as disproving the foreboding offered by West German conservatives in the 1970s about the likely consequences of *détente* and the normalization of intra-German relations, namely, that they would entrench Communist rule; or it could be argued that they were prescient but that a different set of causes and circumstances came into play in the 1980s. More generally, the failure of those accepted as experts to predict the Soviet implosion leads to considerable skepticism about the process by which experts are designated.

Key questions relate firstly to the role of the American arms buildup under President Ronald Reagan (in office 1981–89) and secondly to the impact of Mikhail Gorbachev, who came to power in the Soviet Union in 1985. More generally, a degree of counterfactualism is valuable, as it is overly easy to treat the fall of the Soviet Union as inevitable, which was not how it struck most commentators. In practice, if North Korea could keep ticking over in the 1990s, 2000s, and 2010s, then a state with the resources of the Soviet Union could have kept stumbling along under a Brezhnevite system. While there is little doubt of the weaknesses both of the Communist regimes in Eastern Europe and of the Soviet Union, there is no reason to believe that the course of events was clearcut. As Frederick Pryor noted in 2005, "Most would no doubt agree that if a Soviet leader of the old ruthless mold had taken over . . . in 1985, the regime could have persisted, at least for several decades, despite the problems of long-term viability. . . . A strong case can be made that under the proper political leadership and carefully designed systemic changes, a modified planned economy might have had longer-term political and economic viability."[34]

A lack of inevitability, or indeed predictability, was true both for developments in the Communist bloc, where the trajectory of China over the past half century is very much a reminder of unpredictability, and of the Western response. Indeed, some Western states and political parties, particularly West Germany, thought it appropriate to prop up the Communist regimes to the east, especially through large-scale loans, as part of a policy defended as normalization.

One interpretation of the Soviet collapse very much locates it in terms of an economic confrontation, not least with reference to the Reaganite claim to have won the Cold War by forcing the Soviet Union to admit defeat in the arms race, a claim that plays a continuing role in the politics of American foreign and fiscal policy. This analysis and claim pose a counterfactual—"What if there were no Reagan arms buildup?"; but, in answering, it is important to note that the Soviet commitment to militarism, while in part a product of competition with the West, specifically the United States, also owed much to the particular political and ideological character of the Soviet system. This point returns us to the role of broadly understood cultural factors, and to the extent to which specific political counterfactuals work in this context. The Soviet Union was a military superpower that lacked a solid basis of support. A paranoid sense of vulnerability, which can be traced back certainly to the seventeenth century, but which owed much to the working of the Stalinist political system (predating World War II) and to Communist ideology, encouraged a major stress on military expenditure, which was already high before the Reagan buildup. Although greatly pressed forward by Reagan, the latter was actually initiated by his predecessor, President Jimmy Carter. For example, the overthrow of the Shah led, in early 1980, to the establishment of the Rapid Deployment Task Force, which was to become the basis of Central Command.

Soviet economic difficulties were not only, or mainly, a product of militarism. Totalitarian regimes were command systems that were inherently prone to impose excessive and inefficient direction, and this problem was accentuated by the economic downturn of the mid-1970s to which the government of Leonid Brezhnev lacked an effective response. Heavy investment in armaments was distorting for these economies but, more generally, they suffered from the role of state planning and from the failure to develop the consumer spending that was so important in the United States and Western Europe. This lack of consumer spending had a serious long-term consequence for the stability of the Soviet system, as a lack of popularity, especially in Eastern Europe, made it difficult for governments to view change and reform with much confidence. A further counterfactual here is, "What if it had been possible to prevent access to the Western media and its relentless advertisement of consumer goods?"; such access had a particular impact in East Germany and Estonia. Thus, the degree to which emphasis should be placed on the Reagan buildup is questionable, leaving aside the fact that, combined with KGB paranoia about a probable American attack, this buildup nearly led to a Soviet attack on the West in 1983.

As far as the role of Gorbachev is concerned, it is the case that he precipitated Soviet collapse. Becoming General Secretary of the Communist Party in 1985, his attempts to strengthen the Soviet Union by economic and political reforms instead helped cause economic confusion and a marked increase in criticism that delegitimized the Communist Party and affected the cohesion of the Soviet Union. This confusion and criticism might be seen as an inevitable consequence of any loosening of the inefficient and unpopular Soviet system.

However, as a reminder of the role of contingency, and therefore the place for counterfactuals, there was no protracted attempt in 1989–91 to use the extensive military resources of the Soviet state to prevent the collapse of Communism and of Soviet hegemony in Eastern Europe and the Soviet Union. This point underlines the drawback of preferring structural interpretations, whether based on army size or on economic capability, at the expense of considerations of mood, ideology, and contingency. At the crudest level, in China, in contrast, there was a greater willingness to persist with the use of force in the suppression of dissent. Pro-democracy opposition in Beijing was crushed in June 1989, whereas in Moscow there was no such unity and force behind the maintenance of the Communist order. As a result, when force was used in 1989–91, as in Bucharest, Riga, Vilnius, and Moscow, it was fitful and unsuccessful.

It is not clear how far the different developments reflected contrasting economic paths, political decisions, or social systems, but the events of 1989–91 serve as a powerful reminder of the role of contingency in both China, where popular disturbances were brutally suppressed, and Soviet client states and the Soviet Union, where they were not. An obvious counterfactual focuses on "What if there were no Gorbachev?" for other Soviet leaders might have authorized the use of force in order to keep these regimes in power or to overthrow reform governments, as indeed had happened in Hungary in 1956 and Czechoslovakia in 1968. As a further reminder of the possible use of force, in 1981 the Soviet government decided not to suppress the Solidarity movement in Poland, instead successfully pressing the Polish government to do so; but Marshal Dmitriy Ustinov, the Soviet Defense Minister, was willing to use the Red Army to that end. Mark Almond's counterfactual about 1989 without Gorbachev suggests that a hard line at home and abroad in the late 1980s would have maintained the Soviet system.[35]

There are also the links between developments among different Eastern European states and those within them. Thus, for East Germany in 1989, there is the "What if the Hungarians had not opened their Austrian border, permitting a mass exodus of East Germans that destabilized the state?" as well as such questions as, "Could the East German system have been stabilized by removing the longtime leader, Erich Honecker, earlier, and giving reform Communism a greater chance?"[36] Helmut Kohl, the Christian Democrat Chancellor of West Germany, who played a key role in ensuring German unification, traded subsequently on the counterfactual "What if Kohl had not been in power?" and his reputation helped him win reelection, as Chancellor of the united Germany, in 1994. Such counterfactuals play a major role in election rhetoric, and also are significant for voters weighing the least undesirable of choices.

Aside from the role of contingency, a focus on the weakness of the Soviet government as a result of the arms race with the United States leads to a top-down account of collapse which can be misleading as it directs attention from the views of the populace and the question of consent. To write of the latter, however, can imply a democratic dimension in the collapse of Communist rule, but that was only partly the case, as all consenters were not equal, and the same was true for dissidents. Even more crucial than the lack of popular support manifested in large-scale demonstrations was the disengagement of Communist Party members, whose attempt to create a modified Communist system helped cause its collapse. This process was readily apparent in the Soviet Union and Hungary, but was also the case elsewhere. It is also necessary to consider the role of nationalism, which helped ensure, notably in Poland, hostility to an Eastern Bloc that was perceived as a vehicle for Soviet control. Moreover, nationalism played a key role in causing the breakup of the Soviet Union, Yugoslavia, and, in 1994, Czechoslovakia.

Counterfactuals about the fall of the Soviet Union rest on different assumptions about how the system worked, and highlight the significance and role of these assumptions. This is a potent parallel between counterfactualism and conventional scholarship, as each rests on these assessments and, if they are to be helpful, it is important that these assessments are grounded in a scholarly understanding of the situation. Moreover, the comparative dimension acts as an important corrective to glib accounts, whether counterfactual or not. This dimension indicates that the politics of Communism and of its dissolution varied, and vary, culturally and by conjuncture, as the differing fates of the Soviet Union and China, or of Mongolia and North Korea, or of Hungary and Cuba, exemplify. Attempts to explain these differing fates in economic terms, or with reference to other structural factors, risk offering a misplaced reductionism that fails to give due weight to the element and consequences of consent, and also to the decisions and responses of leaders in particular contingencies.

An emphasis on consent and soft power may seem a rather strange conclusion to a chapter on military history, but the end of the Cold War is considered because it was an important episode in this history which, indeed, is about far more than war. Discussion of the end of the Cold War also indicates that counterfactuals in the fields of military history and international relations need to see hard and soft power not as opposites, but as part of the same equation. As far as power politics are concerned, there is also the need to avoid any overdetermination, both in the standard account and in alternative counterfactuals. Instead, the conditional nature of status as a power is important, not least because of the inherent dependence of power on processes and ideas of negotiation, and on the perceptions of allies and others. Moreover, both during conflicts, at least prior to their outcome, and in the absence of major wars, there is an indeterminacy in power ratios that makes a precise definition of power and a related designation and categorization of great powers misleading and, instead, leaves room for perception and will. Thus, overdetermined explanations, while they offer an attractive clarity, fail to capture a situation in which the understanding of capability, power, success, and victory entail soft as well as hard power, and all involve a high level of subjectivity, variety, and debate. Counterfactuals can most profitably be employed in this light.

The end of the Cold War provides an instance of the way in which developments can alter the parameters within which both earlier historical events and the relevant counterfactuals are considered. For example, the rapid collapse of East Germany offered suggestions about the weakness of the earlier Nazi regime and the possibility of opposition, while that of the Soviet Union suggested that, had Hitler won World War II, a Nazi empire would still have collapsed. The expansion of the potential for comparisons increases the possibilities for discussion.

Discussion may have retrospective interest, but the assessment of strategic choices in the past can also help clarify the present situation, not least by considering whether other outcomes were possible. "They were possible" becomes a route to "They are possible." In 2013, Stephen Biddle and Peter Feaver pointed out, in an assessment of the War on Terror, that logically any judgment rests on implicit counterfactuals, but these are rarely assessed in any depth. They suggested, then, that many of the counterfactual outcomes about alternative American strategies during the War on Terror looked surprisingly close to the situation by 2012, ensuring a degree of "equifinality": similar long-term results of many potential choices.[37] This assessment proved less secure in 2014 when the Sunni fundamentalist group ISIS overran a large part of Iraq and made the country's collapse into sectarian and ethnic units appear possible.

8

INTO THE FUTURE

In his futuristic novel *L'An 2440* (The year 2440), published in 1770, the radical French writer Louis-Sébastien Mercier described a monument in Paris depicting a black man, his arms extended rather than in chains, and a proud look in his eye, surrounded by the pieces of twenty broken scepters. He stands atop a pedestal bearing the inscription, "Au vengeur du nouveau monde" (To the avenger of the New World). Alternative histories deal with the past, but counterfactuals comprehend future histories as well, including, crucially, ones produced in the past foretelling a future era we have now passed. Of course, no future option from the present is yet factual—no option has yet been instantiated—so the question arises as to whether these options can really be counterfactual. However, there are important similarities in the intellectual processes involved in generating alternatives for both past and future. Looked at differently, although it is easier to assess the validity of alternative histories than alternative futures, the issues and methodological problems raised by the latter require discussion, not least, in this context, because they cast some light on alternative histories.

Part of the interest of counterfactuals, indeed, is that, whether located in the past (alternative histories) or the present and future (alternative futures), they suggest the imminence of the future and indeed of a future that can be known, if not controlled, or even countercontrolled, offsetting what appear to be likely developments. That, however, is an aspect of the misleading way in which counterfactuals are frequently used. This is because, at the same time that speculation is normal, it is a dubious exercise to vary the past or fix the present in order to determine a clear onward future; and certainly unless attention is drawn to the process involved.

As with alternative histories, it is valuable to consider what attracts attention in alternative futures. At the current moment, environmental concerns, especially global warming, have come to the fore, and these attract a mixture of futurology and counterfactualism. There is a factual dimension, but also a fictional one, as in popular apocalyptic fiction predicting environmental crisis, such as Kim Robinson's novels *Forty Signs of Rain* (2004) and *Fifty Degrees Below* (2005), in which Washington, DC, faces a flooding threat from melting ice caps. The film *The Day after Tomorrow* (2004) presented an imminent and disastrous freeze, and linked that to then-current American politics, not least in depicting a vice president, clearly modeled on Dick Cheney (vice president from 2001 to 2009), who was portrayed as unwilling to understand the nature and severity of the environmental challenge. It is probable that future counterfactuals will focus more on environmental issues, particularly if calamities attract public interest. Counterfactuals, in the form of alternative scenarios with highly uncertain, but cumulative, effects, seem to be the normal way for environmental scientists to model climate change. Like historical counterfactuals, however, the more they move to the longer term, the more variable become the divergences between possible developments. Among historians, who, as a profession, for long, and certainly as compared with archaeologists, tended to devote insufficient attention to environmentalism,[1] the situation is changing, and this change will probably encourage counterfactuals as they can be readily used. Questions about higher temperatures, or more rapid deforestation, are readily apparent examples, and can be extended to the past. Indeed, at least in this respect, the role of alternative histories may depend on the prominence of alternative futures. There will be more questions about what would have happened if it had not become warmer or colder at different times in the past, for example, "What if there had been no 'Little Ice Age' in the seventeenth century?"—a counterfactual that is sharpened by the argument that climatic deterioration then was due to sunspot activity and, therefore, was far from predictable.[2] There are also questions about specific occasions, for example, "What if the summer of 1529 had not been so wet, delaying Suleyman the Magnificent's advance on Vienna?" or "What if 1941–42 had been a warm winter, as Hitler's weatherman predicted, instead of the harsh winter that hit the German advance on Moscow?"

More generally, environmental concerns have related to a sense of doubt about progressive teleology, indeed about the perfectibility of man. This doubt corresponds to a widespread skepticism about interpretative schema, a skepticism that itself encourages counterfactual speculation. The capacity of human society to tackle problems and secure improvements now appears unclear. In part, this is because the end result of planned and unplanned expansion has been seen to be not only particular drawbacks, such as dams lessening the ability of rivers to "flush out" deltas and estuaries, and also to replenish them with soil, but, more generally, a pernicious assault on an interdependent environment, both at the global level and at regional and local levels.

Despite these doubts, and in part in order to counter the serious problems perceived and envisaged, there continues to be a determination to employ technology, science, and change as a whole to improve the human condition, and that improvement includes the conceptualization of future possibilities. Almost by definition, technological solutions to what appear to be intractable problems are not obvious or apparent until invented. Publicly funded research into biotechnology, fuel-cell technology, information technology, artificial intelligence, and the use of outer space has raised questions about possibilities that underline a latent potential for change in the human condition. Indeed, it is possible to create what has hitherto existed only in the world of fiction.

Moreover, science fiction poses a powerful counterfactual to the real world, offering, in its catastrophist tendency, important clues not only to anxieties, if not paranoias, but also to the hopes of the world. It invites speculation about suspending or transforming the laws of matter and other scientific fundamentals, speculation which can overlap with discussion by physicists of such concepts as parallel universes and other ideas that leave room for counterfactualism. In science fiction as well as engineering, computer science, and biology, the idea of creating new and artificial life forms has become increasingly insistent. In addition to the humanoids of films, such as those in *Metropolis* (1927) and *The Termina-*

tor (1984), came troubling superintelligent computers that seized control from humans, as in *2001: A Space Odyssey* (1968) and *Colossus: The Forbin Project* (1970). Both categories owed something to the depiction of aliens from other planets that might contest the Earth as well as share space. *2001: A Space Odyssey* proposed a new history of man—past, present, and future—with the acquisition by prehistoric man of the ability to use weapons (which certainly occurred) given cosmic significance by the presence of a monolith broadcasting the news across the universe, for which there is absolutely no evidence. This film also provided a classic instance of the extent to which time could be reconceptualized.

The predictive power of the imagination proved very deficient, as no aliens were, or rather have yet been, encountered, despite the massive increase in the human ability to scrutinize other planets, as well as the awareness of successively more distant universes. Not only were no life forms found, as had been anticipated by many, on the Moon or Mars, but the Voyager mission, launched in 1977 to visit the outer planets, sent back pictures that also recorded no signs of life, and the same was true of the cometary probe Deep Impact (2005). The absence of an encounter with extraterrestrial life forms ensured that there was no fundamental questioning of the relative nature of human values. This lack of fundamental questioning was in marked contrast to the predictive power of the imagination, since aliens have frequently appeared in literature and on the screen, as in *Alien* (1979) and *War of the Worlds* (2005). Far from the role of aliens in the human imagination becoming less common with human exploration, it became more pronounced. This role was employed not only to offer adventure, but also to provide alternative narratives of origins, meanings, and futures. Indeed, universes without a deity suggested a strong imaginative challenge to the conventional belief in the divine ordering of life. As a result, religious groups criticized the *Lord of the Rings* trilogy, the *Harry Potter* stories, and the works of Philip Pullman. Indeed, in 2007, some American Catholic organizations denounced the film *The Golden Compass,* which was based on a Pullman novel.

To move from this discussion to the more mundane issues of the here and now is to note that counterfactuals are central not only to the reporting of politics and economics, but also to the planning through which the present is contested in terms of images of the future. This planning is seen not only in the doings of government, but also in individual, corporate, and institutional borrowing. The calculations involved in such borrowing very much include aspects of counterfactualism, not least the consideration of risk. Thus, corporate investment in future productivity entails assessments of likely markets. The same is true of individual economic decisions such as house, insurance, and annuity purchases. There is extensive discussion of the likely shape of the housing market or the probable level of interest rates.

Counterfactual speculation is also involved in investment in lifestyle, such as in higher education or (not to suggest any equivalence) rearranging one's looks through diet, exercise, plastic surgery, hair transplants, and so on. "What would my life be like if I drove this car, or bought this outfit or house?" is transmuted through advertising into "what your life could be when you buy it." To that extent, counterfactualism is crucial to the dissatisfaction and advertising that consumerism requires and uses. The choice, whether of lifestyles or simply of brands, is pushed in terms of counterfactuals. Looked at differently, counterfactuals concern the choices individuals make—choices made, of course, in contexts. Advertising and lifestyle products are about the interaction of consumer choices and the shaping of the response to choice. Consumer choices offer vivid reminders of the role of individual agency in history, which is one of the key points made throughout this book.

Returning to science fiction, which is a central means for the consumption of fantasy, the sense of future possibilities also serves to make comments on the present. This is a key aspect of the presentism to which counterfactualism and futurology consistently lend themselves, however much they may appear separate from the present in theory. This process is not new. Thus, as mentioned above, Mercier depicted a future Paris that would include a statue of a freed slave. More recently, in his novel *The Sixth Commandment* (1979), the popular American writer Lawrence Sanders had the character Dr. Thorndecker set out to "make humans immortal," remarking, "We are so close. You'll see it all within fifty years. Human cloning. Gene splicing and complete manipulation of DNA. New species. Synthesis of human blood and all the enzymes. Solution of the brain's mysteries, and mastery of immunology."[3] According to Sanders's estimate in 1979, we are now, in 2015, over halfway through this timetable. The idea of clones raised underground to provide perfect body parts for their donors in 2019 was the theme of the film *The Island* (2005). Such stories reflect the sense of a greatly altering people, one in which social and governmental factors helped to shape the consequences of rapid and fundamental technological change.

Counterfactualism offers one way to highlight this awareness of change. If the impact of counterfactualism is lessened by its being an aspect of a general sense of flux, at the same time this sense of flux provides more opportunities for counterfactual speculations as it increases the receptivity of the audience. This discussion of the place of counterfactualism offers a more positive account than the suggestion that interest in it is an aspect of conservative antimodernism, or of a modern fashion for irrationality that is the product of a crisis in thought and culture. This crisis is linked by critics to a range of developments, including the questioning of science, the assault on professionalism, the belief in alternative medicines, and other trends.[4] Instead, the suggestion here is that a sense of flux, rather than a departure from rationality, is a key background to the popularity of counterfactualism. This discussion is important to the location and assessment of counterfactualism, and highlights alternatives that critics should consider.

Looking forward, indeed, there is a case for further increasing the number and pace of counterfactuals. Change is integral to the nature of the modern world, and it would be amazing if the twentieth century, which witnessed astonishing developments, were succeeded by a century of stasis. There is no reason in modern culture or scientific capability to envisage such a shift, and the notion of modernity as a constantly changing presence and aspiration will continue. If anything, current trends indicate an acceleration of change and an increase in the sense of flux, as innovations in genetics, neuroscience, and other fields proliferate through the global communications system. The pace of change will be encouraged as the normative value of past and present arrangements declines in most human societies. Counterfactualism, indeed, can be regarded as an aspect of this process.

Acknowledging the role of change is not the same as stating the potency of all changes. This point is relevant when integrating counterfactuals into futurology. Doing so, indeed, indicates some of the problems of using counterfactuals as a guide to the viability of past options. In considering counterfactuals about the future as a basis for the discussion of historical counterfactuals, it is also necessary to understand the extent to which the sense of time, and that of potential in time, were not, are not, and will not be constant.

Turning to the future, in the case of war, it is likely that, at the high end of the conflict spectrum, the weapons, platforms, and weapons systems that dominate at the present moment will remain central for probably two decades and then will be superseded. Aircraft carriers, manned aircraft, and tanks may then appear anachronistic. In their place, new weapons, such as enhanced aerial drones and the development of land and sea equivalents, will need to combine firepower and mobility, but will try to lessen the frictions associated with use. For example, dispensing with manned flight would permit markedly different specifications for aircraft. To look further ahead is to consider the possibility of discovering and using new properties of matter, or at least of particular materials or spectrum ranges. It is also likely that more effort will be devoted to creating effective means to disorientate the minds of opponents. Information jamming will not be restricted to attacks on material systems, and the creation of precision disorientation weapons may be linked to future advances in the understanding of the chemistry and mechanics of the brain. The ability to affect these in a predictable fashion will be developed in medical science, and then there will be a rapid search for military application; indeed, military research may well lead to developments in medical science. In turn, this application will drive a search for countermeasures.

Such suggestions also imply that there will be further discussion about the laws of war. "What if the latter fail to keep pace with technological change?" is an important counterfactual that lawyers and generals need to consider. It is also one that can be clarified by considering history in part as a process of responding to innovations. Looking further into the future, it is possible that cloning will be utilized to produce more "disposable" soldiery, and, as a separate but related issue, that genetic manipulation will be employed to enhance capability. Genetic engineering, however, is likely to be more constrained than developments in the mechanization of war that lead toward more effective robotic soldiers. What if cloned or robotic soldiers are developed? Their use will encourage research in technology designed to interfere with their control systems. Moreover, an awareness of the prospect of continued radical change in soldier and weaponry will affect investment in the platforms from which both are controlled and fired.

At the level of the great powers, counterfactuals today focus on the strength and limitations of American power, and on the possibilities for change in America's status. A move from American great powerdom to hegemony by another state, which at present can only mean China, or to a condition in which there is no such hegemony, would mark more than simply a stage in the cyclical great-power theories of political scientists which frequently place the emphasis on the fact of power, and not on its character. Indeed, in opposition to these theories, the contrasts between the political cultures of individual states are a key element in counterfactuals, because these contrasts ensure that the emphasis is on differing courses if one or another state succeeds. This emphasis takes precedence over the alternative stress on an essential similarity between position and action suggested by the notion that the position in the international system is the prime factor in determining conduct, and that leading states operate in accordance with their position in the system. For example, the response, in the mid-2000s, to the humanitarian crisis in Darfur indicates that there is a relatively benign character to American policy, in terms of liberal antiauthoritarian standards, that is lacking in that of China, the major foreign ally of Sudan and the purchaser of its oil. The same is true of the Chinese response to separatist drives in Tibet and Xinkiang. Chinese policies invite the "What if?" of a move away from one-party dictatorship there, and this possibility suggests comparisons with the fate of the Soviet Union. The Chinese leadership has been very mindful of these counterfactuals and comparisons since the collapse of Eastern European and Soviet Communism in 1989–91.

Again, as a reminder of the values, and value judgments, built into counterfactuals, it is possible to argue that, whereas the United States appears benign if the alternative paths to the future are those of an authoritarian great power (probably China), or a widespread chaos exploited by rogue regimes, American policy can seem less benign if the alternative is proposed in terms of a pluralistic international system supposedly cooperating amicably through institutions, particularly the UN. This alternative was the counterfactual implicit, or indeed explicit, in the critique of the United States offered by many Western European commentators in the 2000s and 2010s, although—to add a clear "What if?"—it is apparent that this criticism only appeared viable because Western Europe was then free from serious Russian pressure. Russian assertiveness in the 2000s and 2010s, for example at the expense of Estonia, Georgia, and Ukraine, and the prospect of more pressure, makes the possibility of a Europe bereft of support from a weakened United States one that should give Europeans reason for concern. "What if the Americans turned to isolationism?" is a pertinent counterfactual, and one given added force by consideration of, "What if the United States *had* turned to isolationism?"

Again, to take the counterfactual of China as a great power, it is unclear whether this would be a revisionist China, seeking to remold the politics of part, or much, of the world, or, instead, a state willing to dominate while accepting the constraints of noninterventionism, specifically the sovereignty of other states. In addition, it is possible that the process by which China might achieve objectives at the expense of its near-neighbors, especially Taiwan, South Korea, Vietnam, and Japan, might involve a degree of intimidation, if not conflict, that ensures that Chinese great-power status is distinctly militaristic. As a result, China might also be continually vigilant in the face of perceived revisionist tendencies on the part of states that have been intimidated or even defeated.[5]

Turning from the United States and China, it is pertinent to ask questions about other powers. "What if India becomes more assertive?" can be linked to other counterfactuals about the country. It is unrealistic to believe that its future options are defined by the experience of its first six decades as an independent state. Moreover, it is pertinent to ask about the possibilities of civil unrest in India. Does democracy lessen or increase these possibilities, and what if comparison is made with China?

History indicates the range of possibilities for Russia. Its armies were in the center of Europe (a difficult and movable concept) in 1716, 1735, 1748, 1814, 1815, 1849, and 1945; it was extremely weak and seemed close to collapse in the late 1910s and the 1990s; and it is assertive anew

under the current leadership of President Vladimir Putin. Many counterfactuals also arise for the European Union. It is unclear how it will
develop and whether it will succeed; and, here, the past is no guide. Thus,
it is pertinent to pose counterfactuals across the range of possibilities.
The appropriateness of doing so is underlined by the extent to which
much of the current debate about the EU, both in Britain and elsewhere,
revolves around possibilities and thus, explicitly or implicitly, counterfactuals. So also, for example, does discussion about the possibilities for,
say, South Africa. "What if it goes the way of Zimbabwe?" into populist
autocracy is a subtext to "Could it go the way of Zimbabwe?" Similar
points could be made about other states, and this emphasizes the relationship between counterfactuals and comparisons, with contingencies
serving as the nexus for this relationship.

Whatever the nature of the distribution of international power in
the future, it is likely that major states will continue to have to plan for
symmetrical and asymmetrical conflict, and for high- and low-tech military operations. It is also necessary, when looking to the future, to accept
that such categories are malleable, and, indeed, may require continual
redefinition. This is a need that counterfactual thought experiments have
to take on board, and, if that is true for present and future, it is also
the case for the past. Conceptual flexibility is particularly necessary, for
military planners and others in different fields, if a task- or opportunity/
problem-based approach to the future is taken, rather than one focused
on developments in capability.

Conflicts give rise to such counterfactual discussion, and it is made
readily available for a mass audience. Thus, John Diamond, a former
intelligence reporter, writing in *USA Today* on April 16, 2008, pressed
the need for a debate on the consequences of a reduction in American
troop levels in Iraq: "There seems to be an assumption that if we draw
down to a level of, say, 40,000 troops . . . chaos and civil war would erupt
and that we would be powerless to stop it. We must test that assumption
thoroughly, the core issue being: Will the resulting chaos be substan-
tially worse than the violence we see in Iraq today, and will the elected
Iraqi government be able to survive?"[6]

A focus on developments in capability (rather than tasking), however, offers a smaller range of options for counterfactual thought exper-

iments, although there are still some significant ones. To take the case of war, as mentioned earlier, it might be dehumanized by entrusting combat to computers, thus apparently taking mechanization to its logical conclusion. Alternatively, the vulnerability of human societies to environmental damage, and of humans to disease, could be exploited in a systematic form, expanding a possibility already seen with bacteriological warfare. In short, there is no reason to believe that the capability of war for adaptation and major change will diminish.

Yet, alongside these ideas, it is more likely that standard aims will continue and that familiar problems will persist. How can states control dissident groups? How can they guarantee stability in an unstable world? How can they use military capability to achieve their objectives short of the unpredictable hazards of war? It is difficult to feel that any of these issues will change, but their relative weight may be transformed, which underlines a problem for counterfactual discussion. All too often, the approach is employed to vary the means (of relative power or particular policies) within a system in which the ends are seen as constant. This approach is mistaken. Instead, and looking not only to the future, the extent to which the ends were, are, and will be unclear and contested is a major problem with analyzing and explaining change, whether or not counterfactual approaches are employed.

This argument returns us to a point made throughout this book, that counterfactuals should not be restricted to the specific and particular, the contingent and the knowable, the last grounded in the availability of sources. Instead, counterfactuals can be employed instructively to consider changes in what in effect are the parameters within which options were, are, and will be considered. This proposition may seem a bridge too far, and clearly many scholars are uneasy about moving beyond the familiar and the readily measurable. However, a sense of goals and attitudes as inherently variable recaptures not only the uncertainty of the past, but also the unpredictability of present and future developments.

9

SKEPTICISM AND THE HISTORIAN

Hitherto, the emphasis in this book has been in part on the place of counterfactualism in widening the scope, and strengthening the appeal, of a properly scholarly history, with all its archival care. This widening has been presented in terms of the stimulus of a more imaginative and flexible conceptualization of past possibilities. In this chapter, I take this argument forward, but also consider counterfactualism as the nemesis of often stuffy and unreflecting academic methods. Counterfactualism certainly challenges conventional scholarly rationales of the management of risk in historical analysis. It explicitly expands the range of explanations by emphasizing the number of possibilities, and, in doing so, there is a danger that a chaos of multiple routes, each mediated by contingency and chance, open up. Counterfactualism, in short, can become a Trojan horse for postmodernist anarchy. Nevertheless, without going so far, multiple routes may make for a fertility in speculation that attracts attention and elicits the interest, even enthusiasm, of the public. Such interest and enthusiasm should be one of the goals of academics, whether or not they are writing for commercial motives.

Yet, this element of possibility or chaos is troubling to many scholars. In part, this response reflects a neo-Platonic quest to focus on accuracy and a supposedly definitive answer; in part, a reasonable sense that counterfactualism lacks discipline; and, in part, a perception that it is not of particular value in individual branches of the subject. There is also concern about the use in counterfactuals of anachronistic ideas which are not appropriate for the period being discussed. These points by no means exhaust the range of criticism. Nevertheless, they capture the extent to which counterfactualism, while applauded by its supporters as a skeptical critique of determinism,[1] is also itself understandably subject to a healthy dollop of skepticism. This skepticism does not necessarily deny counterfactualism's value, but does ensure that it cannot be seen as an equivalent to the discussion of what did occur. Indeed, the lack of any accepted organizing principle for writing counterfactual history is a problem, one that has been highlighted by the greater popularity of this history from the mid-1990s. Historians have always discussed plausible alternatives to crucial decisions, but it is not clear how to structure in detail a journey down "The Road Not Taken," to quote the American poet Robert Frost.

Instead of offering an equivalence or alternative to conventional history, however, counterfactualism can be seen as a valuable secondary approach, and, indeed, one that can help in the elucidation of what did occur. Understood as thought experiments, counterfactual speculations are of great value, although this is possibly less the case for the large-scale quantitative exercises employed by Robert Fogel (see chapter 3). Indeed, what is striking about the latter is that he has had relatively few emulators. Gary Hawke used Fogel's model for his study of British railways,[2] while Nicholas von Tunzelman did the same for the effect of steam engines in Britain,[3] but few others have followed at this scale. The failure to do so may reflect the work required for such quantitative studies, and, possibly, the difficulty of obtaining research grants and approval from colleagues, which are key points for furthering academic research. However, there are also clearly issues and problems as far as economic historians are concerned. In particular, regression analysis, in which the relationships between variables in a data set are studied in order to establish and explain patterns within the data set and to consider the effect of these relationships, appears more valid than counterfactualism, which entails building an alternative model and showing how it pertains. The sense that abstracting an element such as railways from the economy and then measuring the results may be bogus, because of the distorting impact (often highly distorting impact) of the abstraction, is also pertinent. This was a critique of Fogel's work and one that, through that notable prism, influenced academic consideration of counterfactualism.

Nevertheless, abstracting an element can, indeed, be useful. For example, counterfactual work on migration in the nineteenth century suggests that Irish and Continental migration to Britain helped lower British wage rates, which provided an opportunity for enhanced profits for industrialists, but also contributed to poverty in Britain and reduced domestic purchasing power. In turn, this work raises questions about the impact of modern migration, and its consequences for actual and desirable wage rates. In this case, the counterfactual can be useful as a means to widen the past example that is employed in order to understand current developments. In doing so, however, it is necessary to employ a multifaceted analysis, rather than a crude approach, not least by considering the impact of rigidities in the labor market, both in the nineteenth century and today, as well as the extent to which the labor market is comprised of distinct sectors.

For political and military historians, counterfactuals are more helpful. The latter are accustomed to the role of anticipated variables in military planning, not only because of friction, in the Clausewitzian sense, but also because the responses of opponents cannot be fixed, while the progress of campaigning is uncertain. These factors are less central to political history, which may be a reason why counterfactuals play a smaller role in it. Game playing is not after all an aspect of political training, as it is for the military. Indeed, game playing is a modern version of the older staff ride, the visit to the battlefield in order to evaluate options for both sides. Yet, if the training dimension is not present, as it is for the military, the sense of unpredictability in politics, combined with the practice of speculation about options and the future, ensures that counterfactualism has a valuable part to play for historians in recreating the ambience in which decisions were made, whatever its role in evaluating their merit.

Conversely, the use of counterfactualism to evaluate the merit of past decisions is contentious both intellectually and also because this evaluation (not least, but not only, in order to press the case retrospectively for different outcomes) can encourage a feckless failure to understand the very ambience and, in particular, constraints of past decision making. This point is pertinent for the recent as well as the distant past. However, as with other aspects of historical scholarship, poor work should encourage not the jettisoning of the subject, but, instead, more searching effort illuminated by an informed skepticism. Although the nature of the approach and the commercial context make it difficult, counterfactual history, indeed, benefits from being subject to the same disciplined, analytical rules as conventional approaches, in order to exclude anachronism, possibilities without evidence, and unweighed likelihoods. For example, some counterfactuals, while very valuable for opening up debate, can be refuted by an informed consideration of the situation, and thus should encourage such a consideration.

This process can be seen with the argument that British politicians in the 1760s and 1770s failed to appreciate the need for Britain to take an interventionist role in European power politics, and that this failure led to weakness, culminating in British diplomatic isolation, and therefore defeat, in the American War of Independence. A resulting counterfactual—"What if Britain had had allies during that war?"—suggests the possibility of a different outcome. A criticism of the failure to adopt an interventionist role was indeed advanced at the time, notably by those who were angered by the collapse of the British alliance with Frederick II (Frederick the Great of Prussia) in 1762, a collapse that was seen as a failure to sustain and continue the war-winning policies of William Pitt the Elder during the Seven Years' War (1756–63). More recently, scholars have taken up the argument.[4]

This counterfactual is worth probing, firstly, because it is employed as a central theme in a criticism of British foreign policy that is based on the idea that an alternative was viable and desirable; secondly, because it valuably links modern scholarship to the debate of the time; and thirdly, because it can appear to play a role in the current discussion of interventionism. As such, it is a variant of the long-lasting debate about Appeasement in the 1930s.[5] It is notable that Brendan Simms, a highly talented scholar who actively pressed this interventionist counterfactual for the 1760s and 1770s, had previously written, eloquently and critically, in favor of earlier and more vigorous British intervention in the Bosnian crisis of the 1990s.[6]

It is instructive, however, to offer a critique of the argument for interventionism in the 1760s and 1770s, as it indicates the need for care in more generally advancing counterfactual arguments, and, therefore, the problems facing the approach. Moreover, this approach is adopted in this chapter as a foil to that taken in chapter 6. The intention is to demonstrate the weaknesses, as well as the strength, of the method. There are, for example, many dangers in formulating counterfactuals based on simple equations, of the type, Seven Years' War = alliance = success for Britain, whereas War of American Independence = isolation = failure. After all, if a comparative approach is adopted in order to lend substance to the counterfactual argument, it is worth noting that (as is also the case with approaches that are, at least explicitly, not counterfactual) the comparison can be expanded in order to complicate the argument. This expansion acts as a corrective to the approach of allegedly demonstrating proof through simple comparison. Thus, in the case of Britain, it also had allies in the War of the Austrian Succession (in which it was engaged against France in 1743–48 and formally at war in 1744–48), but lacked the degree of success seen during the Seven Years' War, and, in 1748, Britain did not obtain terms comparable to those gained from France and Spain in 1763.

Moreover, the defense of allied territory in the Low Countries (the Austrian Netherlands and the United Provinces—Belgium and the Netherlands) proved a serious drawback for Britain, both militarily and politically, in 1744–48. Conversely, the absence of the need for it was a major help to Britain both during the Seven Years' War (1756–63)—when Britain was not allied to Austria or to the Dutch—and during the War of American Independence, even if it was an aspect of what were, in some respects, serious, but different, strategic situations. The problems with allies were also shown in 1762, when the British found it necessary to send a force to the support of Portugal against Spanish attacks, and were dismayed by the limited help Portugal could produce. In the War of American Independence, in contrast to the Seven Years' War, the British were not obliged to spend money and to send troops to protect the dynasty's German territory of Hanover, nor to help Prussia as had also been the case during the Seven Years' War. In addition, the collapse of the Anglo-Prussian alliance in acrimony in 1762 was not simply due to British policy, whatever critics of the British government might suggest. Alliances could not be simply switched on and off, and discussion, whether counterfactual or not, that assumes that they could be (and therefore should be) is flawed. The counterfactual in this case for the 1760s and 1770s misleadingly presumes a readiness on the part of other states to conform, through alliance and deterrence, with a view of British interests. Such instrumentalism can be a serious problem with counterfactualism: the effects of variations are overdetermined.

In contrast to Simms's counterfactual, the deficiencies of Britain's alliances emerge repeatedly. Prior to the Seven Years' War, a strong alliance system for Britain in Europe had not prevented transoceanic vulnerability to France (especially in North America in 1754), or invasion threats to Britain and Hanover (the latter particularly in 1753), or the collapse of this system itself in 1754–56. Britain had been badly disappointed by its leading ally, Austria, in the latter's attitude toward the Imperial Election Scheme, which was supported by the British government in order to stabilize Germany, and had also been badly disappointed by Austria's attitude toward the need to strengthen the defense of the vulnerable Austrian Netherlands (Belgium). Britain had also found it difficult to win Russia as an ally on acceptable terms. Moreover, Austria and Russia were neither able nor willing to come to the help of Britain in its strategic crisis in 1755 when the French and their Prussian then-ally threatened to broaden Anglo-French hostilities in North America to include an attack on Hanover.

Another criticism of the validity of the interventionist counterfactual for the 1760s and 1770s could be found in events of half a century earlier. The alliance system that George I employed in 1720–21, to try to coerce Peter the Great of Russia into returning his gains from Sweden in the Great Northern War (1700–21), resulted in a total failure of interventionism: Peter was able to retain his gains (Livonia, Ingria, and Estonia), while George's system collapsed. This failure acted as a prelude to a decade in which the desire to master European power politics, by collective security, forceful diplomacy, and the threat of war, ensured that Britain moved from one crisis to another, at considerable cost, and ultimately helped to provoke a serious ministerial and parliamentary crisis in 1729–30.[7] Although, as mentioned earlier, all comparisons face issues of comparability and applicability, this comparison serves to undermine the interventionist counterfactual for the 1760s and 1770s.

At one level, counterfactualism, as often used, represents, as with the support for interventionism in this case, an idealistic approach that, however, is countered by an understanding of the specificity of particular circumstances, the friction of facts, and the nature of the general context. As an instance of all three, cooperation with Prussia worked brilliantly in dissuading French intervention and in supporting Britain's Dutch protégés in the Dutch crisis of 1787, and yet disastrously in the Ochakov crisis four years later in failing to oblige Russia to abandon gains from the Ottoman Empire (Turkey).[8] More generally, the argument for intervention, whether from contemporaries or in subsequent scholarship, was challenged by the growing complexity of European international relations, notably the extent to which the rise of Austria, Prussia, and Russia was such that it ceased to be pertinent for the British to seek to organize these relations in terms of support for, or opposition to, the Bourbons.[9] This development weakened Britain's options insofar as the Continent was concerned, because Britain's strength was most apparent if the Royal Navy could be employed. Simms, in contrast, offered a strongly critical counterfactual in judging the 1760s and 1770s from an interventionist perspective: "Statesmen . . . were less willing than an earlier generation to make concessions in support of a Continental alliance. Contrast, for example, [Thomas, Duke of] Newcastle's heroic efforts to implement the Imperial Election Scheme in the early 1750s, with the steadfast refusal of British statesmen, twenty years later, to agree to the 'Turkish' clause with Russia. The new men seemed unable to grasp that if they wanted European powers to act on Britain's behalf, they would need to offer them something in return."[10]

In practice, however, the thesis that post-1763 Britain should have supported Russian demands on Turkey, with which Russia was at war from 1768 to 1774, or, subsequently, Poland, which Russia helped despoil in the partition of 1772, discounts the problems that would have been created by such an alliance. This thesis also exaggerates what the British state could afford to do, and that at a time when it was struggling with the burden of unprecedented debt and facing serious political problems in Britain and North America over attempts to raise taxation. The last sentence offers a parallel with the present situation for the United States, and thus indicates the interest of considering comparisons and counter-factuals: each in part in light of the other.

Furthermore, even had Britain allied with Austria, Prussia, or Russia after 1763, there is little reason to believe that it would have enjoyed much influence with its ally or allies, or even been consulted by them. This conclusion was suggested by Britain's experience with Austria in 1731–33 and 1748–55, and with Prussia in 1756–63. Moreover, as the three major Eastern European powers were at, or close to, war in 1768–74, 1778–79, and 1782–83, the caution of these British ministers was vindicated. Not only were these conflicts in which Britain had only limited interest, but it was also unlikely that these powers would have been able, or willing, to provide appropriate support to Britain in her confrontations with the Bourbons. Even had they done so, more auxiliaries backing Britain in North America in 1775–83 would have made little more difference than a greater number of French troops supporting Emperor Maximilian in Mexico in the 1860s. In each case, there was a powerful domestic opposition able to sustain resistance, and thus the difficulty of moving from the output of winning victories and conquering territory to the outcome of ending resistance.

What about the "What if?" of Austrian or Prussian pressure on France, or the possibility of this pressure, deterring the latter from helping the Americans from 1778, and thus justifying interventionist British diplomacy in Europe, a variant of the discussion in chapter 6? It is pertinent to ask, however, whether such an alliance would not have led, instead, to a highly damaging British commitment to one side or the other in the Austro-Prussian War of the Bavarian Succession (1778–89). The Seven Years' War, in which Britain had allied with Prussia, was scarcely encouraging in this respect, as it was, initially, far from clear that Britain's involvement in the conflict on the Continent then would work out as favorably as, in the event, happened. In addition, had Britain allied with Austria or Prussia in the War of the Bavarian Succession, then Hanover would presumably have been exposed to attack by its opponent. Hanover was vulnerable, as was repeatedly demonstrated, and had it been overrun, as the French had done in 1757, then its recovery might have jeopardized the military, diplomatic, and political options of the British government. The War of the Bavarian Succession was restricted to two campaigning seasons, but could have been longer, like the Seven Years' War, or speedily resumed, as with the two Austro-Prussian conflicts of the 1740s. Either outcome would have posed problems for Britain.

Moreover, as another critique of the interventionist counterfactual, and, in this case, specifically the argument that it could have deterred French action and thus ensured British victory, the British had, prior to French entry into the war, already failed to translate victories in North America into an acceptable political verdict. French entry was not necessary to stop the British from winning. Thus, the "What if there were no French entry into the war?" is of less moment than might be suggested by a focus on the major French role in the Franco-American defeat of the British at Yorktown in 1781. This point underlines the need to locate speculation about diplomatic options in a context of understanding strategic possibilities. This understanding is insufficiently pursued in the case of some work on the eighteenth century, as well as in some of the discussion of Appeasement.

Goals also need to be borne in mind: it is always a problem if counterfactuals are not adequately grounded in an understanding of contemporary objectives and political culture. Britain was a "satisfied" power after 1763, and, as a consequence, it was difficult, if not dangerous, to try to strengthen the status quo through alliances with powers that wished to overturn it. There was also no significant domestic constituency for an interventionist diplomacy, and notably none for any particular interventionist course of action. Aside from the practicalities of British power, and the nature of British politics, the Western question—the fate of Western Europe, more particularly the Low Countries, the Rhineland, and Italy—had been settled diplomatically in the 1750s, by the Austrian alliances with Spain and then France, removing both the need and the opportunity for British intervention. This shift in power politics was crucial, for the public support for interventionism was fragile, if not weak, unless the Bourbons (the rulers of France and Spain) were the target. Indeed, the domestic coalition of interests and ideas upon which public backing for foreign policy rested was heavily reliant on the consistency offered by the resonance of the anti-Bourbon beat.[11] This dependence helped ensure a continuum (and yet also contrasts) between this misleading public consistency and ministers facing a more complex reality but sometimes having recourse to simple, if not dated, notions.

To turn from the specific to the pedagogic, counterfactualism is a means of discussion that is particularly appropriate for encouraging engagement with the past. Counterfactual perspectives are certainly popular with many students, a point made by a number of academics with whom I discussed the topic. Teaching helps to focus and amplify the "Why" question. Counterfactual history is exciting to students (maybe even excessively so) because it can help to underline the possibilistic view of history. However, it is not so easy to pose the right questions. What if Emperor Frederick III of Germany, the father of Wilhelm II and a known liberal and admirer of Britain, had not died in 1888? Then Bismarck would not have been sacked in 1890 and Germany would not have started up its maritime expansion program—or would it? No World War I, perhaps, and a big war between France and Britain, aided by Germany, over the possession of colonies in Africa instead, for example as a result of the Fashoda crisis of 1898? What if Charles I of Austria-Hungary had been successful in resisting the shipment of Lenin and his like to Russia in 1917? What if the Stauffenberg attack on Hitler in 1944 had been successful? "Tell me, what would have happened?" asks the student.

Having taught a Special Subject on World War II at Exeter on several occasions, I am struck by how frequently counterfactual issues and perspectives help seminars to come alive, and also serve the valuable goal of underlining the extent of options, the impact of contingency, and the difficulty of judgment. Moreover, the same is true of courses that cover broader periods. Counterfactuals give real weight to the comparative dimension—between periods and between states—that is employed to try to explain issues. For example, standard explanations of the French Revolution in terms of social divisions and strains can be countered by asking why it broke out in 1789 and not earlier, when social divisions and strains were also apparent. Again, what if revolution had broken out in Spain, not France? What would be the conclusion? What if, for example, this leads us to argue that social division in France is not the key issue? More generally, counterfactuals based on the varied explanations for the outbreak and course of the French Revolution can be posed, as also for the American Revolutionary War.

The students' "What ifs?" can share with the teacher's use of the same approach the encouragement of a humane skepticism toward glib explanations. The Oxford medievalist John Blair tells me that he finds counterfactual questions a useful way to encourage his students to focus on the essentials, not least by considering how far a different result in the battle of Hastings in 1066 would have affected social, economic, and ecclesiastical developments in England. This teaching method of course simply makes explicit the practice in research and writing of thinking in counterfactual terms before establishing and arguing that something was decisive or an absolutely necessary precondition for something else. In the absence of Harold's defeat by the Normans under William the Conqueror at Hastings, Bob Higham has raised the question of an Anglo-Saxon feudalism and of Anglo-Saxon castle building.[12] The major role of counterfactualism in military education has already been referred to. These studies then inform military history, as in discussion of the likely consequences had the Spaniards, French, and Germans invaded southern England in 1588, 1805, and 1940, respectively.

Possibly this emphasis on teaching and, indeed, the public interest in counterfactual approaches, can encourage, as a counterfactual, asking about the possibility of a different form of academe and a contrasting academic culture. Indeed, this question might be seen as a point of this book. The academic profession is, in many respects, seriously ahistorical in its general assumption that its current norms and power structures have a timeless and universal validity. This assumption downplays not simply the extent to which interpretations and academic practices change, but also the degree to which academic structures should be understood, at least in part, in terms of a politics and sociology of knowledge.[13]

Such an understanding offers a different location for academic criticisms of approaches judged unacceptable, such as counterfactualism. These criticisms can be seen, at least to some extent, as an expression of current power structures, rather than the presentation of a supposedly translucent truth. The awareness of change in academe, and thus of transience in judgments and a long-term subjectivity in methods, can be taken further by suggesting that, in the next few decades, the role of academics in defining and discussing, narrating and explaining, the past will decline as part of a further democratization of opinion through the internet and related developments. Irrespective of the desirability of these changes (and they provide a field for serious concern as well as a major source of opportunity), it is appropriate to consider the likely lineaments of this popular history and the extent to which scholars can engage with it: counterfactualism offers an approach that can be employed for each issue.

To consider counterfactualism in terms of a discussion of the very structure of the profession, and the latter in terms of counterfactualism, underlines the controvertible, not to say ultimately transient, character of an academic power structure that claims distinctive authority, as well as definitive status for its works, and the opposite for those outside this power structure. In particular, there is generally a lack of engagement on the part of academe with popular history, as opposed to a scholarly scrutiny of it as a subject. From this background, the academic critique of counterfactualism, which is seen most prominently as a form of popular history, and criticized accordingly, is scarcely surprising, as is the snobbery, even arrogance, with which this critique can be expressed. Nevertheless, the validity of this critique is questionable. As this chapter has sought to show, the target for criticism should not be counterfactualism itself. Rather, the target should be work that, however thought provoking, also reflects a limited knowledge and understanding of the past.

10

CONCLUSIONS

You will not find a serious student of history, or any commonplace man of intelligence, for the matter of that, who, if you asked, would it not have been God's blessing for the world if Buonaparte [Napoleon] had been assassinated on his return from Egypt [in 1799]? would not answer without hesitation, Yes. But we—we are murderers.

Manfred, one of "The Four Just Men," employing a counterfactual to discuss the response to their plan to assassinate the British Foreign Secretary.[1]

Counterfactualism is valid under a number of heads. Firstly, it helps return us to the uncertainties and contingencies of the world as experienced by contemporaries, and of the events we study. In one light, counterfactualism thereby indicates the fallacy of drawing lessons from the past.[2] Instead, there is no firm past from which to dictate to the future. That conclusion emerges from the study of periods and cultures for which evidence is plentiful, and can also be suggested for others for which there is not comparable evidence.

As the lengthy counterfactual in chapter 6 indicates, an emphasis on uncertainty may be particularly interesting for societies, such as eighteenth-century Britain, that had a mechanistic notion of activity and change. Drawing on Newtonian physics, this notion encouraged attempts to assess different forces and options with a clear and explicit evaluation of consequences, as in the French government's debate in 1778 about whether or not to help the Americans against British rule. However, although the contemporary concepts of national interests and the balance of power might seem to limit policy options, these concepts were regarded as normative, and not as descriptive, and thus it was understood that rulers and ministers could depart from their apparently obvious consequences.[3]

Indeed, the habit of discussing policy in these terms led to the focus of counterfactuals on the views of rulers and ministers. These individuals were regarded as having the free will to enable them to defy the normative character of the policies that should derive from an understanding of national interests.[4] This focus on the free will of rulers encouraged the counterfactualism inherent in the consideration of monarchical systems, with a particular emphasis on the prospect of the royal succession. There were enough abrupt changes of policy after new rulers came to the throne—for example that of Russia toward Prussia after Peter III succeeded Elizabeth in 1762,[5] or, less famously, of Spain away from aggression after Ferdinand VI succeeded Philip V in 1746, and toward war with Britain after Charles III, in turn, succeeded him in 1758—to encourage counterfactuals on that theme all the time.

At the same time as counterfactuals are thereby a study in, and of, uncertainty, they also provide a degree of greater understanding in that it is essential for historians to recover, as far as possible, the preoccupations, influences, and pressures acting upon decision makers and groups at the specific junctures in history at which crucial decisions were made. For that, it is necessary to appreciate the range of possibilities as they appeared to the actors at the time, an approach that captures the sense of indeterminacy, and the observation of unpredictable and uncertain linkages, held by contemporaries. Counterfactualism is an aspect of this process, and some application of counterfactuals is essential for the understanding of the motivations of decision makers in the past. This is easier in some circumstances than others. There are cross-cultural issues, as it is difficult if commentators lack the empathetic cultural knowledge necessary to make accurate assessments and formulate reasonable scenarios. This problem arises not only between countries but also within them if there are fundamental changes in political culture, as in twentieth-century China.

Secondly, counterfactual studies make explicit the role of the scholar as interpreter. Leaving aside the authorial voice, historians, by simply identifying an episode or development or indeed scholarly approach as important, whether in narrative or in analysis, imply that others are less significant. This process is generally left silent for reasons of space, but also because the very process of consideration invites a debate that is unwelcome to many, not least due to the reality that a large number of scholars work on the basis of "truth by declaration."[6] This argument by assertion does not invite debate or qualification. In contrast, the argument here is that the silent comparative judgment is best addressed explicitly. Offering a counterfactual is one way to do so, although such explicit methods are not part of the dominant academic culture, and, indeed, there is considerable uneasiness about their use.

Thirdly, the questions "How?" and "Why?" should be in dialogue with "What if?" if these explanations are to be true to their historical moments. Aside from returning us to the possibilities latent in both "How?" and 'Why?" this dialogue, more specifically, also enables us to focus on political traditions as, in practice, an accretion or deliberate consequence of choices made from among contingencies. Such a presentation of political traditions underlines the extent to which forms of government and structures of politics were far from fixed, and the same point can be made about other fields. Indeed, as this book has indicated, choices can be seen across the range of human activities, not that choice exhausts the possibilities present in the counterfactual approach. To take one of my particular interests, war—the subject of chapter 7—is all about choice: in terms of force structure, tasking, strategy, doctrine, etc. Few of these choices were clear to contemporaries.

If historical scholarship involves judgments, as it tends to do, then it is important to consider the options faced by people in the past, the way in which they considered these options, and the reasons for their choices. Counterfactuals, in short, make us think and should motivate us to dig deeper or to dig further under the often-too-readily-accepted explanatory surface. Moreover, counterfactual speculations can be used to isolate causal elements for purposes of assessment. For some questions, this focuses on choices between alternatives, but for others, there is a more complex relationship, with such choices discussed alongside the issues posed by the context. Thus, in the case of legal history, there may appear to be the simple choice posed by questions such as "What if this judgment had not been made or piece of legislation passed?" but the choices can most profitably be discussed by considering them in relation to the nature of society, not least the willingness to implement particular laws. To propose a "What if?" in terms of the implications, especially in case law systems, of an individual judgment or law requires also considering whether it could have been enforced.[7] Thus, the assessment involves two different types of counterfactuals, and appreciating the complex relationship between them entails scholarly understanding.

In short, counterfactual discussion, and notably of this type, calls on the same qualities as other scholarly questions. That, of course, does not mean that only academics are capable of answering them, but scholars certainly offer insights that cannot be provided by such active employers of counterfactuals as politicians and war gamers. Moreover, counterfactualism offers a variety of different advantages for academics: principally as an ancillary scholarly tool of analysis; as a valuable teaching method, used to indicate the complexities of past situations and choices; and as a more disciplined version of a widespread public need to appropriate and reflect on the past.

Dealing, as it does, with what did not happen, counterfactualism cannot, of course, equate with scholarship that seeks to recover what did, but it is mistaken to go on to argue that counterfactualism has no value, and indeed cannot help in this recovery; it is also wrong to presume that established scholarly practices are without serious problems. Counterfactualism indeed can be seen as providing, at least in part, what history lacks when compared to many of the sciences, namely, an ability to repeat experiments in order to test propositions. The counterfactual thought-experiments can be presented as alternative hypotheses employed in order to permit a repetition of the experiments.

Furthermore, there is scientific discussion based on the idea that the thoughts of scientists help determine their theories while their perspectives affect their observations, which thus limits the concept of separate objective reality. In addition, physicists and biologists in particular are keen to probe different perspectives on development, for example the notion of parallel universes, and, in doing so, employ counterfactualism. Again, this helps suggest comparisons, rather than stark contrasts, between history and science. In a particular modern vista, counterfactualism possibly emerges as a ripple effect of quantum physics into the field of history, and is an aspect of a broader emphasis in science on chaos, random changes, and "punctuated equilibrium."[8]

To turn in a different direction, there is a possible overlap between counterfactualism and certain types of artistic depiction. Thus, *capricci* (fantasy scenes or fanciful views), which were common in early modern Italy, and indeed many other cultures, were a popular form of landscape painting there in the eighteenth century. Frequently these scenes incorporated recognizable buildings or archaeological monuments rearranged in juxtapositions not meant to be topographically accurate. The *capricci* were considered to be a higher form of art than the simple views depicting what was actually in a scene, since they did not merely imitate nature but, instead, required an exercise of the intellect and the imagination, an approach also adopted by those who praised British landscape gardening. As an instance of such *capricci, A Capriccio of the Roman Forum* (1741), by Giovanni Paolo Panini (ca. 1692–1765),[9] is based on a view of the Forum Romanum seen from the west, including the ruins of the Arch of Titus and the Temples of Castor and Pollux, Saturn, and the Divine Vespasian. Interspersed with these landmarks are fragments of classical sculpture from various Roman collections and figures emblematic of the transitory nature of human endeavor. The invented view in Canaletto's *Capriccio: A Circular, Domed Church* (1740s)[10] is similarly instructive.

Likewise, Henry Fielding insisted that his novels, such as *Tom Jones* and *Joseph Andrews,* were "true histories" in that they revealed the truth of behavior, as was also allegedly the case with William Styron's *Sophie's Choice* (1979) and *The Confessions of Nat Turner* (1967). The overlap between counterfactualism and certain types of artistic depiction provides an interesting parallel to that with scientific discussion, and each encourages an open-endedness in terms of definition that is appropriate in the discussion of counterfactualism. That does not mean that all forms are of equal merit. As a philosophical discussion to throw light on actual events, counterfactualism clearly has its place: dialectic and counter examples are very useful tools. As a way to test ideas, it is always useful to question, and, in doing so, to provide the antithesis, if not the counterfactual. Questioning accepted facts and interpretations has to form part of the methodology necessary to establish a thesis. That is at the core of historical debate, and necessarily as a means to explore an acceptable version of the truth—even, or especially, as multiple truths can exist, depending on the viewpoint. However, if part of the conspiracy school of thought, counterfactualism is perhaps more akin to historical fiction than scholarly research.

Counterfactual analyses are often striking but always debatable. Whether or not one is struck by them, they make us much more aware of the role of the contingent and of the importance of decision making, and of how fragile a process it sometimes is. Counterfactualism is central to the process of clarifying, and thus assessing, not only the options of the past but also the way in which choices and changes had particular consequences. To adopt this approach does not imply any distinctive political agenda, and it does not need to be foolish. There is a silly element—"Would the history of the world have been different if Napoleon had been hit by a meteorite?" etc.—but by asking the "What if?" question, we can illuminate what did happen, and better prepare ourselves to make judgments.

11

POSTSCRIPT

This book is an invitation to debate, one addressed not only to academics and others concerned with the subject of history as conventionally taught and studied, but also to specialists in other fields who are interested in the past and in the processes of change through time. Other specializations have much to offer historians. We should welcome this, not least because an understanding of the validity of different viewpoints ought to be part of academic history understood as a humane subject. As such, there is scant comfort here for the notion that academic history can provide definitive accounts of the past. This point provides room for reflection, indeed counterfactuals, at both professional and personal levels. As far as the former is concerned, it can be asked whether the search for definitive history is not misleading, indeed a conceit that tells us more about the pretensions of particular intellectual, academic, and publishing systems than about the extent to which our understanding of the past is always a work in progress, and indeed, because of the number of possible interpretations, an interim report. Counterfactualism may demonstrate this variety, but, in doing so, it simply underlines a situation that would exist even if counterfactuals were not pursued.

Ultimately, there is a puzzle with counterfactualism. Why is the academic profession on the whole so resistant to a practice that is so well established at the personal and social levels, as individuals and groups consider outcomes and tell stories predicated on the assumption that life might well have been different? I, indeed, am writing this in a hospital Accident and Emergencies department after an accident that probably should not have occurred (whatever "probably" and "should" mean in this context), and wondering what the immediate and longer-term consequences might and will be. And so for others. Such counterfactuals play a role in biographies and autobiographies, but there is something particularly disappointing about how, when a broader group is considered, there is no such engagement. This situation may reflect a difficulty in considering counterfactuals that rely on choice, and thus alternative choices, when looking at the level of many choosers, but such is the analysis adopted for many problems. "Why did Scots, but not Spaniards, support the Reformation?" is an approach that invites different outcomes as a central element in the analysis. So also with controversies over the response by "ordinary Germans" to the Nazi regime and, thereby, the degree and character of their complicity in the Holocaust.[1] Possibly, it is the writing out of these alternatives and outcomes that creates uneasiness, but it is scarcely different from the process of hypothesis in many other subjects.

The focus of disapproval may therefore be on the literary manifestation of such work and what can appear to be a melding of history and fiction. Such disapproval, however, neglects the extent to which there is an overlap, notably in the nature of narrative. Moreover, the popular character of historical writing frequently relies on the dramatic counterpointing of alternatives in order to argue the significance of turning points and decisive leaders and events. Such an approach clashes with that of much academic scholarship, notably over the last ninety years, and particularly since the 1960s. However, there is no inherent reason why academic practices, themselves frequently in part a matter of disciplinary trends and power structures, should dominate the wider public engagement with the past. The latter involves the desire for explanation and entertainment, and, therefore, the need to provide both. Counterfactualism is a bridge between the two, and this linkage apparently can irritate those who prefer a heavier emphasis on explanation. However, the extent to which history offers entertainment and is seen as a source of it will sustain this particular type of literature. Indeed, it may well be the case that, as with other types, for example detective fiction, it will spread from Anglophone countries to others.

From the political dimension, there may also be pressure to deploy counterfactual arguments as the need to reconsider the origin account of states increases because the legitimacy derived from success in winning independence or changing governing system recedes and is compromised. South Africa is an instance of this process. Indeed, the political context of counterfactualism is more varied and complex than that offered by critics who present it as a response by conservatives. Thus, counterfactualism emerges as an intellectual tool providing a good way of thinking about historical necessity and its absence, a literary device, and a record of political trends as well as historical developments.

I consider the personal level in chapter 2 because I think historiography and historical method would be more pertinent if they focused on present (not past) historical writing and on the treatment of historians as individuals rather than as members of groups. To mention my own case, then, reflects not vanity but the simple point that I am able to write about it with greater authority. There is great pressure, in career, institutional, and professional terms, to write supposedly definitive history, and I have certainly produced heavyweight archival and detailed tomes that might well be fatal if dropped from any height, as well as many instances of telephone kiosk history, that is, you could fit all those who would be interested into a kiosk. Yet, I am aware that such methods are not possible when tackling broader topics; and indeed the aspiration to be definitive is misleading and unhelpful. Instead, it is valuable to engage explicitly with the range of intelligent approaches and views that are available, and to offer them to the reader as part of a two-way process of engagement. This method, in part, rests on the idea that to appear to explain all is to mislead, because it represents a claim to a panoptic vision that the scholar in truth lacks. Indeed, ultimately, one of the values of counterfactualism is that, although it can be self-indulgent or whimsical, it can also challenge any sense of all-knowingness. This humility is one that we should try to communicate. To study is to understand the difficulties of analysis and the problems of exposition. That is a knowledge and wisdom we must seek to convey.

Notes

1. INTRODUCTION

1. P. Simons, "Crucial D-Day Forecast Was Luck, Not Science," *Times* (London), May 16, 2014, 33; reporting findings of Anders Persson.

2. J. D. Fearon, "Counterfactuals and Hypothesis Testing in Political Science," *World Politics* 43 (1991) 169–95; G. Hawthorn, *Plausible Worlds: Possibility and Understanding in History and the Social Sciences* (Cambridge, 1991); A. Demandt, *History That Never Happened: A Treatise on the Question, What Would Have Happened If*, 3rd ed. (Jefferson, NC, 1993); P. E. Tetlock, R. N. Lebow, and G. Parker, eds., *Unmaking the West: "What-If?" Scenarios That Rewrite World History* (Ann Arbor, MI, 2006); S. L. Morgan and C. Winship, *Counterfactuals and Causal Inference: Methods and Principles for Social Research* (Cambridge, 2007). See also R. Martin, Historical Counterexamples and Sufficient Causes," *Mind* 88 (1979) 59–73. The extended introduction to *Uchronia: The Alternate History List* (http://www.uchronia.net) offers valuable guidance on the types of counterfactualism. The list is a bibliography of over 2,800 novels, stories, essays, and other printed material involving the "What ifs?" of history. Robert B. Schmunk runs the site.

3. Morgan and Winship, *Counterfactuals and Casual Inference*.

4. P. A. Cohen, *History in Three Keys: The Boxers as Event, Experience, and Myth* (New York, 1997).

5. G. Rosenfeld, "Why Do We Ask 'What If?': Reflections on the Function of Alternative History," *History and Theory* 41, no. 4 (December 2010): 90–103.

6. L. Beehner, "A Brave New World . . . Without Us," *USA Today*, March 26, 2008, A11.

7. The frequent, often polemical use made of the 1930s' Appeasement of the dictators is a prime instance.

8. D. Kahneman, P. Slovic, and A. Tversky, *Judgment under Uncertainty: Heuristics and Biases* (New York, 1982); N. J. Roese, "The Functional Basis of Counterfactual Thinking," *Journal of Personality and Social Psychology* 66 (1994): 805–18; N. J. Roese and J. M. Olson, eds., *What Might Have Been: The Social Psychology of Counterfactual Thinking* (Mahwah, NJ, 1995); L. J. Sanna, "Defensive Pessimism, Optimism, and Simulating Alternatives: Some Ups and Downs of Prefactual and Counterfactual Thinking," *Journal of Personality and Social Psychology* 71 (1996): 1020–36; M. N. McMullen, "Affective

Contrast and Assimilation in Counterfactual Thinking," *Journal of Experimental Social Psychology* 65 (1999): 812–21; D. R. Mandel, "Counterfactuals, Emotions and Context," *Cognition and Emotion* 17 (2003): 139–59; D. R. Mandel, D. J. Hilton, and P. Catellani, *The Psychology of Counterfactual Thinking* (London, 2005).

9. D. R. Addis, A. T. Wong, and D. L. Schacter, "Remembering the Past and Imagining the Future: Common and Distinct Neural Substrates during Event Construction and Elaboration," *Neuropsychologia* 45 (2007): 1363–77; D. Hassabis, D. Kumaran, S. D. Vann, and E. A. Maguire, "Patients with Hippocampal Amnesia Cannot Imagine New Experiences," *Proceedings of the National Academy of Science* 104 (2007): 1726–31; D. L. Schacter and D. R. Addis, "The Ghosts of Past and Future," *Nature* 445 (January 4, 2007): 27; D. Hassabis and E. A. Maguire, "Deconstructing Episodic Memory with Construction," *Trends in Cognitive Sciences* 11, no. 7 (2007): 299–306; A. Zeman, *Portrait of the Brain* (New Haven, CT, 2008).

10. P. A. Cohen, *History and Popular Memory: The Power of Story in Moments of Crisis* (New York, 2014), 202–206; J. Gottschall, *The Storytelling Animal: How Stories Make Us Human* (Boston, 2012).

11. B. Kilbourn, *Disappearing Persons: Shame and Appearance* (Albany, NY, 2002).

12. R. Grusin, *Premediation: Affect and Mediality in America after 9/11* (Basingstoke, 2010), 146.

13. R. M. Brás, "*Chaimite:* Premediation and Remediation of Pre-Colonial War Rebellions" (paper presented to the Fifth CECC International Conference on Culture and Conflict, Lisbon, December 2013). I would like to thank Brás for discussing the topic with me.

14. M. Quinlan, "We Must Question the Case for Aircraft Carriers," *Financial Times,* February 20, 2008, 13.

15. Ex inf. Peter Luff, minister for defense procurement, 2010–13.

16. For a very different and thoughtful approach to determinism, R. J. Evans, *Altered Pasts: Counterfactuals in History* (Waltham, MA, 2014), 47–70.

17. N. N. Taleb, *The Black Swan: The Impact of the Highly Improbable,* 2nd ed. (London, 2010), 196–200.

18. J. Black, *The Curse of History* (London, 2008), 119–20, 128–29.

19. E. H. Carr, *What Is History?* (London, 2001), 91–93; E. P. Thompson, *The Poverty of Theory and Other Essays* (London, 1978), 108. See also E. Hobsbawn, *On History* (London, 1997), 113–15.

20. G. Rosenfeld, *The World Hitler Never Made: Alternate History and the Memory of Nazism* (Cambridge, 2005), 3.

21. D. N. McCloskey, "History, Differential Equations, and the Problem of Narration," *History and Theory* 30 (1991): 34.

22. J. Tosh, *Why History Matters* (Basingstoke, 2008), 50.

23. E. Showalter, *Hystories: Hysterical Epidemics and Modern Culture* (London, 1997); M. Shermer, *Why People Believe Weird Things* (London, 2002); F. Wheen, *How Mumbo-Jumbo Conquered the World* (London, 2004). For particular criticisms of false history, J. Williams, *Fantastic Archaeology: The Wild Side of North American Prehistory* (College Park, PA, 1991); M. Lefkowitz, *Not Out of Africa: How Afrocentrism Became an Excuse to Teach Myth as History* (London, 1996); C. E. Walker, *We Can't Go Home Again: An Argument about Afrocentrism* (Oxford, 2001).

24. D. Thompson, *Counterknowledge* (London, 2008), 48, 69.

25. For Richard Bernstein's sympathetic review, see "The Promise and the Perils of 'What If?,'" H-Law, H-Net Reviews, January 2000, http://www.h-net.org/reviews /showrev.php?id=3721.

26. R. J. Evans, lecture at Queen's University Belfast, October 2002; abbreviated in "Telling It Like It Wasn't," *BBC History,* December 2002, and *Historically Speaking* 5, no. 4 (March 2004): 11–15, 28–31; reprinted as part of an exchange in D. A. Yerxa, ed., *Recent Themes in Historical Thinking: Historians in Conversation* (Columbia, SC, 2008), 120–30; Evans, *Altered Pasts.*

27. As examples of a larger number, R. N. Lebow, *Archduke Franz Ferdinand Lives! A World without World War I* (New York, 2014); I. Morris, *War! What Is It Good for? Conflict in Civilisation, from Primates to Robots* (London, 2014), 236–38. For an emphasis on the role of individuals in the causes of the war, T. G. Otte, *July Crisis: The World's Descent into War, Summer 1914* (Cambridge, 2014), 505–24.

28. E. H. Carr, *From Napoleon to Stalin* (London, 1989), 262–63.

29. *Deus ex machina* is "a God from a machine," a device in ancient Greek theater that leads to a sudden intervention.

30. F. Fernández-Armesto, review of *Altered Pasts: Counterfactuals in History,* by R. J. Evans, *Times* (London), March 29, 2014.

31. J. Buchan, *The Causal and the Casual in History* (Cambridge, 1929), 35; W. Moore, *Bring the Jubilee* (New York, 1953); P. Patton, "Lee Defeats Grant," *American Heritage* 50 (September 1999), 39–45.

32. W. S. Churchill, "If Lee Had Won the Battle of Gettysburg," in *If It Happened Otherwise: Lapses into Imaginary History,* ed. J. C. Squire (London, 1931), 259–84.

33. R. Fogel, *Railroads and American Economic Growth: Essays in Econometric History* (Baltimore, MD, 1964) and "The New Economic History: Its Findings and Methods," *Economic History Review,* 2nd ser., 19 (1966): 642–56; S. L. Engerman, "Counterfactuals and the New Economic History," *Inquiry* 23 (1980), 157–72.

34. M. Powell and J. Stewart, "Counterfactuals and Contingencies in Historical Policy Learning" (paper presented to the 36th Annual Conference of the Social Policy Association, Teesside University, Middlesbrough, UK, July 15–17, 2003); R. Neustadt and E. May, *Thinking in Time: The Uses of History for Decision Makers* (New York, 1986).

35. Jeff Horn, e-mails to the author, March 20, 2014.

36. T. W. Perry, *Public Opinion, Propaganda, and Politics in Eighteenth-Century England: A Study of the Jew Bill of 1753* (Cambridge, MA, 1962).

37. A. Wohl, "'Dizzi-Ben-Dizzi': Disraeli as Alien," *Journal of British Studies* 34 (1995): 375–411.

38. I. D'Israeli, *Curiosities of Literature,* vol. 2 (Paris, 1835), 369–78.

39. A. J. Toynbee, *A Study of History,* vol. 2, *The Geneses of Civilisations, Part 2* (Oxford, 1934).

40. P. Fouracre, *The Age of Charles Martel* (London, 2000); J. France, "Poitiers," in *The Seventy Great Battles of All Time,* ed. J. Black (London, 2005), 49–50; H. Kennedy, *The Great Arab Conquests: How the Spread of Islam Changed the World We Live In* (London, 2007), 320–23.

41. B. Strauss, *The Battle of Salamis: The Naval Encounter That Saved Greece—and Western Civilization* (New York, 2004), concluding chapter; and Strauss, "The Resilient West," in Tetlock, Lebow, and Parker, *Unmaking the West,* 90–118.

42. For example in the series of books edited by Robert Cowley, of which the first is *What If? The World's Foremost Military Historians Imagine What Might Have Been* (New York, 1999). Other influential collections include J. C. Squire, ed., *If It Happened Otherwise: Lapses into Imaginary History* (London, 1932); D. Snowman, ed., *If I Had Been . . . : Ten Historical Fantasies* (London, 1979); J. M. Merriman, ed., *For Want of a Horse: Choice and Chance in History* (Lexington, MA, 1985); N. Ferguson, ed., *Virtual History: Alternatives and Counterfactuals* (London, 1997).

43. For military and nonmilitary turning points of World War I, I. F. W. Beckett, *The Making of the First World War* (New Haven, CT, 2012), especially 4–11, and for the relevant counterfactuals, 238–39.

44. A reference to the changes introduced by Peter the Great (r. 1689–1725).

45. E. Gibbon, *The History of the Decline and Fall of the Roman Empire*, ed. J. B. Bury (London, 1776–88; London, 1897–1901), 4:166–67. Citations refer to the later edition.

46. D. B. Ralston, *Importing the European Army: The Introduction of European Military Techniques and Institutions into the Extra-European World, 1660–1914* (Chicago, 1990).

47. Gibbon, *The History of the Decline and Fall*, 4:166; J. Black, "Gibbon and International Relations," in *Edward Gibbon and Empire*, ed. R. McKitterick and R. Quinault (Cambridge, 1997), 217–46.

48. H. H. Herwig, "Hitler Wins in the East but Germany Still Loses World War II," in Tetlock, Lebow, and Parker, *Unmaking the West*, 323–360.

49. K.-H. Harbeck, *Die Zeitschrift für Geopolitik 1924–44* (Kiel, 1963).

50. G. Ó Tuathail, *Critical Geopolitics* (London, 1996).

51. M. J. Oakeshott, *Experience and Its Modes* (Cambridge, 1933) and *Rationalism in Politics and Other Essays* (New York, 1962); L. O'Sullivan, *Oakeshott on History* (Exeter, 2003).

52. On these, see, repeatedly, P. Furtado, ed., *Histories of Nations: How Their Identities Were Forged* (London, 2012).

53. This argument is probed at length in J. Black, "Confessional State or Elect Nation? Religion and Identity in Eighteenth-Century England," in *Protestantism and National Identity: Britain and Ireland, c. 1650–c. 1850*, ed. T. Claydon and I. McBride (Cambridge, 1998), 53–74.

54. P. W. Schroeder, *The Transformation of European Politics, 1763–1848* (Oxford, 1994). The nearest German equivalent is more alive to contingencies: H. Duchhardt, *Balance of Power und Pentarchie, 1700–1785* (Paderborn, 1997).

55. J. Black, *European International Relations, 1648–1815* (Basingstoke, 2002).

2. A PERSONAL NOTE ON LIFE AND TIMES

1. R. J. Evans, "Telling It Like It Wasn't," *BBC History*, December 2002.

2. E.g., J. Black, *From Louis XIV to Napoleon: The Fate of a Great Power* (London, 1999), 217, 229.

3. J. Black, *European International Relations, 1648–1815* (Basingstoke, 2002), especially 5–49.

4. D. Frum, "The Chads Fall Off in Florida," in *What Might Have Been: Leading Historians on Twelve "What Ifs" of History*, ed. A. Roberts (London, 2004), 179–88; J. Nicholas, "What If Al Gore Had Won the US Presidential Election of November 2000?" in *President Gore and Other Things That Never Happened*, ed. D. Brack (London, 2006), 305–22;

J. Greenfield, *43: When Gore Beat Bush—A Political Fable* (San Francisco, CA, 2012); *Then Everything Changed: Stunning Alternate Histories of American Politics; JFK, RFK, Carter, Ford, Reagan* (New York, 2011); and *If Kennedy Lived: The First and Second Terms of President John F. Kennedy; An Alternate History* (New York, 2013).

5. S. Heffer, "The Brighton Bomb Kills Margaret Thatcher," in Roberts, *What Might Have Been,* 166–78.

6. For others for this era, D. Brack and I. Dale, eds., *Prime Minister Portillo and Other Things That Never Happened* (London, 2003).

7. K. Dawson et. al., "Congress of Vienna," in *Simulation in the Classroom,* ed. J. L. Taylor and R. Walford (Harmondsworth, 1972), 106.

8. A. Wilson, *War Gaming* (London, 1970; previously published as *The Bomb and The Computer,* 1968), 35–39. Based on papers in NA, WO. 33/364, A1017. For American and Japanese war planning in the 1920s and 1930s, E. S. Miller, *War Plan Orange: The U.S. Strategy to Defeat Japan, 1897–1945* (Annapolis, MD, 1991); A. A. Nofi, *To Train the Fleet for War: The U.S. Navy Fleet Problems, 1923–1940* (Newport, RI, 2010); I. Hata, "Admiral Yamamoto and the Japanese Navy," in *From Pearl Harbor to Hiroshima: The Second World War in Asia and the Pacific, 1941–45,* ed. I. S. Dockrill (New York, 1994), 58.

9. John Maurer, in conversation with the author, March 25, 2008.

10. Peter Lorge, e-mail to the author, June 8, 2014.

11. Giovanni Zamboni to Landgrave of Hesse-Darmstadt, January 19, 1748, Darmstadt, Staatsarchiv, E1 M10/6.

12. For an argument about the rise of consensus and balancing policies, D. Croxton, *Westphalia: The Last Christian Peace* (New York, 2013).

13. Charles VI, the Habsburg ruler. His lack of male heirs ensured that the Habsburg succession caused a bitter war in the 1740s.

14. The Infanta, who had been intended as a bride for Louis XV of France.

15. Roman god of war.

16. A reference to Elizabeth Farnese, queen of Spain, the wife of Philip V of Spain, uncle of Louis XV.

17. Louis-Henri, Duke of Bourbon, first minister of France, 1723–26.

18. André Hercule Fleury, bishop of Frejus, first minister of France, 1726–43.

19. The Alliance of Hanover.

20. Correctly so.

21. The emperor's transoceanic trading company which clashed with British objectives.

22. John Perceval to Edward Southwell, January 12, 1726, BL, Add. 47031, fols 73–74. See, more generally, J. Black, *Politics and Foreign Policy in the Age of George I, 1714–1727* (Farnham, 2014) and *British Politics and Foreign Policy, 1727–1744* (Farnham, 2014).

23. S. R. Williamson and E. R. May, "An Identity of Opinion: Historians and July 1914," *Journal of Modern History* 79 (2007): 335–87. For counterfactuals, see e.g. 359.

24. R. Toye, "Winston Churchill's 'Crazy Broadcast': Party, Nation, and the 1945 Gestapo Speech," *Journal of British Studies* 49 (2010): 655–80.

25. I. Kershaw, *Fateful Choices: Ten Decisions That Changed the World, 1940–1941* (London, 2007), 6. For limiting the value of counterfactual analysis to relatively short-term predictions, J. S. Levy, "Counterfactuals and Case Studies," in *The Oxford Handbook of Political Methodology,* ed. J. M. Box-Steffensmeier, H. E. Brady, and D. Collier (New York, 2008), 642.

26. I have benefited from discussing this point with Richard Overy.

27. C. Paullin, *Atlas of the Historical Geography of the United States* (Washington, DC, 1932), xiii.

28. First published in 1877. A. Wolf, "What Can the History of Historical Atlases Teach? Some Lessons from a Century of Putzger's *Historischer Schul-Atlas*," *Cartographica* 28, no. 2 (1991): 21–37; J. Black, "Mapping the World: Richard Overy and the *Times Atlas of World History*," in *Rethinking History, Dictatorship and War: New Approaches and Interpretations,* ed. C. C. W. Szejnmann (London, 2009), 27–37.

29. I. Porciani, "Mapping Institutions, Comparing Historiographies: The Making of a European Atlas," *Storia della Storiografia* 50 (2006): 27–58.

30. E.g., "India, 1756–1805," in *The New Cambridge Modern History: XIV Atlas,* ed. H. C. Darby and H. Fullard (Cambridge, 1970), 267.

31. J. P. Diggins, "The National History Standards," in *Reconstructing History: The Emergence of a New Historical Society,* ed. E. Fox-Genovese and E. Lasch-Quinn (London, 1999), 253–75; G. B. Nash, C. Crabtree, and R. E. Dunn, *History on Trial: Culture Wars and the Teaching of the Past* (New York, 1997).

32. Alexandra Molano Avilan and Sebastian Crankshaw, letter, *Guardian,* March 13, 2008, 27.

33. For a flawed approach that is useful in citing newspaper material, Robert Guyver, "Michael Gore's History Wars 2010–2014: The Rise, Fall and Transformation of a Neoconservative Dream," *Agora* (Sungraphô), 45, 4 (2014): 4–11.

3. TYPES OF HISTORY

1. The translation is from the Loeb edition: Livy, *History of Rome,* trans. B. O. Foster, vol. 4, *Books 8–10* (Cambridge, MA, 1926), 9.17.

2. R. Moreno, "Livy's Alexander Digression: Counterfactuals and Apologetics," *Journal of Roman Studies* 92 (2002): 62–85; S. P. Oakley, *A Commentary on Livy, Books 6–10,* vol. 3, *Book 9* (Oxford, 2005), 184–261.

3. The translation is from the Loeb edition: Herodotus, *The Persian Wars,* trans. A. D. Godley, vol. 3, *Books 5–7* (Cambridge, MA, 1922), 6.109.

4. Ibid., 7.138–39.

5. I have benefited from discussing these points with Peter Wiseman and Mike Dobson.

6. S. Levine, ed., *New Zealand as It Might Have Been* (Wellington, 2006), back cover.

7. P. Hart, "On the Necessity of Violence in the Irish Revolution," in *Shadows of the Gunmen: Violence and Culture in Modern Ireland,* ed. D. Farquharson and S. Farrell (Cork, 2007), 14–37; L. Kennedy, "Was There an Irish War of Independence?," in *Hearts and Minds: Irish Culture and Society under the Act of Union,* ed. B. Stewart (Gerrards Cross, 2002), 188–229.

8. Ronald Hutton, e-mail to the author, December 9, 2013.

9. Ex inf. Colin Imber.

10. Ex inf. Tim May.

11. M. R. Peattie, *Ishiwara Kanji and Japan's Confrontation with the West* (Princeton, NJ, 1975).

12. Although see a noted medievalist, G. Tellenbach, "'Ungeschehene Geschichte' und ihre heuriotische Funktion," *Historische Zeitschrift* 258 (1994): 297–316.

13. Gijs Rommelse, e-mail to the author, June 8, 2014. For examples, T. von der Dunk and J. D. snel, *Buren? Eeen alternatieve geschiedenis van Nederland* (Amsterdam, 2005); and T. van der Meer, ed., *Wat als Pim Fortuyn niet was vermoord: Wat als de geschiedenis heel anders was gelopen?* (Amsterdam, 2011).

14. K. O. von Aretin, *Das alte Reich 1648–1806*, 3 vols. (Stuttgart, 1993–97); R. J. W. Evans, M. Schaich, and P. H. Wilson, eds., *The Holy Roman Empire 1495–1806* (Oxford, 2011); J. Whaley, *Germany and the Holy Roman Empire, 1495–1806*, 2 vols. (Oxford, 2012).

15. C. M. Clark, *Iron Kingdom: The Rise and Downfall of Prussia, 1600–1947* (London, 2006).

16. F. Cochet, *La grande guerre* (Paris, 2014), 36.

17. J. M. Sardica, *Twentieth Century Portugal: A Historical Overview* (Lisbon, 2008), 15, 100. I have benefited from discussing the issue with Sardica.

18. R. N. Lebow, *Forbidden Fruit: Counterfactuals and International Relations* (Princeton, NJ, 2010).

19. Ronald Hutton, e-mail to the author, December 2, 2013.

20. C. Wickham, *Framing the Early Middle Ages: Europe and the Mediterranean, 400–800* (Oxford, 2005), 386, 428–33.

21. R. M. Page, "Another Thirteen Years of Labour, 1951–1964: From Socialist Commonwealth to Welfare 'Progressivism'?," *Social Policy and Society* 4 (2005): 313–20.

22. R. M. Page, "Attlee versus Blair: Labour Governments and Progressive Social Policy in Historical Perspective," in *Social Policy Review 16: Analysis and Debate in Social Policy, 2004*, ed. N. Ellison, L. Bauld, and M. Powell (Bristol, 2004), 143–66.

23. E.g., R. Briggs, *The Witches of Lorraine* (Oxford, 2007), 371–72.

24. R. Overy, *The Bombing War: Europe 1939–1945* (London, 2013), 584, 615; F. Taylor, *Dresden: Tuesday, 13 February 1945* (London, 2004); W. Kansteiner, *In Pursuit of German Memory: History, Television, and Politics after Auschwitz* (Athens, OH, 2006).

25. S. Pollard, *Britain's Prime and Britain's Decline: The British Economy, 1870–1914* (Cambridge, 1988); W. D. Rubinstein, *Capitalism, Culture and Decline in Britain, 1750–1990* (London, 1990).

26. K. Pomeranz, *The Great Divergence: China, Europe, and the Making of the Modern World Economy* (Princeton, NJ, 2000). See also chapter 5.

27. M. Overton, J. Whittle, D. Dean, and A. Hann, *Production and Consumption in English Households, 1600–1750* (London, 2004), 143–47.

28. W. H. McNeill, "What If Pizarro Had Not Found Potatoes in Peru?," in *More What If? Eminent Historians Imagine What Might Have Been*, ed. R. Cowley (London, 2003), 413–27, quotations from 415, 427.

29. T. Burnard, "'The Countrie Continues Sicklie': White Mortality in Jamaica, 1655–1780," *Social History of Medicine* 12 (1999): 45–72.

30. D. B. Quinn, *European Approaches to North America, 1450–1640* (Aldershot, 1998), 329–31.

31. The bubonic plague had already hit Northeast China in the early 1330s.

32. For a more mainstream account, R. N. Lebow, *Archduke Franz Ferdinand Lives! A World without World War I* (New York, 2014).

33. R. J. Evans, *Altered Pasts: Counterfactuals in History* (Waltham, MA, 2014), 47–48, 54–55, 136–37.

34. P. E. Tetlock and A. Belkin, eds., *Counterfactual Thought Experiments in World Politics: Logical, Methodological, and Psychological Perspectives* (Princeton, NJ, 1996).

35. A. G. Dickens, *The English Reformation* (London, 1964); R. Rex, *Henry VIII and the English Reformation* (Basingstoke, 1993); E. Duffy, *The Stripping of the Altars* (New Haven, CT, 1992); G. W. Bernard, *The King's Reformation: Henry VIII and the Remaking of the English Church* (New Haven, CT, 2005); and *The Late Medieval English Church: Vitality and Vulnerability on the Eve of the Break with Rome* (New Haven, CT, 2012).

36. B. Pascal, *Pensées,* 1669, 2.162; G. W. Bernard, *Anne Boleyn: Fatal Attractions* (New Haven, CT, 2010); J. B. Bury, "Cleopatra's Nose," in *Selected Essays of J. B. Bury,* ed. H. Temperley (Cambridge, 1930), 60–69; J. Buchan, *The Causal and the Casual in History* (Cambridge, 1929), 21; J. Ober, "Not by a Nose," in Cowley, *More What If?,* 30; J. M. Carter, *The Battle of Actium: The Rise and Triumph of Augustus Caesar* (London, 1970).

37. Pascal, *Pensées,* 3.206, 4.277.

38. R. Beaumont, *The Nazis' March to Chaos. The Hitler Era through the Lenses of Chaos-Complexity Theory* (Westport, CT, 2000), 10.

39. J. Gleick, *Chaos: Making a New Science* (New York, 1987); M. Waldrop, *Complexity: The Emerging Science at the Edge of Order and Chaos* (New York, 1992); G. A. Reisch, "Chaos, History and Narrative," *History and Theory* 30 (1991): 1–20; D. N. McCloskey, "History, Differential Equations, and the Problem of Narration," *History and Theory* 30 (1991): 21–36. For an argument for structured contingency, S. Morillo, "Contrary Winds: Theories of History and the Limits of *Sachkritik,*" in *The Medieval Way of War: Studies in Medieval Military History in Honor of Bernard S. Bachrach,* ed. G. Halfond and D. Bachrach (Farnham, forthcoming). I would like to thank Stephen Morillo for sending me a copy of this.

40. J. Barrow-Green, *Poincaré and the Three Body Problem* (London, 1996); P. Galison, *Einstein's Clocks, Poincaré's Maps: Empires of Time* (New York, 2003).

41. The film's English-language title is *Happenstance.*

42. J. D. Barrow, *Impossibility: The Limits of Science and the Science of Limits* (London, 1998). For a criticism of the applicability of chaos theory to history, Evans, *Altered Pasts,* 66.

43. H. Husemann, "When William Came; If Adolf Had Come: English Speculative Novels on the German Conquest of Britain," *Anglistik & Englischunterricht* 29–30 (1986): 57–83.

44. P. Novick, *That Noble Dream: The "Objectivity Question" and the American Historical Profession* (Cambridge, 1988); K. Jenkins, *The Postmodern History Reader* (London, 1997); A. Munslow, *The New History* (London, 2003); B. Southgate, *Postmodernism in History: Fear or Freedom?* (London, 2003).

45. See, for example, J. Cañizares-Esguerra, *How to Write the History of the New World: Histories, Epistemologies, and Identities in the Eighteenth-Century Atlantic World* (Stanford, CA, 2001); N. L. York, *Fiction as Fact: The Horse Soldiers and Popular Memory* (Kent, OH, 2001).

46. E. R. May, *"Lessons" of the Past: The Use and Misuse of History in American Foreign Policy* (Oxford, 1973); J. Record, *Making War, Thinking History: Munich, Vietnam, and Presidential Uses of Force from Korea to Kosovo* (Annapolis, MD, 2002).

47. A. D'Agostino, "The Revisionist Tradition in European Diplomatic History," *Journal of the Historical Society* 4 (2004): 258.

48. J. Ramsden, review of *Churchill: A Study in Greatness,* by Geoffrey Best, *English Historical Review* 118 (2003): 1023.

49. D. R. Massam, "British Maritime Strategy and Amphibious Capability, 1900–1940 (DPhil diss., Oxford University, 1995).

50. T. Travers, *Gallipoli 1915* (Stroud, 2001); C. Bell, *Churchill and Sea Power* (Oxford, 2012).

51. J. Buchan, *The Causal and the Casual in History*, 37–42; G. Bailey, "The Narrow Margin of Criticality: The Question of the Supply of 100-Octane Fuel in the Battle of Britain," *English Historical Review* 123 (2008): 351–78.

52. Churchill to General Alexander, September 14, 1943, LH, Alanbrooke Papers, 6/2/18.

53. J. L. Gaddis, *The Cold War: A New History* (London, 2005), 48–50. I would like to thank John Gaddis for discussing this passage with me.

54. *Times* (London), March 14, 2014, 29.

55. E. T. Linenthal and T. Englehardt, eds., *History Wars: The Enola Gay and Other Battles for the American Past* (New York, 1996); S. M. Jager and R. Mitter, eds., *Ruptured Histories: War, Memory, and the Post-Cold War in Asia* (Cambridge, MA, 2007).

56. J. Kurth, "Europe's Identity Problem and the New Islamist War," *Orbis* 50 (2006): 555–57.

57. J. Black, "The British Attempt to Preserve the Peace in Europe, 1748–1755," in *Zwischenstaatliche Friedenswahrung in Mittelalter und Früher Neuzeit,* ed. H. Duchhardt (Cologne, 1991), 227–43.

58. J. Black, *Debating Foreign Policy in Eighteenth-Century Britain* (Farnham, 2011).

59. Holdernesse to Yorke, September 13, 1754, NA, SP 84/467.

60. J, Black, *Parliament and Foreign Policy in the Eighteenth Century* (Cambridge, 2004), 196; L. Stewart, *The Rise of Public Science: Rhetoric, Technology, and Natural Philosophy in Newtonian Britain, 1660–1750* (Cambridge, 1992).

4. POWER AND THE STRUGGLE FOR IMPERIAL MASTERY

1. R. J. Evans, *Altered Pasts: Counterfactuals in History* (Waltham, MA, 2014), 192.

2. J. Black, *War and Technology* (Bloomington, IN, 2013).

3. J. Black, *War: The Cultural Turn* (Cambridge, 2011).

4. C. M. N. Eire, "Pontius Pilate Spares Jesus," in *More What If? Eminent Historians Imagine What Might Have Been,* ed. R. Cowley (London, 2003), 48–67; and "The Quest for a Counterfactual Jesus: Imagining the West without the Cross," in *Unmaking the West: "What-If?" Scenarios That Rewrite World History,* ed. P. E. Tetlock, R. N. Lebow, and G. Parker (Ann Arbor, MI, 2006), 119–42.

5. J. Black, *The Power of Knowledge: How Information and Technology Made the Modern World* (New Haven, CT, 2014).

6. I. Kershaw, "The Persecution of the Jews and German Popular Opinion in the Third Reich," *Leo Baeck Institute Yearbook* 26 (1981): 261–89; R. Gellately, *Backing Hitler: Consent and Coercion in Nazi Germany* (Oxford, 2001); G. Eley, "Hitler's Silent Majority? Conformity and Resistance under the Third Reich," *Michigan Quarterly Review* 42 (2003): 389–425.

7. M. J. Rodríguez-Salgado, *The Changing Face of Empire: Charles V, Philip II and Habsburg Authority, 1551–1559* (Cambridge, 1988).

8. A. R. Lewis, *The American Culture of War* (New York, 2007).

9. J. Glete, *War and the State in Early Modern Europe: Spain, the Dutch Republic and Sweden as Fiscal-Military States, 1500–1660* (London, 2001).

10. A. I. Johnston, *Cultural Realism: Strategic Culture and Grand Strategy in Chinese History* (Princeton, NJ, 1995); E. Ringmar, *Identity, Interest and Action: A Cultural Explanation of Sweden's Intervention in the Thirty Years War* (Cambridge, 1996).

11. S. Morillo, "The Sword of Justice: War and State Formation in Comparative Perspective," *Journal of Medieval Military History* 4 (2006): 1–17.

12. N. Jordan, "Strategy and Scapegoatism: Reflections on the French National Catastrophe, 1940," in *The French Defeat of 1940: Reassessments*, ed. J. Blatt (Oxford, 1998), 22–29; W. Murray, "May 1940: Contingency and Fragility of the German RMA," in *The Dynamics of Military Revolution, 1300–2050*, ed. M. Knox and W. Murray (Cambridge, 2001), 154–74; B. Bond and M. Taylor, eds., *The Battle of France and Flanders: Sixty Years On* (Barnsley, 2001); J. A. Gunsburg, "The Battle of Gembloux—14–15 May: The 'Blitzkrieg' Checked," *Journal of Military History* 64 (2000): 97–140.

13. J. Jackson, *The Fall of France: The Nazi Invasion of 1940* (Oxford, 2003).

14. J. Darwin, *Unfinished Empire: The Global Expansion of Britain* (London, 2012), 342–85.

15. A. Roberts, "Prime Minister Halifax," in Cowley, *More What If?*, 279–90.

16. R. Jervis, *Perception and Misperception in International Politics* (Princeton, NJ, 1976); J. Kugler and M. Arbetman, "Choosing among Measures of Power: A Review of the Empirical Record," in *Power in World Politics*, ed. R. J. Stoll and M. D. Ward (Boulder, CO, 1989), 49–77.

17. A. Fraser, "The Gunpowder Plot Succeeds," in *What Might Have Been: Leading Historians on Twelve "What Ifs" of History*, ed. A. Roberts (London, 2004), 27–39. See also W. H. Sewell, "Historical Events as Transformation of Structures," *Theory and Society* 26 (1996): 841–81.

18. G. Modelski and W. R. Thompson, *Leading Sectors and World Powers: The Coevolution of Global Politics and Economics* (Columbia, SC, 1996).

19. J. Collins, *The State in Early Modern France* (Cambridge, 1995).

5. THE WEST AND THE REST

1. E. L. Dreyer, *Zheng He: China and the Oceans in the Early Ming Dynasty, 1405–1433* (New York, 2007).

2. For an introduction, S. Morillo, J. Black, and P. Lococo, *War in World History* (New York, 2008), 1:293–96.

3. T. J. Barfield, *The Perilous Frontier: Nomadic Empires and China, 221 BC to AD 757* (Oxford, 1989).

4. J. Glete, *Warfare at Sea, 1500–1650: Maritime Conflicts and the Transformation of Europe* (London, 2000), and *War and the State in Early Modern Europe: Spain, the Dutch Republic and Sweden as Fiscal-Military States, 1500–1660* (London, 2002); J. Black, *Kings, Nobles and Commoners: States and Societies in Early Modern Europe; A Revisionist History* (London, 2004).

5. P. C. Perdue, *China Marches West: The Qing Conquest of Central Eurasia* (Cambridge, MA, 2005).

6. M. Zelin, *The Magistrate's Tael: Rationalising Fiscal Reform in Eighteenth Century Ch'ing China* (Berkeley, CA, 1992).

7. R. Bin Wong, *China Transformed: Historical Change and the Limits of European Experience* (Ithaca, NY, 1997); K. Pomeranz, *The Great Divergence: China, Europe, and the*

Making of the Modern World Economy (Princeton, NJ, 2000); P. K. O'Brien, "Making the Modern World Economy," *History* 87 (2002): 552.

8. For example, B. Guy, *The French Image of China, before and after Voltaire* (Geneva, 1963); A. Thomson, *Barbary and Enlightenment: European Attitudes towards the Maghreb in the 18th Century* (Leide, 1987).

9. C. de la Porte, P. Pochet, and G. Room, "Social Benchmarking, Policy Making and New Governance in the EU," *Journal of European Social Policy* 11 (2001): 291–307.

10. M. Powell and J. Stewart, "Counterfactuals and Contingencies in Historical Policy Learning" (paper presented to the 36th Annual Conference of the Social Policy Association, Teesside University, Middlesbrough, UK, July 15–17, 2003).

11. C. Bekar and R. Lipsey, "Science, Institutions and the Industrial Revolution," *Journal of European Economic History* 33 (2004): 709–53.

12. M. Gladwell, *The Tipping Point: How Little Things Can Make a Big Difference* (Boston, 2000).

13. D. R. Headrick, *When Information Came of Age: Technologies of Knowledge in the Age of Reason and Revolution, 1700–1850* (Oxford, 2000).

14. K. Pomeranz, "Re-Thinking the Late Imperial Chinese Economy: Development, Disaggregation and Decline, circa 1730–1930," *Itinerario* 24 (2000): 49–66.

15. K. Pomeranz, "Without Coal? Colonies? Calculus? Counterfactuals and Industrialisation in Europe and China," in *Unmaking the West: "What-If" Scenarios That Rewrite World History*, ed. P. E. Tetlock, R. N. Lebow, and G. Parker (Ann Arbor, MI, 2006), 248.

16. S. Subrahmanyam, "'Un grand dérangement': Dreaming an Indo-Persian Empire in South Asia, 1740–1800," *Journal of Early Modern History* 4 (2001): 337–78.

17. M. Axworthy, *Sword of Persia: Nader Shah, from Tribal Warrior to Conquering Tyrant* (London, 2006); E. Tucker, *Nadir Shah's Quest for Legitimacy in Post-Safavid Iran* (Gainesville, FL, 2006). I have benefited from discussing Nadir Shah with Michael Axworthy.

18. C. A. Bayly, *Imperial Meridian: The British Empire and the World 1780–1830* (Harlow, 1989).

19. P. P. Barua, "Maritime Trade, Seapower, and the Anglo-Mysore Wars, 1767–1799," *Historian* 73 (2011): 28–29.

20. R. G. S. Cooper and N. K. Wagle, "Maratha Artillery: From Dalhoi to Assaye," *Journal of the Ordnance Society* 7 (1995): 58–78.

21. For Napoleon's weaknesses in 1815 and at Waterloo, including counterfactuals, T. Lentz, *Nouvelle histoire du premier empire IV: Les cent-jours 1815* (Paris, 2010), 246, 406. For the role of Providence at Waterloo, V. Hugo, *Les Misérables*. See also G. M. Trevelyan, "If Napoleon Had Won the Battle of Waterloo," in *Clio: A Muse, and Other Essays* (London, 1913), 184–200.

22. A. Attman, *American Bullion in European World Trade, 1600–1800* (Gothenburg, 1986).

23. A. Crosby, *The Columbian Exchange: Biological and Cultural Consequences of 1492* (Westport, CT, 1969), and *Ecological Imperialism: The Biological Expansion of Europe, 1500–1900* (London, 1986).

24. J. Black, *War and the World: Military Power and the Fate of Continents, 1450–2000* (New Haven, CT, 1998), and *Great Powers and the Quest for Hegemony: The World Order since 1500* (Abingdon, 2008).

6. BRITAIN AND FRANCE, 1688–1815

1. This is not an exhaustive list of dates. 1940 is discussed in chapter 7.

2. For the argument, from a historian keen on the methods of international relations specialists and prone to emphasize systemic interpretations, that it would have made scant difference, P. W. Schroeder, "Embedded Counterfactuals and World War I as an Unavoidable War," in *Systems, Stability, and Statecraft: Essays on the International History of Modern Europe* (New York, 2004), 157–91. For a different view, R. N. Lebow, *Archduke Franz Ferdinand Lives! A World without World War I* (New York, 2014).

3. R. Cowley, "Benedict Arnold Wins the Revolutionary War for Britain"; N. Stone, "Archduke Franz Ferdinand Survives Sarajevo"; A. Roberts, "Lenin Is Assassinated at the Finland Station"; in *What Might Have Been: Leading Historians on Twelve "What Ifs" of History,* ed. A. Roberts (London, 2004), 59–78; 105–18; 119–33. See also G. Feifer, "No Finland Station," in *More What If? Eminent Historians Imagine What Might Have Been,* ed. R. Cowley (London, 2003), 210–35.

4. H. J. Mackinder, "The Geopolitical Pivot of History," *Geographical Journal* 23 (1904): 421–37.

5. T. M. Otte, "'A Very Internecine Policy': Anglo-Russian Cold War before the Cold War," in *Britain in Global Politics,* vol. 1, *From Gladstone to Churchill,* ed. C. Baxter, M. L. Dockrill, and K. Hamilton (Basingstoke, 2013), 17–49.

6. P. W. Schroeder, *The Transformation of European Politics, 1763–1848* (Oxford, 1994); B. Simms, *Europe: The Struggle for Supremacy, from 1453 to the Present* (New York, 2013).

7. The choice of descriptive terms is instructive. "Percolate," "ramify," and "operate" all have different meanings and connotations.

8. R. F. Hamilton, *President McKinley, War and Empire,* vol. 1, *President McKinley and the Coming of War, 1898* (New Brunswick, NJ, 2006), 253.

9. Amongst the massive literature on this subject, it is worth noting D. R. Weir, "Tontines, Public Finance, and Revolution in France and England, 1688–1789," and E. N. White, "Was There a Solution to the Ancien Régime's Financial Dilemma?," *Journal of Economic History* 49 (1989): 124, 545–68.

10. K. Chase, *Firearms: A Global History to 1700* (Cambridge, 2003).

11. H. Kleinschmidt, *The Nemesis of Power: A History of International Relations Theories* (London, 2000).

12. A. Stanziani, *Bâtisseurs d'empires: Russie, Chine et Inde à la croisée des mondes, XVe–XIXe siècle* (Paris, 2012), and *After Oriental Despotism: Eurasian Growth in a Global Perspective* (London, 2014).

13. A. D. Lublinskaya, *French Absolutism: The Crucial Phase, 1620–1629* (Cambridge, 1968); D. Parker, *La Rochelle and the French Monarchy: Conflict and Order in Seventeenth-Century France* (London, 1980); J. Bergin, *The Rise of Richelieu* (New Haven, CT, 1991).

14. G. Parker, *The Thirty Years' War,* 2nd ed. (London, 1997).

15. J. Adamson, "King Charles I Wins the English Civil War," in Roberts, *What Might Have Been,* 40–58.

16. J. Black, *A System of Ambition? British Foreign Policy, 1660–1793,* 2nd ed. (Stroud, 2000), xii.

17. R. G. S. Cooper, *The Anglo-Maratha Campaigns and the Contest for India: The Struggle for the South Asian Military Economy* (Cambridge, 2004).

18. J. A. Henretta, *"Salutary Neglect": Colonial Administration under the Duke of Newcastle* (Princeton, NJ, 1972).

19. A. T. Patterson, *The Other Armada: The Franco-Spanish Attempt to Invade Britain in 1779* (Manchester, 1994).

20. J. F. Bosher, "French Colonial Society in Canada," *Transactions of the Royal Society of Canada,* 4th ser., 19 (1981): 156.

21. Further details and references for the following section can be found in J. Black, *From Louis XIV to Napoleon: The Fate of a Great Power* (London, 1999). See also A. Reese, *Europäische Hegemonie und France d'outre-mer: Koloniale Fragen in der französüschen Aussenpolitik, 1700–1763* (Stuttgart, 1988).

22. J. Black, *Fighting for America: The Struggle for Mastery in North America, 1519–1871* (Bloomington, IN, 2011), 178–396.

23. X. de Planhol, *An Historical Geography of France* (Cambridge, 1994).

24. J. Pritchard, *In Search of Empire: The French in the Americas, 1670–1730* (Cambridge, 2004), 421.

25. C. Duffy, *Prussia's Glory: Rossbach and Leuthen* (Chicago, 2003).

26. J. Dull, *A Diplomatic History of the American Revolution* (New Haven, CT, 1985).

27. M. Price, "The Dutch Affair and the Fall of the *Ancien Régime,* 1784–1787," *Historical Journal* 38 (1995): 880.

28. B. Stone, *The Genesis of the French Revolution: A Global-Historical Interpretation* (Cambridge, 1994); O. T. Murphy, *The Diplomatic Retreat of France and Public Opinion on the Eve of the French Revolution, 1783–1789* (Washington, DC, 1998).

29. D. C. M. Platt, *Latin America and British Trade, 1806–1914* (London, 1972).

30. Report by Broglie, A E, C P, Ang. 348 fol. 56.

31. E. A. Wrigley, "The Divergence of England: The Growth of the English Economy in the Seventeenth and Eighteenth Centuries," *Transactions of the Royal Historical Society,* 6th ser., 10 (2000), 117–41.

32. C. Mukerji, *Territorial Ambitions and the Gardens of Versailles* (Cambridge, 1997).

33. G. J. Ames, *Colbert, Mercantilism, and the French Quest for Asian Trade* (DeKalb, IL, 1996).

34. J. Black, *British Foreign Policy in an Age of Revolutions, 1783–1793* (Cambridge, 1994).

35. C. Esdaile, *Napoleon's Wars: An International History, 1803–1815* (London, 2007).

36. Its return to France under the peace treaty of the previous year.

37. In the West Indies, for example Barbados.

38. Vernon to Sir Francis Dashwood, July 29, 1749, M S D. D. Dashwood B11/12/6, Bodleian Library, University of Oxford.

39. J. Black, *The War of 1812 in the Age of Napoleon* (Norman, OK, 2009).

40. J.-M. Lafont, *French Administrators of Maharaja Ranjit Singh* (Delhi, 1988), and *La présence Française dans le royaume Sikh du Penjab* (Paris, 1992).

41. J. Black, *Convergence or Divergence? Britain and the Continent* (London, 1994).

42. For problems with the concept of overstretch, J. Black, "The Limits of Empire: The Case of Britain," in *The Limits of Empire: European Imperial Formations in Modern World History,* ed. T. Andrade and W. Reger (Farnham, 2012), 175–81.

43. J. Childs, *The Army, James II, and the Glorious Revolution* (Manchester, 1980), 168–98.

44. The extensive literature on this rising includes J. Prebble, *Culloden* (London, 1961); W. A. Speck, *The Butcher: The Duke of Cumberland and the Suppression of the '45* (Oxford, 1981); F. J. McLynn, *The Jacobite Army in England* (Edinburgh, 1983), and *Charles Edward Stuart: A Tragedy in Many Acts* (London, 1988); J. Black, *Culloden and the '45* (Stroud, 1990); S. Reid, *1745: A Military History of the Last Jacobite Rising* (Staplehurst, 1996); C. Duffy, *The '45: Bonnie Prince Charlie and the Untold Story of the Jacobite Rising* (London, 2003). For an assessment of the consequences of Jacobite success, C. Petrie, "If: A Jacobite Fantasy," in *If: Or, History Rewritten*, ed. J. C. Squire (New York, 1931).

45. J. M. Hill, "Gaelic Warfare 1453–1815," in *European Warfare 1453–1815*, ed. J. Black (London, 1999), 201–23; J. P. C. Laband and P. S. Thompson, *Field Guide to the War in Zululand and the Defence of Natal, 1879* (Pietermaritzburg, 1983); I. Knight, *The Anatomy of the Zulu Army: From Shaka to Cetshwayo, 1818–1879* (London, 1995).

46. Ossian, a third-century Highland bard who was the creation of James Macpherson, was the central figure in a Scottish literary sensation of the 1760s in which claims to have discovered ancient Celtic epics were made. These fictions won a Europe-wide reputation.

47. S. Conway, *The War of American Independence 1775–1783* (London, 1995), 23–40. For a challenge to the notion of political modernity, J. C. D. Clark, *The Language of Liberty 1660–1832: Political Discourse and Social Dynamics in the Anglo-American World* (Cambridge, 1993).

48. G. Satterfield, *Princes, Posts and Partisans: The Army of Louis XIV and Partisan Warfare in the Netherlands, 1673–1678* (Leiden, 2003).

49. J. Lynn, *The Bayonets of the Republic. Motivation and Tactics in the Army of Revolutionary France, 1791–94*, 2nd ed. (Boulder, CO, 1996).

50. G. Parker, *The Military Revolution: Military Innovation and the Rise of the West, 1500–1800*, 2nd ed. (Cambridge, 1996).

51. F. J. McLynn, "Sea Power and the Jacobite Rising of 1745," *Mariner's Mirror* 67 (1981): 163–72.

52. E. Cruickshanks, "The Revolution and the Localities: Examples of Loyalty to James II," in *By Force or by Default? The Revolution of 1688–1689*, ed. E. Cruickshanks (Edinburgh, 1989), 28–43.

53. E. Cruickshanks, *Political Untouchables: The Tories and the '45* (London, 1979).

54. J. Pritchard, *Anatomy of a Naval Disaster: The 1746 French Naval Expedition to North America* (Montreal, 1995).

55. F. J. McLynn, *France and the Jacobite Rising of 1745* (Edinburgh, 1981).

56. J. Black, *British Foreign Policy in the Age of Walpole* (Edinburgh, 1985).

57. J. Dull, *The French Navy and American Waters 1775–1783* (Aldershot, 1989); D. Syrett, *The Royal Navy in American Waters 1775–1783* (Aldershot, 1989).

58. D. McCullough, "What the Fog Wrought: The Revolution's Dunkirk, August 29, 1776," in *What If? America: Eminent Historians Imagine What Might Have Been*, ed. R. Cowley (London, 2004), 43–54. For a more varied list, T. Fleming, "Unlikely Victory," in Cowley, *What If? America*, 155–86.

59. C. Carr, "William Pitt the Elder and the Avoidance of the American Revolution," in Cowley, *What If? America*, 17–42.

60. J. Black, *War for America: The Fight for Independence 1775–1783* (Stroud, 1991).

61. J. Black, *Pitt the Elder*, 2nd ed. (Stroud, 1999), 158–70.

62. J. C. D. Clark, "British America: What If There Had Been No Atlantic Revolution?," in *Virtual History: Alternatives and Counterfactuals,* ed. N. Ferguson (London, 1997), 125.

63. On the plasticity of America's geographic evolution, D. W. Meinig, *The Shaping of America,* vol. 1, *Atlantic America, 1492–1800* (New Haven, CT, 1986).

64. F. Fernández-Armesto, *The Americas: A Hemispheric History* (New York, 2003), 121–27.

65. P. Lawson, *The Imperial Challenge: Quebec and Britain in the Age of the American Revolution* (Montreal, 1989).

66. V. T. Harlow, *The Founding of the Second British Empire 1763–1793,* vol. 2, *New Continents and Changing Values* (London, 1964).

67. R. Hutton, "The Making of the Secret Treaty of Dover, 1668–1670," *Historical Journal* 29 (1986): 297–318.

68. J. Black, "The Revolution and the Development of English Foreign Policy," in Cruickshanks, *By Force or by Default?,* 135–58.

69. P. P. Hill, *French Perceptions of the Early American Republic, 1783–1793* (Philadelphia, 1988).

70. G. Parker, "Martin Luther Burns at the Stake, 1521," in Cowley, *More What If?,* 117.

71. For an example, N. Ferguson, "Afterword: A Virtual History, 1646–1996," in Ferguson, *Virtual History,* 416–40.

72. Black, *British Foreign Policy in an Age of Revolutions,* 400.

73. H. C. Syrett, ed., *The Papers of Alexander Hamilton,* vol. 7 (New York, 1963), 70–74; J. P. Boyd, *Number 7: Alexander Hamilton's Secret Attempts to Control American Foreign Policy* (Princeton, NJ, 1964), 4–13.

74. Anthony Merry, British envoy, to Henry, Lord Mulgrave, foreign secretary, March 29, April 29, August 4, November 25, 1805, NA, FO 5/45 fols 128–32, 192–93, 259, 322–31.

75. C. A. Bayly, *Imperial Meridian: The British Empire and the World, 1780–1830* (Harlow, 1989).

76. G. Plank, *An Unsettled Conquest: The British Campaign against the Peoples of Acadia* (Philadelphia, 2004).

77. S. P. Sen, *The French in India, 1763–1816* (Calcutta, 1958), 530.

7. COUNTERFACTUALISM IN MILITARY HISTORY

1. A. Horne, "Ruler of the World: Napoleon's Missed Opportunities," in *What If? The World's Foremost Military Historians Imagine What Might Have Been,* ed. R. Cowley (New York, 1999), 215.

2. J. Black, *Fighting for America: The Struggle for Mastery in North America, 1519–1871* (Bloomington, IN, 2011).

3. C. Holland, "The Death That Saved Europe," in Cowley, *What If?,* 105.

4. Brian Melland to Liddell Hart, May 17, 1961, LH, Liddell Hart papers, 4/31.

5. Molony to Liddell Hart, October 7, 1958, LH, Liddell Hart papers, 4/32.

6. Liddell Hart to Major-General Ian Playfair, January 23, 1954, October 27, 1956, November 12 and 19, 1956, December 4, 1956, reply November 28, 1956, LH, Liddell Hart papers, 4/32.

7. D. Rowland, *The Stress of Battle: Quantifying Human Performance in Combat* (London, 2006), 106–41.

8. J. M. McPherson, "If the Lost Order Hadn't Been Lost: Robert E. Lee Humbles the Union, 1862," in *What If? America: Eminent Historians Imagine What Might Have Been,* ed. R. Cowley (London, 2004), 101.

9. For an emphasis on contingency, J. M. McPherson, *The Battle Cry of Freedom: The Civil War Era* (New York, 1988), 858.

10. N. Ferguson, "The Kaiser's European Union: What If Britain Had 'Stood Aside' in August 1914?," in *Virtual History: Alternatives and Counterfactuals,* ed. N. Ferguson (London, 1997), 228–80.

11. C. Duggan, review of *Mussolini and the Rise of Fascism,* by Donald Sassoon, in *Literary Review,* February 2008, 5.

12. J. T. Sumida, "'The Best Laid Plans': The Development of British Battle-Fleet Tactics, 1919–1942," *International History Review* 14 (1992): 682–700.

13. J. P. Harris, *Men, Ideas and Tanks: British Military Thought and Armoured Forces, 1903–1939* (Manchester, 1995).

14. J. Black, *War and Technology* (Bloomington, IN, 2013).

15. D. Healey, *The Time of My Life* (London, 1990), 276–77.

16. F. J. McHugh, *The United States Naval War College Fundamentals of War Gaming* (Newport, RI, 1966); P. P. Perla, *The Art of Wargaming* (Annapolis, MD, 1990); R. B. Myerson, *Game Theory: Analysis of Conflict* (Cambridge, MA, 1991); T. J. Gzerwinski, *Coping with the Bounds: Speculations in Nonlinearity in Military Affairs* (Washington, DC, 1998); B. Gilad, *Business War Games* (Franklin Lakes, NJ, 2009); on the Naval War College today, S. Carpenter, e-mail to the author, June 9, 2014.

17. I. Hata, "Admiral Yamamoto and the Japanese Navy," in *From Pearl Harbor to Hiroshima: The Second World War in Asia and the Pacific, 1941–45,* ed. S. Dockrill (New York, 1994), 58; A. N. Caravaggio, "'Winning' the Pacific War: The Masterful Strategy of Commander Minoru Genda," *Naval War College Review* 67 (2014): 85–118; M. Vlahos, *The Blue Sword: The Naval War College and the American Mission, 1919–1941* (Newport, RI, 1980), esp. 113–55. For later war games, H. M. Friedman, "Blue versus Orange: The United States Naval War College, Japan, and the Old Enemy in the Pacific, 1945–1946," *Journal of Military History* 78 (2014): 211–31.

18. J. A. Gunsburg, "*La Grande Illusion:* Belgian and Dutch Strategy Facing Germany, 1919–May 1940," *Journal of Military History* 78 (2014): 129.

19. W. Murray, "The War of 1938," in *More What If? Eminent Historians Imagine What Might Have Been,* ed. R. Cowley (London, 2003), 261.

20. N. Smart, *British Strategy and Politics during the Phony War* (Westport, CT, 2003); T. C. Imlay, *Facing the Second World War: Strategy, Politics, and Economics in Britain and France, 1938–40* (Oxford, 2003).

21. W. Murray and A. R. Millett, eds., *Military Innovation in the Interwar Period* (Cambridge, 1996).

22. H. H. Herwig, "Innovation Ignored: The Submarine Problem—Germany, Britain, and the United States, 1919–1939," in Murray and Millett, *Military Innovation in the Interwar Period,* 227–64.

23. I. Kershaw, *Fateful Choices: Ten Decisions That Changed the World, 1940–1941* (London, 2007), esp. 471–83. See also J. Lukacs, *Five Days in London: May 1940* (London, 2001).

24. For the variant of a papal protest leading Hitler to change direction, R. Katz, "Pius XII Protests the Holocaust," in Cowley, *More What If?,* 317–32.

25. H. H. Herwig, "Hitler Wins in the East but Germany Still Loses World War II," in *Unmaking the West: "What-If?" Scenarios That Rewrite World History,* ed. P. E. Tetlock, R. N. Lebow, and G. Parker (Ann Arbor, MI, 2006), 331; M. Burleigh, "Nazi Europe: What If Nazi Germany Had Defeated the Soviet Union?," in Ferguson, *Virtual History,* 321–47.

26. S. S. Montefiore, "Stalin Flees Moscow in 1941," in *What Might Have Been: Leading Historians on Twelve "What Ifs" of History,* ed. A. Roberts (London, 2004), 134–53.

27. For a counterfactual, Louis Geoffroy, *Napoléon apocryphe, 1812–1832: Histoire de la conquête du monde et de la monarchie universselle* (Paris, 1836).

28. Among the extensive literature, S. B. Erdheim, "Could the Allies Have Bombed Auschwitz?," *Holocaust and Genocide Studies* 11 (1997): 129–70; and M. J. Neufeld and M. Berenbaum, eds., *The Bombing of Auschwitz: Should the Allies Have Attempted It?* (New York, 2000).

29. A. Iriye, *The Origins of the Second World War in Asia and the Pacific* (Harlow, 1986).

30. C. Black, "The Japanese Do Not Attack Pearl Harbor," in Roberts, *What Might Have Been,* 153–65.

31. R. B. Frank, "No Bomb: No End," in Cowley, *More What If?,* 366–81.

32. B. J. Bernstein, "Compelling Japan's Surrender Without the A-Bomb, Soviet Entry, or Invasion: Reconsidering the US Bombing Survey's Early-Surrender Conclusions," *Journal of Strategic Studies* 18 (1995): 101–48; T. B. Allen and N. Polmar, *Code-Name Downfall: The Secret Plan to Invade Japan—and Why Truman Dropped the Bomb* (New York, 1995); R. B. Frank, *Downfall: The End of the Imperial Japanese Empire* (New York, 1999); T. Hasegawd, *Racing the Enemy: Stalin, Truman, and the Surrender of Japan* (Cambridge, MA, 1999).

33. A. Waldron, "China without Tears," in Cowley, *What If?,* 377–92; R. L. O'Connell, "The Cuban Missile Crisis: Second Holocaust," in Cowley, *What If? America,* 251–72.

34. F. L. Pryor, "The Rise and Fall of Marxist Regimes: An Economic Overview," *Orbis* 49 (2005): 137.

35. M. Almond, "1989 without Gorbachev: What If Communism Had Not Collapsed?," in Ferguson, *Virtual History,* 392–415. See also R. English, "Perestroika without Politics: How Realism Misunderstands the Cold War's End," in *Explaining War and Peace: Case Studies and Necessary Condition Counterfactuals,* ed. G. Goertz and J. S. Levy (New York, 2007), 237–60.

36. A. J. McAdams, *Germany Divided: From the Wall to Reunification* (Princeton, NJ, 1993), 194.

37. S. Biddle and P. D. Feaver, "Assessing Strategic Choices in the War on Terror," in *How 9/11 Changed Our Ways of War,* ed. J. Burk (Stanford, CA, 2013), 27–55.

8. INTO THE FUTURE

1. This is not a critique of the excellent work by environmental historians, but, simply, a criticism of the limits of its impact on most historical scholarship.

2. For a key historical work that also comments, more problematically, on the present and future, G. Parker, *Global Crisis: War, Climate Change and Catastrophe in the Seventeenth Century* (New Haven, CT, 2013).

3. L. Sanders, *The Sixth Commandment* (New York, 1979; repr., New York, 1980), 110.

4. D. Thompson, *Counterknowledge* (London, 2008).

5. D. Rapkin and W. R. Thompson, "Power Transition Theory and the Rise of China," *International Interactions* 29 (2003): 315–42; A. L. Friedberg, "The Future of U.S.-China Relations: Is Conflict Inevitable?," *International Security* 30 (2005): 7–45; A. Goldstein, *Rising to the Challenge: China's Grand Strategy and International Security* (Stanford, CA, 2005); J. Kurlantzick, *Charm Offensive: How China's Soft Power Is Transforming the World* (New Haven, CT, 2007).

6. J. Diamond, "Are We Ready for Iraq to End?," *USA Today,* April 16, 2008, A11.

9. SKEPTICISM AND THE HISTORIAN

1. J. C. D. Clark, *Our Shadowed Present: Modernism, Postmodernism, and History* (Stanford, CA, 2004), 28–29.

2. G. R. Hawke, *Railways and Economic Growth in England and Wales 1840–1870* (Oxford, 1970).

3. N. von Tunzelman, *Steam Power and British Industrialization to 1860* (Oxford, 1978).

4. M. Roberts, *Splendid Isolation, 1763–1780* (Reading, 1970); H. M. Scott, *British Foreign Policy in the Age of the American Revolution* (Oxford, 1990); B. Simms, *Three Victories and a Defeat: The Rise and Fall of the First British Empire, 1714–1783* (London, 2007).

5. For the repeated tendency to draw on Appeasement for lessons, Institut National d'Études Slaves, *Munich 1938: Mythes et réalités* (Paris, 1970); D. Chuter, "Munich, or the Blood of Others," in *Haunted by History: Myths in International Relations,* ed. C. Buffet and B. Heuser (Oxford, 1998), 65–79; J. Record, *Making War, Thinking History: Munich, Vietnam, and Presidential Uses of Force from Korea to Kosovo* (Annapolis, MD, 2002), and "The Use and Abuse of History: Munich, Vietnam and Iraq," *Survival* 49 (2007): 163–80. For other instances of historical analogy see, for example, E. R. May, *"Lessons" of the Past: The Use and Misuse of History in American Foreign Policy* (New York, 1973); R. Jervis, *Perception and Misperception in International Politics* (Princeton, NJ, 1976), 217–82; Y. F. Khong, *Analogies at War: Korea, Munich, Dien Bien Phu, and the Vietnam Decisions of 1965* (Princeton, NJ, 1992); R. E. Neustadt and E. R. May, *Thinking in Time: The Use of History for Decision Makers* (New York, 1986); C. Hemmer, *Which Lessons Matter? American Foreign Policy Decision Making, 1979–1987* (Albany, NY, 2000).

6. B. Simms, *Unfinest Hour: Britain and the Destruction of Bosnia* (London, 2001).

7. J. Black, *Politics and Foreign Policy in the Age of George I, 1714–1727* (Farnham, 2014).

8. J. Black, *British Foreign Policy in an Age of Revolutions, 1783–93* (Cambridge, 1994).

9. H. M. Scott, *The Emergence of the Eastern Powers, 1756–1775* (Cambridge, 2001).

10. Simms, *Three Victories and a Defeat,* 677.

11. J. Black, *A System of Ambition? British Foreign Policy 1660–1793,* 2nd ed. (Stroud, 2000).

12. R. Higham and P. Barleet, *Timber Castles* (London, 1992), 39–40.

13. For example, for nineteenth-century Germany, W. Clark, *Academic Charisma and the Origins of the Research University* (Chicago, 2006).

CONCLUSIONS

1. E. Wallace, *The Four Just Men* (London, 1936), 120.

2. R. N. Lebow, *Archduke Franz Ferdinand Lives! A World without World War I* (New York, 2014), 238.

3. H. Kleinschmidt, *The Nemesis of Power* (London, 2000), 114–70, and "Systeme und Ordnungen in der Geschichte der internationalen Beziehungen," *Archiv für kulturgeschichte* 82 (2000): 433–54.

4. Germain-Louis de Chauvelin, French foreign minister, about Austro-Spanish alliance, 1725, AE, CP, Autriche 165, fol. 129.

5. C. S. Leonard, *Reform and Regicide: The Reign of Peter III of Russia* (Bloomington, IN, 1993).

6. R. F. Hamilton, *President McKinley, War and Empire,* vol. 1, *President McKinley and the Coming of War, 1898* (New Brunswick, NJ, 2006), 252. For a contrary defense, making good points about the problems of footnote citation in wide-ranging books, C. A. Bayly, *The Birth of the Modern World, 1780–1914* (Oxford, 2004), xxiii.

7. I am most grateful to Anthony Musson for his advice on this point.

8. For a brief discussion of an Oxford conference, S. Begley, "Putting Time in a (Leaky) Bottle," *Newsweek,* July 30, 2007, 49. For lengthier discussion, F. A. Wolf, *The Yoga of Time Travel* (Wheaton, IL, 2004), esp. 95–135; the counterfactual past and the time traveler's possibility wave are discussed on 129–33. See also N. Herbert, *Quantum Reality* (New York, 1985) and D. Deutsch, *The Fabric of Reality: The Science of Parallel Universes—and Its Implications* (New York, 1997).

9. Yale University Art Gallery, New Haven, CT, 1964.41.

10. Worcester Art Museum, Worcester, MA, 1923.211.

POSTSCRIPT

1. D. J. Goldhagen, *Hitler's Willing Executioners: Ordinary Germans and the Holocaust* (New York, 1996); C. R. Browning, *Ordinary Men: Reserve Police Battalion 101 and the Final Solution in Poland* (New York, 1992); M. Mann, "Were the Perpetrators of Genocide 'Ordinary Men' or 'Real Nazis'? Results from Fifteen Hundred Biographies," *Holocaust and Genocide Studies* 14 (2000): 331–66.

Selected Further Reading

Brack, D., and I. Dale, eds. *Prime Minister Portillo and Other Things That Never Happened.* London: Politicos, 2003.

Bulhof, J. "What If? Modality and History." *History and Theory* (1999): 145–68.

Bunzl, M. "Counterfactual History: A User's Guide." *American Historical Review* 109 (2004): 845–68.

Cowley, R., ed. *What If? The World's Foremost Military Historians Imagine What Might Have Been.* New York: Putnam, 1999.

Demandt, A. *History That Never Happened: A Treatise on the Question, What Would Have Happened If . . . ?* 3rd ed. Jefferson, NC: McFarland, 1993.

Dolezel, L. *Possible Worlds of Fiction and History: The Postmodern Stage.* Baltimore: Johns Hopkins University Press, 2010.

Elster, J. *Logic and Society: Contradictions and Possible Worlds.* New York: Wiley, 1978.

Evans, R. J. *Altered Pasts: Counterfactuals in History.* Waltham, MA: Brandeis University Press, 2014.

Ferguson, N., ed. *Virtual History: Alternatives and Counterfactuals.* London: Picador, 1997.

Fogel, R. *Railroads and American Economic Growth: Essays on Econometric History.* Baltimore: John Hopkins University Press, 1964.

Goertz, G., and J. S. Levy, eds. *Explaining War and Peace: Case Studies and Necessary Condition Counterfactuals.* New York: Routledge, 2007.

Hassig, R. "Counterfactuals and Revisionism in Historical Explanations." *Anthropological Theory* 1 (2003): 57–72.

Hawthorn, G. *Plausible Worlds: Possibility and Understanding in History and the Social Sciences.* Cambridge: Cambridge University Press, 1991.

Hellekson, K. *The Alternate History: Refiguring Historical Time.* Kent, OH: Kent State University Press, 2001.

Lebow, R. N. *Forbidden Fruit: Counterfactuals and International Relations.* Princeton, NJ: Princeton University Press, 2010.

Lewis, D. *Counterfactuals.* Cambridge, MA: Harvard University Press, 1987.

Morgan, S. L., and C. Winship. *Counterfactuals and Causal Inference: Methods and Principles for Social Research.* Cambridge: Cambridge University Press, 2007.

Renouvier, C. *Uchronie (L'Utopie dans l'histoire): Esquisse historique apocryphe du développement de la civilisation européenne tel qu'il n'a pas été, tel qu'il aurait pu être* [Uchronia (utopia in history): An apocryphal sketch of the development of European

civilization not as it was but as it might have been]. Paris: Bureau de la Critique Phi-
losophique, 1876.

Roberts, A., ed. *What Might Have Been: Leading Historians on Twelve "What Ifs" of History*. London: Weidenfeld & Nicolson, 2004.

Rodiek, C. *Erfundene Vergangenheit: Kontrafaktische Geschichtsdarstellung (Uchronie) in
der Literatur (Analecta Romana)* [Fictional past: Counterfactual presentation of history (utopia) in the literature]. Frankfurt: Klostermann, 1997.

Roese, N. J., and J. M. Olson, eds. *What Might Have Been: The Social Psychology of Counterfactual Thinking*. Mahwah, NJ: Psychology Press, 1995.

Rosenfeld, G. *The World Hitler Never Made: Alternate History and the Memory of
Nazism*. Cambridge: Cambridge University Press, 2005.

Schroeder, P. W. "Embedded Counterfactuals and World War I as an Unavoidable War."
In *Systems, Stability, and Statecraft: Essays on the International History of Modern Europe*, 157–91. New York: Palgrave Macmillan, 2004.

Snowman, D., ed. *If I Had Been . . . : Ten Historical Fantasies*. London: Robson Books,
1979.

Squire, J. C. *If It Had Happened Otherwise: Lapses into Imaginary History*. London:
Longmans, Green, 1931.

Tetlock, P. E., and A. Belkin, eds. *Counterfactual Thought Experiments in World Politics:
Logical, Methodological, and Psychological Perspectives*. Princeton, NJ: Princeton University Press, 1996.

Tetlock, P. E., and R. N. Lebow. "Poking Counterfactual Holes in Covering Laws: Cognitive Styles and Historical Reasoning." *American Political Science Review* 95 (2001):
829–43.

Tetlock, P. E., R. N. Lebow, and G. Parker, eds. *Unmaking the West: "What If?" Scenarios
That Rewrite World History*. Ann Arbor: University of Michigan Press, 2006.

Waugh, C. G., and M. H. Greenberg. *Alternative Histories: Eleven Stories of the World as It
Might Have Been*. New York: Taylor & Francis, 1986.

Index

JEREMY BLACK is Professor of History at the University of Exeter. He is author of more than one hundred books, including *War and Technology* (IUP, 2013), *Fighting for America: The Struggle for Mastery in North America, 1519–1871* (IUP, 2011), and *War and the Cultural Turn*. Black received the Samuel Eliot Morison Prize from the Society for Military History in 2008.